Praise for *Cryptoassets* and Chris Burniske and Jack Tatar

Anyone with a practical or theoretical interest in financial markets should know about cryptoassets. Burniske and Tatar do an excellent job explaining this brave new world to us.

—HARRY MAX MARKOWITZ, winner of the Nobel Prize
in Economics and founder of Modern Portfolio Theory

Cryptoassets is an outstanding overview of the state of digital currencies and assets. Highly recommended for those who want to understand where finance is going.

—BALAJI S. SRINIVASAN, CEO of 21.co
and board partner at Andreessen Horowitz

Burniske and Tatar have delivered a seminal guide to what may be the biggest investment opportunity since the Internet. Informative and actionable, *Cryptoassets* is a must-read for crypto-enthusiasts and capital market investors alike.

—ARTHUR B. LAFFER, chairman of Laffer Associates,
member of President Reagan's Economic Policy Advisory Board,
and creator of the Laffer Curve

As we hurtle into a new, decentralized economy, Burniske and Tatar have laid down something of immense importance: a coherent logic, a new science even, for investing in the assets that will define that coming world.

—MICHAEL J. CASEY, senior advisor to the Digital Currency
Initiative at MIT Media Lab and coauthor of *The Age of
Cryptocurrency*

In this sweeping and lucid work, Burniske and Tatar make a compelling case that cryptoassets are foundational to the second generation of the Internet and represent a once-in-a-generation opportunity for the innovative investor. Required reading for anyone wanting to understand the future of finance, business, and more.

—ALEX TAPSCOTT, CEO of NextBlock Global
and coauthor of *Blockchain Revolution*

Poised to be one of the most profound inventions in history, blockchain technology may change everything—just as the wheel and the Internet did. Chris and Jack will help you understand blockchains and the cryptoassets within them. If you're a financial advisor, this book will help you serve your clients better.

—RIC EDELMAN, three-time #1 Independent Financial Advisor
(*Barron's*) and *New York Times* bestselling author of
The Truth About Your Future

Investors are always seeking new assets to diversify their portfolios, and the emergence of cryptoassets provides such an opportunity. Burniske and Tatar offer the first detailed analysis of cryptoassets from the perspective of a portfolio investment.

—CAMPBELL R. HARVEY, former president of the American
Finance Association and professor of finance at the Fuqua School
of Business at Duke University

Cryptoassets is the definitive guide that comes just in time to introduce you to a radically new era of innovative investment. This book tells you all you need to know to invest in this supreme opportunity of our time: replacing the porous top-down "winner-take-all" Internet with a safe and cornucopian cadastre of trust and opportunity that makes us all potential winners.

—GEORGE GILDER, cofounder of the Discovery Institute
and author of *The Scandal of Money*

The growth and importance of cryptocurrency and cryptocomputing rivals the early growth of the commercial Internet and web, and the technical and economic revolution that will result is perhaps even more significant than the first phase of the Internet. *Cryptoassets* is an excellent introduction to this breakthrough in technology and finance, and a tremendous resource for those eager to get their heads around what can be a daunting and complex subject.

—JEREMY ALLAIRE, CEO and founder of Circle

This is an extremely well-researched and timely "state of the nation" treatise on cryptoassets. I'm excited that the knowledge base of our industry is continuing to expand with such high-quality thought leadership and insights.

—VINNY LINGHAM, cofounder and CEO of Civic.com,
Shark on *Shark Tank South Africa*, and board member
of the Bitcoin Foundation

Since Bitcoin's creation, people have been wondering why it and other crypto-assets have any value. Chris Burniske and Jack Tatar give the most compelling case for why, with sharp, detailed analysis that reflects their deep understanding of the technology and their strong finance background. Beginners as well as more seasoned crypto investors will find new insights and sensible tips in this practical guide.

> —LAURA SHIN, senior editor at *Forbes* and host of *Unchained*

Cryptoassets is a fascinating introduction to this new space of the digital economy. The authors surface many historical examples to remind us that in times of excitement, it is even more important to pay attention to the teams and talent behind each project.

> —CHRISTIAN CATALINI, Theodore T. Miller Career
> Development Professor at MIT and assistant professor of
> technological innovation, entrepreneurship, and strategic
> management at the Sloan School of Management at MIT

Cryptoassets is a must-read for all financial services executives and investors who want to understand the fundamentals and future directions of this burgeoning new asset class. Delivered by two of the foremost authorities in the nascent, multibillion-dollar space, this is the most extensive guide on crypto-assets currently available.

> —SANDRA RO, former head of digitization at CME Group

As renowned industry thought leaders, it's no surprise that Chris and Jack have delivered what is likely the most thoughtful and in-depth framework for evaluating cryptoassets. Within this book, they've rolled up their sleeves to provide helpful historical context and a valuation framework that readers will find intellectually stimulating and illuminating for understanding this rapidly emerging world of cryptoassets.

> —SPENCER BOGART, managing director
> and head of research at Blockchain Capital

Chris is at the forefront of the important work to better understand and analyze this emerging class of assets. In this book, he and Jack have encapsulated years of their thinking in an easy-to-digest manner.

> —DAVID KINITSKY, VP of research and innovation
> at Fidelity Labs

For the uninitiated, the world of cryptocurrencies is fraught with risks and pitfalls. No one should venture into this world without preparation. *Cryptoassets* explains, in simple to understand terms, the full paradigm of Bitcoin and its successor currencies, and it provides everything needed to explore this exciting world.

—JOHN MCAFEE, founder of McAfee Associates

A thorough, balanced, and easy read. I would recommend this to anyone who considers building a portfolio of cryptoassets.

—RYAN SELKIS, former director of investments at Digital
Currency Group and managing director of CoinDesk

Serious investment professionals should read *Cryptoassets* if they want to understand and value the first new asset class of the twenty-first century. Chris and Jack explain this new-age investment opportunity comprehensively, artfully, and masterfully.

—CATHERINE WOOD, founder and CIO
of ARK Investment Management

A rare combination of quantitative analysis and first principles-based thinking—this is insightful, original content.

—ADAM WHITE, vice president of Coinbase
and general manager of GDAX

In an increasingly digital world, it is only a matter of time until enormous amounts of value are transmitted and secured via blockchains, including the value of music and creative works. *Cryptoassets* makes blockchains accessible to the nontechnical by exploring their varied origin stories, use cases, and fundamental value. If you're looking for a grounded, first-principles approach to the next wave of Internet innovation, then this is a great book to read.

—JESSE WALDEN, founder of Mediachain Labs
and blockchain lead at Spotify

Chris and Jack show us the future of cryptoassets today. Their outlook is pointed and perceptive. A must-read to understand the next era in wealth and value creation.

—WILLIAM MOUGAYAR, general partner at Virtual Capital
Ventures and author of *The Business Blockchain*

Young, Stanford-trained blockchain analyst and investor Chris Burniske has teamed up with financial planning expert and author Jack Tatar to provide the first comprehensive guide to understanding the fastest growing, most exciting asset class under the sun. While many investors are still waking up to the opportunity, these assets have already provided outsized returns, as the overall market is now hovering around $100 billion, which is 10x from a year ago and 100x from four years ago. Collectively referring to these investments as "cryptoassets," Burniske and Tatar provide a solid background on how the technology arose, what problems it solves, and how, like the Internet itself, it's going to have a dramatic impact on not only the venture capital process but on investing itself. Don't think of rebalancing your portfolio without reading this book.

—MICHAEL TERPIN, founder of Transform Group,
organizer of CoinAgenda, and cofounder of BitAngels

While the cryptoasset space has witnessed exponential growth, to achieve its full potential, it has to be broadly integrated into the real world. With consistent objectivity and clarity, Chris and Jack's book details cryptoassets as an asset class, and will prove influential in driving institutional investor adoption of this groundbreaking opportunity.

—JENNIFER ZHU SCOTT, founding partner of Radian Partners
and member of the Future of Blockchain Council of the World
Economic Forum

Cryptoassets provides a great introduction to and overview of the young yet rapidly growing universe of all things blockchain. This industry, asset class, and overall idea will make you ponder why abstract concepts like money, identity, and business function like they do in the world today, and how the innovation we're seeing will completely reshape the economy of tomorrow. From setting the stage to diving into specific protocols and projects to sharing practical knowledge on how to invest in these emerging assets, Chris and Jack's combination of expertise and familiarity with the complex topics at hand are testament to why I have considered them some of the best resources throughout my journey of falling deeper and deeper down the crypto rabbit hole.

—ALEX SUNNARBORG, research analyst at CoinDesk
and cofounder of Lawnmower.io

From inception to the latest phase, *Cryptoassets* explores the past, present, and future of this new asset class. It's not a hard read yet delves into much of the detail needed for a complete understanding of the benefits, and risks, of bitcoin, blockchain, and more. Chris and Jack have written a book I highly recommend to investors in this burgeoning field!

—PAT BOLLAND, former business editor at CNBC, CBC, BNN

Cryptoassets is the bible for all things crypto. Whether you're a beginner or expert, you will walk away with a deeper understanding of the entire ecosystem after reading this book.

—GREG ROSEN, principal at BoxGroup

Chris and Jack provide a holistic view of the origin, evolution, and analysis of cryptoassets. It goes through their very short but intense history, talks about methods for analyzing their value, and identifies the ones with potential. I'd recommend it to anyone who wants to dive into investing and understanding how cryptoassets will shape the future of society and the creation of value.

—LUIS CUENDE, cofounder of Aragon and Stampery

Those of us who work in the blockchain industry have long realized that the rise of cryptocurrencies as a legitimate asset class was inevitable. But most traditional investors have been slow on the uptick. Chris was the first buy-side analyst to focus exclusively on this emerging asset class, and Jack was one of the earliest financial journalists to stress its importance. For years, Chris has been working hard to bring Wall Street's rigorous analytical methodologies to cryptocurrencies, while Jack has been busy explaining the benefits of cryptocurrencies to audiences around the world. Now, with *Cryptoassets*, they describe, as nobody has before, why every investor should incorporate bitcoin, ether, and new blockchain-based assets into their portfolios, and how to analyze these tokens in order to make the right investments.

—TRAVIS SCHER, investment associate at Digital Currency Group

Chris and Jack have written our generation's *A Random Walk Down Wall Street*. This book is required reading for anyone looking to get involved with and profit from the cryptoassets boom.

—PATRICK ARCHAMBEAU, VP of engineering at CoinDesk
and cofounder of Lawnmower.io

Chris and Jack have been fellow travelers in the blockchain space since way before it was a polite cocktail party topic. Over the years, we've laughed and marveled together at how the space has evolved. This book could not be more timely in describing an emerging $100+ billion financial market and all of the chaos and promise it brings. The authors capture not only the technical and market analysis you need to know to invest in these projects but also the ethos and excitement of the people pushing the envelope. Savor this book. It's a time-capsule view of the birth of an amazing technology.

—PETER KIRBY, cofounder and CEO of Factom, Inc.

Burniske and Tatar thread the needle between an approachable guide for new-comers and thought-provoking insights for seasoned investors. I will surely be assigning it to my graduate students as we cover cryptoassets.

—STEPHEN MCKEON, associate professor of finance at the Lundquist College of Business at the University of Oregon

Token-based fund-raising is here to stay, and this book offers the best way to value cryptoassets that I've seen. The book provides background and the potential impacts of ICOs, offering insightful knowledge to both those entering the space and experienced investors like myself. I would recommend this book for any crypto reading arsenal!

—PAUL VERADITTAKIT, partner at Pantera Capital

Burniske and Tatar have now given me an easy response when people ask how to get started with cryptoassets—this book!

—ARI PAUL, CIO of BlockTower Capital

This is a seminal work in the evolution of the cryptosphere as digital money moves mainstream. The book covers the full potential and array of what this technology offers in piercing the veil to an Internet of value with all the new innovations and crossovers from the traditional realm of finance. Chris and Jack have brought a wealth of knowledge and cross-disciplinary methods to bear from their respective fields and broken new ground in their analysis of this exciting new space.

—CHARLIE HAYTER, cofounder and CEO of CryptoCompare

Cryptoassets is a tour de force. Burniske and Tatar are able to leverage their deep industry experience to condense a complex, continually evolving topic into a concise and informative guide for investors looking to be on the cutting edge of a new asset class. *Cryptoassets* will serve as the entry point to the space for retail investors for years to come.

—PIETER GORSIRA, software engineer at CoinDesk
and cofounder of Lawnmower.io

In a world where issuing digital assets becomes as easy as creating a website, Chris and Jack provide a comprehensive guide that will help you separate the wheat from the chaff.

—DEMIAN BRENER, cofounder and CEO of Zeppelin Solutions

As we enter the next great evolution in global financial markets, Chris Burniske and Jack Tatar have authored a unique and much-needed volume. It offers not only a foundational understanding of cryptoassets and digital currencies but also serves as a reference for evaluating and participating in a cryptoasset future. A new asset class has emerged, and *Cryptoassets* is the definitive guide.

—RON QUARANTA, chairman of the Wall Street
Blockchain Alliance

This book is very accessible, comprehensive, and easy to read for any size investor. One of its strengths is its ability to be valuable to the novice and the experienced professional alike.

—JARED HARWAYNE-GIDANSKY, founding board member
of the Blockchain Association of Australia

Chris and Jack have created a book that not only explains the world of crypto-assets but provides a framework for how to invest in it and become part of what may be the greatest investment opportunity since the Internet.

—NED SCOTT, founder and CEO of Steemit

Cryptoassets is an intelligent and well-organized introduction to the world of cryptoassets. The book adapts classic finance pricing models to the challenging task of valuing cryptoassets, offering the reader a solid head start to investing in this new exciting asset class.

—ALESSIO SARETTO, assistant professor of finance
at the University of Texas at Dallas

If you want to know how cryptoassets work, get *Mastering Bitcoin* by Andreas Antonopoulos, but if you want to know how and why you should be investing in this new asset class, get yourself a copy of *Cryptoassets*.

—TRON BLACK, investor and principal developer
at Medici Ventures

Newcomers often try to wiggle their way into the world of accepted financial tools. Most fail miserably. But cryptocurrency and its accompanying blockchain technology have made their mark and will likely have an ongoing impact on how we all do business. Burniske and Tatar have written an incredibly comprehensive book that explains what you need to know about this new asset class.

—DOUGLAS GOLDSTEIN, CFP, author of *Rich as a King*

By explaining the various crypto investments, from coins to tokens to commodities, and providing the tools to perform investment analysis, *Cryptoassets* is the best crypto investment novices, professionals, and business leaders can make.

—RON KOCHMAN, former president and CEO of
Volt Information Sciences and cryptoasset angel investor

Cryptoassets provides a one-stop shop for learning about this new asset class. You'll learn about their colorful histories, how to apply fundamental valuation techniques, and practical tips to navigate the at-times turbulent markets.

—MATTHEW GOETZ, CEO of BlockTower Capital

With investing, people always want to know about the next big thing. For curious minds who want to know about emerging technologies or even those who already have an understanding of blockchains, Chris and Jack leave no stone unturned. From the origins, to an explanation of how it works, to what's next, the reader will leave excited about the possibilities of investing money and time in this exciting adventure.

—TOM SZAKY, founder and CEO of TerraCycle

This book is a must-read for any financial advisor who wants to stay on top of the shifting asset and technological landscape. Advisors would be wise to familiarize themselves with cryptoassets before their innovative clients approach them for an intelligent cryptoasset discussion!

—FRED PYE, president and CEO of 3iQ Corp.

What will a technology that validates the order of entries in an electronic ledger without a centralized administrator bring? Time will tell. If you can't wait until then, read Chris and Jack's book. It will give you a great start.

—FRANCOIS GADENNE, chairman and executive director
of the Retirement Income Industry Association

The most complete and informational piece of literature on the subject today. Chris Burniske and Jack Tatar steer the reader through a torrent of unknowns, illuminating the complicated world of cryptoassets and their underlying technology, which will more than likely become our generation's most important innovation.

—RYAN LANCELOT, coauthor of *What's the Deal with Bitcoins?*

A must-read to appreciate the Bitcoin network effect and the wave of innovation that it launched through the community of people who played critical roles in creating all the distributed ecosystems that are transforming business models.

—CRISTINA DOLAN, cofounder and COO of InsureX

Crypto trading and the FinTech innovations unlocked by blockchains will do to Wall Street what personal Internet publishing and blogging did to media empires. This power shift is inevitable. Capital allocation no longer needs to be managed by powerful institutions which have proven to be corrupt and reckless. Regulation and regulatory capture is putting the U.S. at risk of losing out in the transition. Chris Burniske and Jack Tatar give you, the individual, the tools to evaluate these new cryptoassets and take advantage of what I believe will be the greatest rebalancing of wealth and power that the world has ever seen.

— DR. PATRICK BYRNE, CEO of Overstock.com

CRYPTOASSETS

CRYPTOASSETS

The Innovative Investor's Guide to Bitcoin and Beyond

CHRIS BURNISKE & JACK TATAR

New York   Chicago   San Francisco   Athens
London   Madrid   Mexico City   Milan
New Delhi   Singapore   Sydney   Toronto

3 4 5 6 7 8 9   LCR   22 21 20 19 18 17

ISBN   978-1-260-02667-2
MHID   1-260-02667-1

e-ISBN   978-1-260-02668-9
e-MHID   1-260-02668-X

This publication is designed to provide accurate and authoritative information in regard to the subject matter covered. It is sold with the understanding that neither the author nor the publisher is engaged in rendering legal, accounting, securities trading, or other professional services. If legal advice or other expert assistance is required, the services of a competent professional person should be sought.

> —*From a Declaration of Principles Jointly Adopted*
> *by a Committee of the American Bar Association*
> *and a Committee of Publishers and Associations*

Library of Congress Cataloging-in-Publication Data

Names: Burniske, Chris, author. | Tatar, Jack, author.
Title: Cryptoassets : the innovation investor's guide to bitcoin and beyond /
    by Chris Burniske and Jack Tatar
Description: New York : McGraw-Hill, [2018] | Includes bibliographical references
    and index.
Identifiers: LCCN 2017031956 | ISBN 9781260026672 (alk. paper) | ISBN
    1260026671
Subjects: LCSH: Bitcoin. | Electronic funds transfers. | Investments.
Classification: LCC HG1710 .B86 2018 | DDC 332.1/78—dc23
LC record available at https://lccn.loc.gov/2017031956

McGraw-Hill Education books are available at special quantity discounts to use as premiums and sales promotions, or for use in corporate training programs. To contact a representative, please visit the Contact Us page at www.mhprofessional.com.

To Dad, who taught me how to write,
and to Mom, who made me believe I could
—CB

To Eric and Grace, you are the future
—JT

Contents

Part II   WHY

Part III   HOW

Authors' Note

When we started writing this book in December 2016, bitcoin was in the $700s, ether was in the $7s, and the aggregate network value of cryptoassets was just north of $10 billion. Over the ensuing months of writing we watched bitcoin push past $4,000, while ether crossed $400, and the aggregate network value of cryptoassets punched through $100 billion. Cryptoassets went from being esoteric dark web material to mainstream topics of conversation and enthusiasm.

When embarking on our literary journey, we recognized the difficulty in documenting arguably the world's fastest moving markets. These markets can change as much in a day—up or down—as the stock market changes in a year. Nonetheless, we were continually asked the same question: "What should I read to get the full picture of what's going on in these markets?" The frequency of this question grew to a clamor as the markets rose through the first half of 2017, and yet information channels remained stubbornly fragmented among Reddit, Twitter, Telegram, Slack, Medium, news sites, and more.

While we recognize the difficulty in covering the *full picture* of the ever-moving cryptoasset markets, we believe that this book provides a comprehensive view of the history, technology, and marketplace dynamics of bitcoin and beyond. We have crafted the book to be as evergreen as possible with regard to the background and methodologies laid forth, so that even as the markets change, the book retains its value. We recognize that by the time you read this, some asset prices may seem like the distant past, and some teams may be indignant that we didn't cover their story. We couldn't possibly have covered every price change and every story, or we would never have published the book.

Our hope is to serve as a starting point and means to understanding, so that we can all study and experience this space together. It is a history that is still in its earliest stages of being written.

Foreword

When I first learned about bitcoin, I was convinced it would fail. Based on a few articles and two decades of experience as a skeptical trader, I loudly—and now regrettably—declared on CNBC's *Fast Money* that bitcoin would not survive. How could it? It was not backed by any entity; it did not have a central bank; it was not accepted for taxes; and it did not have an army to enforce its use. What's more, it was extremely volatile and had a bad reputation—all of which would contribute surely to its premature demise. I have never been more incorrect in my entire career.

Somewhere in the CNBC archives exists an awkward video of me railing against this "magic Internet money." If you're reading this and have access to the video, treat it with the respect it deserves and destroy it! Since those unenlightened days, I have come to understand that bitcoin—and the blockchain beneath it—is a technological advancement that has the potential to revolutionize financial services the same way email did to the post office.

Once I realized that blockchain technology was a disruptive force, I sought out people who shared my view. I met Chris Burniske at the very first Wall Street Blockchain Alliance holiday party, and we immediately found common interest in the potential for blockchain-based assets, or cryptoassets, to become a new asset class for investors. At the time, very few people saw bitcoin's potential, but Chris did, and it was clear to me that he possessed rare leadership and vision.

Jack Tatar is an expert in retirement planning who has spent over two decades in the financial industry and brings a much-needed perspective of finance and investment knowledge to the cryptoasset world. New technology can be confusing and intimidating, but through his engaging writing, Jack possesses the unique ability to distill a complex subject into an easily digestible serving. As a result of their combined perspectives, *Cryptoassets* is a book that will satisfy the most curious minds and engage those approaching the subject for the first time.

Readers will benefit not only from Chris and Jack's vision but also their deep knowledge of the topic. As the manager of a hedge fund that invests in digital assets, I am constantly researching this asset class's investment potential, and when I get stumped, my first call is to Chris Burniske. While I am thrilled that Chris is sharing his unique insights in this book, I am selfishly reluctant to lose my secret go-to resource. Layer on Jack's experience as one of the first financial journalists to write about bitcoin, and you have a powerful combination. Let them be your resource as well.

The beauty of this book is that it takes the reader on a journey from bitcoin's inception in the ashes of the Great Financial Crisis to its role as a diversifier in a traditional investment portfolio. Those who want to look under the hood of blockchain technology will be thrilled with the skillful description of the elegant architecture that powers this technology, and financial historians, like myself, will find the discussion of investment bubbles instructive. Chris and Jack artfully apply financial history lessons to the cryptoasset investment world. Spoiler alert: even though blockchain technology is disrupting traditional financial market structures, fear and greed remain uniquely human traits that can and will find a place in cryptoassets. Thankfully, Chris and Jack give readers the tools and knowledge to know what to look out for when bubbles do occur.

Armed with this knowledge, the reader can then use the valuation framework laid out in Chapters 12 and 13 to find the most promising cryptoassets. Valuing cryptoassets is done unlike traditional investments; they typically do not have revenue or cash flows and thus present a conundrum for those evaluating their merits. Here, Chris and Jack present groundbreaking work on how to properly value an asset based on the network effect and teams of decentralized developers. Everyone who is even thinking about investing in cryptoassets needs to read these chapters.

One of the most fascinating outcomes of the blockchain revolution is how cryptoassets are disrupting the disruptors. As Chris and Jack explain, the venture capital business model is being turned on its head by crowdfunding efforts that include initial cryptoasset offerings, or ICOs. Cryptoassets are made of code, and because they easily track and convey ownership, they can be used as fund-raising tools for startups. In the last two years, there has been a wave of entrepreneurs that bypassed venture capitalists and instead chose to raise startup capital via these methods.

As with any new model, there are questions about legality and sustainability, but the Silicon Valley ethos of "break things first, then ask for forgiveness" has found its way to Wall Street. Professionals who are involved in all aspects of fund-raising—from venture capital to capital markets—will find the discussion of these new methods of raising capital riveting, maybe even a little frightening.

The final chapter of my book *The Bitcoin Big Bang* was titled "Everything You Know About Business Is Wrong," and it previews what Chris and Jack have identified as a game-changing development in the way capital is raised and distributed. Self-funded, decentralized organizations are a new species in the global economy that are changing everything we know about business. A cryptoasset as the fuel for a decentralized organization not only changes the organizational chart, it also rearranges incentive structures.

These new organizations are altering the way software is developed. Cryptoassets have inverted the value creation structure that worked so well during the development of the Internet. These so-called fat protocols are self-funding development platforms that create and gain value as applications are built on top. This is an entirely new paradigm for open-source projects that incentivizes developers to build socially useful projects.

When I started working on Wall Street, the Internet was something on a computer at the end of the trading desk. Amazon, eBay, and Google did not exist—but within five years, these companies had changed the world. As a greenhorn trader, I was too young and inexperienced to recognize that the Internet was a once-in-a-generation investment opportunity. I was convinced that I would not see another exponential investment opportunity for the rest of my career—until I discovered blockchain technology. Blockchain technology is one of the most important innovations in the history of finance. It is changing the way we transact, distribute capital, and organize our companies. If you're like me and missed investing in the Internet, read this book so you can take advantage of the biggest investment opportunity since the Internet.

—BRIAN KELLY, CNBC Contributor and
Manager of the BKCM Digital Asset Fund

Acknowledgments

Thanks first and foremost to the best literary partner one could have—the great Karen Lacey. This truly was a three-person production, and we thank you for helping us define, refine, and execute on our vision. Not only did you hone our thinking, but you dove deep down the cryptoasset rabbit hole too! Anyone looking to work with a gifted and patient literary partner can find Karen at www.theuncommonoctopus.com.

Thanks to our wonderful editor at McGraw-Hill, Casey Ebro, and our literary agent, Marilyn Allen.

Special thanks to all of those in the cryptoasset and financial community who provided ideas, advice, and commentary, especially the awesome trio of Alex Sunnarborg, Patrick Archambeau, and Pieter Gorsira, as well as Charles Bovaird, Balaji Srinivasan, Arthur Laffer, Michael Casey, Alex Tapscott, Ric Edelman, Campbell Harvey, George Gilder, Jeremy Allaire, Vinny Lingham, Laura Shin, Christian Catalini, Sandra Ro, Spencer Bogart, David Kinitsky, John McAfee, Ryan Selkis, Adam White, Jesse Walden, William Mougayer, Michael Terpin, Jennifer Zhu Scott, Pat Bolland, Greg Rosen, Luis Cuende, Travis Scher, Peter Kirby, Stephen McKeon, Paul Veradittakit, Ari Paul, Charlie Hayter, Demian Brener, Ron Quaranta, Jared Harwayne-Gidansky, Ned Scott, Alessio Saretto, Tron Black, Douglas Goldstein, Matthew Goetz, Tom Szaky, Fred Pye, Ryan Lancelot, Cristina Dolan, Ryan Strauss, Jack Hough, and of course to Brian Kelly for his support, friendship, and assistance. We appreciate the support of the worldwide cryptoasset community and if we forgot to list anyone who was there for us during this journey, please forgive us—it's because of the crypto-community that this book exists!

—CB and JT

Thanks to Dad, who was a writer himself, and from a young age had me journaling, writing summer book reports, and submitting essays to justify the purchase of gadgets. He taught me the importance of never having a TV in the house, that all creativity comes at the cost of maintenance, and that excellence should never be compromised.

Thanks to Mom, who has been a fountain of belief and support through the good and the bad. While she may not know much about blockchains (yet), she loves them because I love them. She is the most positive person I know and the one who has taught me how to find silver linings in the clouds. Thanks to my brother, Justin, who resisted the urge to strangle me when Mom was away, and taught me that power doesn't always have to corrupt.

Thank you to Cathie Wood, who plucked me from a fishmongership and taught me that not all finance is bad. In a few years, Cathie taught me more about economics, the markets, and how the world works than I learned in my time at Stanford. In a world where mentors are increasingly rare, Cathie's guidance has been pivotal in my life. Thank you to Rob Wood, the friendly giant who introduced us.

Thanks to Brett Winton, who has taught me how to approach the most complex of problems and that maybe I'm not as dense as I fear. To Joel Monegro, who has been my thematic torchbearer in the world of crypto, thank you. There's no one I look forward to brainstorming with more than you. Thanks to James Wang, who taught me to love Twitter, and that valuation matters.

Last but not least, thanks to Jack, who has been the driving force behind this book. If not for a fateful lunch at Consensus and Jack's relentless enthusiasm, this book never would have happened.

—CB

Thanks to the great Harry Markowitz for his advice and insight. One of the wonderful results of this book has been my ability to gain the friendship of this wonderful man. Thanks, Harry! I'm humbled by your assistance.

Special thanks to my bubbie, Stu Sharoff, for taking the dive into this wacky world, his advice on the cover, and for being a brother to me for so many years.

Thanks to Stu Rosenberg for also taking the dive and providing such great support and friendship over the years.

Special thanks for my angel investing partner and dear friend, Ron Kochman, for his honest insight into the book and for making this journey so much more entertaining. Also to Steve Katz, who we miss every day.

Thanks to the great John Gioia for his advice and insight throughout the entire process of creating this book. Thanks to Irene Cibas for just being herself and putting up with John and me for *so* many years. Thanks also to Bill Bonomo, John Barbera, and David Fink for their help and support during the years when I needed it. Of course, thanks to the legendary Sam Kirk for his assistance throughout this process.

To my Mom and Dad, who may not be here physically, but inspire and direct me each and every day.

Most of all, thanks to my family, who put up with me during this process. I couldn't have done any of it without you. To my children, Eric and Grace, I could never fully articulate how important and valuable your advice and support has been to me. You're my inspiration for everything.

Finally, to the reason for my being and the love of my life, my Maudee Ann. No one knows better than you what crazy schemes and ideas I've had in my life, and you've endured them and supported me throughout. I thank God for allowing me the opportunity to live my life with you, and I thank you for, well, everything. I love you more than words can tell . . . always!

And of course, to my terrific coauthor, Chris, who brings intellect, humor, compassion, and honesty to everything he does. The best part of this book was making your friendship.

—JT

Introduction

Books, TV shows, and movies have been making futuristic predictions for decades, many of which were originally considered absurd. *Star Trek* featured several that proved to be not so outlandish: the indispensable handheld communicators have become today's smartphones, the personal access display device is now our tablet, and a universal translator exists, of which there are several apps to choose. Edward Bellamy's enigmatically titled 1887 book *Looking Backward* predicted debit and credit cards, and *2001: A Space Odyssey* imagined forms of social media, though nothing on the scale that we currently have. Alvin Toffler's *Future Shock* gripped readers in the 1970s as it predicted the exponential change destined to shake our society, and issued a warning: "In the three short decades between now and the twenty-first century, millions of ordinary, psychologically normal people will face an abrupt collision with the future." This future would create "the shattering stress and disorientation that we induce in individuals by subjecting them to too much change in too short a time."

Exponential change has now become a buzzword, but the power of an exponential curve is rarely considered. Each year will entail greater change than the year before. Such a concept differs drastically from a linear rate of change, where the future will change just as quickly as the past did (see Figure I.1.) The two may appear similar in the early days of change, but when the exponential curve starts to inflect it quickly, and at times violently, distinguishes itself.

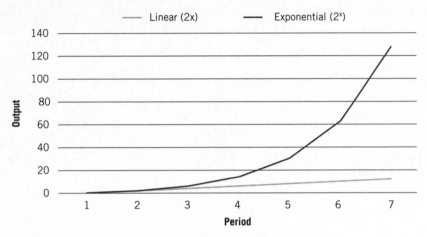

Figure I.1 ■ Exponential versus linear rates of change

While year 1 exhibits the exact same value for linear and exponential change in Figure I.1, as does year 2, by year 7 an exponential rate has progressed nearly tenfold more than the corresponding seventh period of linear change. We often operate with the rough assumption that the rate of change over the next year or two will be roughly equal to that over the prior years, which is a linear world view. That works for the early stage of change, but not when the exponential curve starts to bend like a hockey stick. Unfortunately, most investment portfolios are being managed with a linear world view, with indices that are pegged to the past guiding our future investments. Nothing could be more shortsighted or potentially dangerous in a time of exponential change.

The Internet has irrevocably changed the world, and it continues to do so as developers build on the platform of connection it creates. Thus far, the World Wide Web has been the greatest meta-application to leverage the underlying fiber of the Internet. The indexed web contains at least 4.73 billion pages, nearing the point where there will be one page for every human.[1]

The beginning of the Internet is commonly associated with the 1990s, with Tim Berners-Lee stumbling upon the idea of the World Wide Web while trying to create an information management system for CERN, and Marc Andreessen developing the first widely used web browser, which ultimately became Netscape. Although the accomplishments of Berners-Lee and Andreessen were linchpins to mainstream adoption, the web and the ability to browse it were the first killer apps built on top of the Internet, not to be conflated with the creation of the Internet itself. We are likely still in the early stages of leveraging the potential of the Internet and building meta-applications atop it.

The Internet was first conceptualized in the early 1960s to create resilient communication systems that would survive a nuclear attack on the United States. According to one of the Internet's progenitors, Paul Baran, the key to accomplishing such resilience was decentralization.[2] J. C. R. Licklider proselytized the concept of an "Intergalactic Computer Network," convincing his colleagues at DARPA—which is responsible for investigating and developing new technologies for the U.S. military—of its importance.[3] Leonard Kleinrock, an MIT professor, was doing work on packet switching—the technology underpinning the Internet—that would lead to the first book on the subject: Communication Nets. Ironically, though they were all working on a means to connecting the world, many of the early researchers in this period were unaware of one another.

But their dream has been realized. Every day more than 3.5 billion Google search queries are made,[4] 18.7 billion text messages are sent (that doesn't even include WhatsApp and Facebook Messenger, which combine for more than 60 billion messages per day),[5] and 269 billion emails are sent.[6] Interestingly, however, the Internet has become increasingly centralized over time, potentially endangering its original conception as a "highly survivable system."

Human ingenuity often surfaces when it's most needed, and now, a new technology is emerging that returns to the decentralized ethos of the original Internet with the potential to revolutionize our computational and transactional infrastructure: blockchain technology. Every second, millions of packets of information are *transacted* between humans and machines using the Internet, and blockchain technology is forcing us to rethink the costs, security, and ownership of these transactions.

Blockchain technology came from Bitcoin. In other words, Bitcoin is the mother of blockchain technology. Bitcoin, with a capital *B*, is a platform that carries upon it programmable money, known as bitcoin with a lowercase *b*. The technological foundation to this platform is a distributed and digital ledger referred to as a blockchain. In January 2009, when Bitcoin was first released, it embodied the first working implementation of a blockchain the world had seen.

Since then, people have downloaded the open-source software that is Bitcoin, studied its blockchain, and released different blockchains that go far beyond Bitcoin. Blockchain technology can now be thought of as a general purpose technology, on par with that of the steam engine, electricity, and machine learning.

To quote a May 2016 article in *Harvard Business Review* by Don and Alex Tapscott: "The technology most likely to change the next decade of business is not the social web, big data, the cloud, robotics, or even artificial intelligence. It's the blockchain, the technology behind digital currencies like bitcoin."[7]

Incumbents are sensing the inherent creative destruction, especially within the financial services sector, understanding that winners will grow new markets and feast off the disintermediated. Many startups are eyeing these middlemen with the oft-flickering thought that has been credited to Amazon's Jeff Bezos: "Your fat margins are my opportunity."[8]

If financial incumbents don't embrace the technology themselves, Bitcoin and blockchain technology could do to banks what cell phones did to telephone poles. Nearly every global bank, exchange, custodian, and financial services provider is part of some blockchain consortium, investing in the potential disruptors or internally building its own team. These players include JP Morgan, Goldman Sachs, Citibank, the New York Stock Exchange, NASDAQ, Banco Santander, Barclays, UBS, South African Reserve Bank, Bank of Tokyo Mitsubishi, Mizuho, China Merchants Bank, Australian Stock Exchange, and more.

Financial incumbents are aware blockchain technology puts on the horizon a world without cash—no need for loose bills, brick-and-mortar banks, or, potentially, centralized monetary policies. Instead, value is handled virtually, through a system that has no central authority figure and is governed in a decentralized and democratic manner. Mathematics force order in the operations. Our life savings, and that of our heirs, could be entirely intangible, floating in a soup of secure 1s and 0s, the entire system accessed through computers and smartphones.

Technology providers smell the disruption as well, with Microsoft and IBM most vocally leading the charge. Microsoft provides Blockchain as a Service (BaaS) for developers within its Azure cloud platform. Marley Gray, its director of technology strategy, has said, "We want, and frankly our customers want, access to every blockchain. It could be two guys in a garage that forked bitcoin and had this genius idea and people want to try that out. We don't want to have any barriers. We're open to all. We help even the smallest players onboard."[9]

Just as the Internet and World Wide Web changed how we live our lives and interact with others, it also made millionaires out of the innovators who began companies based on these technologies—and the investors who invested in them. Those with the foresight to have bought Google during its "Initial Public

Offering" (IPO) would have seen a 1,800 percent appreciation by August 2016, and those who bought Amazon's IPO would have seen a 1,827 percent appreciation.[10]

Blockchain architectures and their native assets are well on their way to becoming the next great meta-application to leverage Internet infrastructure. They already provide services that include global currencies, world computers, and decentralized social networks, among hundreds of others.

The native assets historically have been called cryptocurrencies or altcoins, but we prefer the term cryptoassets, which is the term we will use throughout the book. The terms *cryptocurrencies* and *altcoins* convey only a fraction of the innovation that is occurring in the cryptoasset economy. Not all of the 800 existing cryptoassets are currencies. We are not just witnessing the decentralized creation of currencies but also of commodities and polished digital goods and services, as blockchains meld technology and the markets to build Web 3.0.

It's early enough in the life of blockchain technology that no books yet have focused solely on public blockchains and their native cryptoassets from the investing perspective. We are changing that because investors need to be aware of the opportunity and armed both to take advantage and protect themselves in the fray.

Inevitably, innovations of such magnitude, fueled by the mania of making money, can lead to overly optimistic investors. Investors who early on saw potential in Internet stocks encountered the devastating dot-com bubble. Stock in Books-A-Million saw its price soar by over 1,000 percent in one week simply by announcing it had an updated website. Subsequently, the price crashed and the company has since delisted and gone private. Other Internet-based high flyers that ended up crashing include Pets.com, Worldcom, and WebVan.[11] Today, none of those stocks exist.

Whether specific cryptoassets will survive or go the way of Books-A-Million remains to be seen. What's clear, however, is that some will be big winners. Altogether, between the assets native to blockchains and the companies that stand to capitalize on this creative destruction, there needs to be a game plan that investors use to analyze and ultimately profit from this new investment theme of cryptoassets. The goal of this book is not to predict the future—it's changing too fast for all but the lucky to be right—but rather to prepare investors for a variety of futures.

Bitcoin, the most widely known cryptoasset, has been riding a roller coaster. If one had invested $100 in bitcoin in October 2009—the first time an exchange rate was established for the nascent digital currency—one would now have over $100 million. In November 2013, if one had invested that same $100 in bitcoin, one would have endured an 86 percent drop by January 2015. There are nearly 800 other stories to tell, considering there are over 800 cryptoassets floating on globally connected and ever-on markets. At the end of 2016, a list of the top 50 included:[12]

> Bitcoin, Ethereum, Ripple, Litecoin, Monero, Ethereum Classic, Dash, MaidSafeCoin, NEM, Augur, Steem, Iconomi, Dogecoin, Factom, Waves, Stellar Lumens, DigixDAO, Zcash, Lisk, Xenixcoin, E-Dinar Coin, Swiscoin, GameCredits, Ardor, BitShares, LoMoCoin, Bytecoin, Emercoin, AntShares, Gulden, Golem, Tether, ShadowCash, Xaurum, Storjcoin, Stratis, Nxt, Peercoin, I/O Coin, Rubycoin, Bitcrystals, SingularDTV, Counterparty, Agoras Tokens, Siacoin, YbCoin, BitcoinDark, SysCoin, PotCoin, and Global Currency Reserve.

This book will be the first of its kind to dive deep into a number of these. While many have slipped under the mainstream radar, the opportunities they present may be just as great as bitcoin.

We hope to transform today's intelligent investor into an innovative investor by providing a guide that explains what cryptoassets are, why they should be considered, and how to invest in them. Written by Benjamin Graham, *The Intelligent Investor* is a seminal work on value investing that Warren Buffet crowned as "the best book about investing ever written."[13] While we can only hope to achieve a fraction of the success Graham had in educating investors, our goals are very similar. We have chosen to focus on an asset class that didn't exist in Graham's day, and one that serves as a nice hedge against the exponential change that increasingly will disrupt existing portfolios over time.

One of the keys to Graham's book was always reminding the investor to focus on the inherent value of an investment without getting caught in the irrational behavior of the markets. Just as he aimed to arm the intelligent investor with the tools to make an investment decision based on fundamental analysis, we hope to do the same for the innovative investor who is considering adding cryptoassets to his or her portfolio.

This is not a get-rich-quick book with the latest hot tips. Rather it's a book that grounds this new asset class in the context of its own history, common investment strategies, the history of financial speculation, and more. Investors who follow through on their interest in cryptoassets and examine them in the context of their overall financial goals and portfolio strategies will become innovative investors.

We've written this book for the novice and the expert. We've divided it into three parts: *What*, *Why*, and *How*. The *What* lays the foundation for this new asset class, providing a concise explanation of the technology and history of cryptoassets. The *Why* dives into why portfolio management matters, as well as why we think this is a whole new asset class that offers great opportunity—as well as great risk. The *How* details how to approach adding a cryptoasset to a portfolio, including a framework for investigating the merits of a new asset, and the logistical grit of acquisition, storage, taxes, and regulation. Each chapter effectively can stand alone.

The world of cryptoassets may at times feel like science fiction; we imagine that when the Internet was first explained and discussed, people felt the same way. For many, change sparks fear. We understand that. But it also kindles opportunity, and we hope to prepare the reader to recognize, understand, and act on the opportunities available in the world of cryptoassets.

Tomorrow inevitably becomes today. Exponential change isn't going away. This book will help the innovative investor not only survive but thrive. Let's dive in.

CRYPTOASSETS

Part I

WHAT

Chapter 1

Bitcoin and the Financial Crisis of 2008

I n 2008, Bitcoin rose like a phoenix from the ashes of near Wall Street collapse. From August to October 2008, an unprecedented series of changes occurred: Bitcoin.org was registered, Lehman Brothers filed for the largest bankruptcy in American history, Bank of America bought Merrill Lynch for $50 billion, the U.S. government established the $700 billion Troubled Asset Relief Program (TARP), and Satoshi Nakamoto published a paper that founded Bitcoin and the basis of blockchain technology.[1]

The entwinement of the financial collapse on the one hand and the rise of Bitcoin on the other is hard to ignore. The financial crisis cost the global economy trillions of dollars and burned bridges of trust between financial titans and the public.[2] Meanwhile, Bitcoin provided a system of decentralized trust for value transfer, relying not on the ethics of humankind but on the cold calculation of computers and laying the foundation potentially to obviate the need for much of Wall Street.

WHO IS SATOSHI NAKAMOTO?

Referring to Satoshi as "he" is simply a matter of convenience because to this day no one knows exactly who or even what Satoshi is. He, she, they, or it remains totally anonymous. On a profile page Satoshi created for the P2P Foundation—which he used to communicate with others as he spun up Bitcoin—he wrote that he was a 37-year-old male living in Japan.[3]

3

Yet outside of Japan, fact digging has led people to believe Satoshi resided in the United Kingdom, North America, Central America, South America, or even the Caribbean. People point to his impeccable written English or occasionally British phrases as proof of U.K. residence,[4] while others cite his posting patterns as being indicative of living in geographies in Eastern or Central time zones.[5] A number of phony Satoshis have appeared, too, as the media is all too eager to present a solution to such a juicy puzzle. An Australian, Craig Wright, claimed to be Satoshi in May 2016 and momentarily grabbed the attention of publications such as *The Economist*[6] and *Wired*[7] before being debunked.[8]

Claims of Satoshi's origin now cover five continents, leading us back to the possibility that maybe Satoshi isn't even a single person but rather a group of people. The mastery Satoshi showcased across a wide scope of topics—including cryptography, computer science, economics, and psychology—and the ability to communicate it all fluidly seems to support the hypothesis that Satoshi is more than one person. But who would they be? While the mystery may never be solved, Satoshi most certainly was aware of Wall Street's growing instability.

THE FINANCIAL CRISIS OF 2008

For financial titans, 2008 proved a slowly unfolding nightmare. In March of that year, the first major Wall Street institution—Bear Stearns—acquiesced to its demons. After weathering every type of market for 85 years, Bear Stearns was finally dragged under by a slumping housing market. On March 16, JPMorgan Chase & Co. bought it for $2 a share, about 1 percent of the value of its $170 per share price from a year prior.[9] To catalyze the deal, the Federal Reserve agreed to facilitate the purchase of $29 billion in distressed assets from Bear Stearns.[10] Yet disturbingly, a month after the buyout, John Mack and Lloyd Blankfein, CEOs of Morgan Stanley and Goldman Sachs Group Inc., respectively, told shareholders the housing market crisis was going to be short-lived and nearing a close.[11]

Much of this crisis was born of irresponsible lending, known as *subprime loans*, to Americans who couldn't repay their debts. Historically, when a bank issued a loan, the bank was on the hook for ensuring that the borrower repaid the funds. However, in the case of many subprime loans, once these loans were issued to borrowers, they were then packaged, or *securitized*, into complex instruments known as collateralized mortgage obligations (CMOs). These

CMOs were then sold to other investors, effectively passing on the risk like a hot potato through the financial markets, with purchasers lured by the promise of high returns combined with low risk, due to purported diversification.

What people didn't realize, including Wall Street executives, was how deep and interrelated the risks CMOs posed were. Part of the problem was that CMOs were complex financial instruments supported by outdated financial architecture that blended analog and digital systems. The lack of seamless digital documentation made quantifying the risk and understanding exactly what CMOs were composed of difficult, if not impossible. Furthermore, as these CMOs were spread around the world, global investors were suddenly interconnected in a web of American mortgages.[12] In the summer of 2008, despite the lack of financial transparency but emboldened by access to funds from the Federal Reserve in case of further distress, Richard Fuld Jr., the CEO of Lehman Brothers, eerily claimed, "We can't fail now."[13]

As a storm brewed around unknowing Wall Street executives, Satoshi Nakamoto was busy fleshing out the concept of Bitcoin. On August 18, 2008, Bitcoin.org, the home website for information on Bitcoin, was registered.[14] Whether as an individual or an entity, what's now clear is that Satoshi was designing a technology that if existent would have likely ameliorated the toxic opacity of CMOs. Due to the distributed transparency and immutable audit log of a blockchain, each loan issued and packaged into different CMOs could have been documented on a single blockchain. This would have allowed any purchaser to view a coherent record of CMO ownership and the status of each mortgage within. Unfortunately, in 2008 multiple disparate systems—which were expensive and therefore poorly reconciled—held the system together by digital strings.

On the morning of Wednesday, September 10, 2008, Fuld and other senior management faced a different reality from Fuld's confident summer proclamation. Management struggled to explain to a group of critical analysts $5.3 billion worth of write-downs on "toxic assets" and a quarterly loss of $3.9 billion.[15] The call ended abruptly, and analysts signed off unconvinced of the measures Lehman was taking. The markets had already punished Lehman the day before, dropping its stock price 45 percent, and on Wednesday it dropped another 7 percent.[16]

Two days later, on Friday afternoon, the CEOs of Merrill Lynch, Morgan Stanley, and Goldman Sachs met at the New York Federal Reserve, along with the Federal Reserve Chairman, the U.S. Treasury Secretary, and the president of the New York Federal Reserve. The afternoon's topic was what to do about

Lehman Brothers. It was clear the situation had become critical. Initially it appeared either Barclays or Bank of America would come to the rescue of Lehman Brothers, but that likelihood quickly evaporated.

On Saturday, as the same group met again at the New York Fed, John Thain, Merrill Lynch's CEO, had an unsettling thought. During the briefing on Lehman's situation, he realized his company might only be a few steps from the same catastrophe. "This could be me sitting here next Friday,"[17] he said. Thain quickly moved to find suitors for Merrill, the most promising option being Bank of America, which had already been in talks to buy Lehman. With talks secretly progressing between Merrill Lynch and Bank of America, Lehman Brothers held Barclays as its only suitor hope.

By Sunday, September 14, Barclays was ready to approve a deal to buy Lehman Brothers. Lehman only needed the U.S. or British government to back its trading balances for a couple of days, enough time for Barclays to conduct a shareholder vote for final approval. Neither government was willing to step in, and the likelihood of a deal began to melt. With only a few hours left until Asian markets opened for trading, the U.S. government questioned Lehman on its only remaining option: bankruptcy.

Harvey Miller, a well-regarded bankruptcy lawyer at Weil, Gotshal & Manges, had been working quietly since Thursday night to lay the groundwork for this worst-case bankruptcy scenario. When asked by a senior Fed official if Mr. Miller felt Lehman was ready to file for bankruptcy, he responded: "This will cause financial Armageddon."

If Lehman filed for bankruptcy, financial firms that did business with Lehman would also lose billions, potentially triggering a domino effect of bankruptcy.

Later that evening, Bank of America inked a deal to buy Merrill Lynch for $50 billion, and a couple of hours later, in the early hours of Monday morning, Lehman Brothers filed for Chapter 11 bankruptcy protection, making it the biggest bankruptcy in U.S. history. So came to an end a 164-year-old firm born from a dry-goods store that had evolved into the fourth largest U.S. investment bank. It signaled the end of an era.[18]

Lehman's bankruptcy and Merrill's buyout proved to be only the beginning. On Tuesday, the Federal Reserve Bank of New York was authorized to lend up to $85 billion to the American International Group (AIG), the biggest insurer in America, as the behemoth organization began to teeter.[19] It was mid-September and darker clouds loomed on the horizon for Wall Street and global financial markets.

THE BIRTH OF BITCOIN

Six and a half weeks later, on October 31, 2008, Satoshi released the Bitcoin white paper, which serves as the genesis for every single blockchain implementation deployed today and forevermore. In the concluding paragraph of his foundational paper, Satoshi wrote: "We have proposed a system for electronic transactions without relying on trust."[20]

By the time he released the paper, he had already coded the entire system. In his own words, "I had to write all the code before I could convince myself that I could solve every problem, then I wrote the paper."[21] Based on historical estimates, Satoshi likely started formalizing the Bitcoin concept sometime in late 2006 and started coding it around May 2007. In this same time span, many regulators began to believe that the U.S. housing market was overextended and likely in for a rough ride.[22] It's hard to believe someone with such breadth of knowledge as Satoshi would be working in isolation from what he was witnessing in global financial markets.

The day after publishing his white paper, Satoshi sent an email to "The Cryptography Mailing List" with a link to his paper.[23] The list was composed of subscribers focused on cryptography and its potential applications. Satoshi's email sparked a chain of responses.

On Friday, November 7, 2008, in reply to his increasingly passionate group of followers, he wrote: "You will not find a solution to political problems in cryptography . . . but we can win a major battle in the arms race and gain a new territory of freedom for several years. Governments are good at cutting off the heads of centrally controlled networks like Napster, but pure P2P networks like Gnutella and Tor seem to be holding their own."[24] It's clear from this quote that Satoshi was not creating Bitcoin to slip seamlessly into the existing governmental and financial system, but instead to be an alternative system free of top-down control, governed by the decentralized masses. Such decentralized autonomy was foundational to the early days of the Internet as well, where each node on the network was an autonomous agent that corresponded with other agents through shared protocols.

On November 9, the Bitcoin project was registered on SourceForge.net, a website geared toward facilitating open-source software development. In response to a growing number of inquiries and interest on The Cryptography Mailing List, Satoshi wrote on November 17: "I'll try and hurry up and release the source code as soon as possible to serve as a reference to help clear up all these implementation questions."[25]

Then Satoshi went quiet for a couple months as Wall Street continued to crumble. The Emergency Economic Stabilization Act of 2008 had done little to ameliorate the meltdown that ensued after Lehman's bankruptcy. Passed by Congress and signed by President George W. Bush on October 3, the emergency act had established the $700 billion TARP. As a result of TARP, the U.S. government acquired preferred stock in hundreds of banks as well as massive companies such as AIG, General Motors, and Chrysler. The stock didn't come for free, though. It took $550 billion in investments to stabilize those teetering mammoths.[26]

In the opening moments of Bitcoin's life as a public network, Satoshi made clear he was attuned to the failings of the global financial system. In the first instance of recording information on Bitcoin's blockchain, Satoshi inscribed: "The Times 03/Jan/2009 Chancellor on brink of second bailout of banks,"[27] in reference to an article that appeared in the British publication *The Times* on the U.K.'s likely need to assist more banks in staying afloat.[28] Many years later people would realize that one of the most powerful use cases of blockchain technology was to inscribe immutable and transparent information that could never be wiped from the face of digital history and that was free for all to see. Satoshi's choice first to employ this functionality by inscribing a note about bank bailouts made it clear he was keen on never letting us forget the failings of the 2008 financial crisis.

AN ALTERNATIVE FINANCIAL SYSTEM

Nine days after this poignant inscription, the first ever transaction using bitcoin took place between Satoshi Nakamoto and Hal Finney, an early advocate and Bitcoin developer. Nine months later the first exchange rate would be set for bitcoin, valuing it at eight one-hundredths of a cent per coin, or 1,309 bitcoin to the dollar.[29] A dollar invested then would be worth over $1 million by the start of 2017, underscoring the viral growth that the innovation was poised to enjoy.

Diving deeper into Satoshi's writings around the time, it becomes more apparent that he was fixated on providing an alternative financial system, if not a replacement entirely. After the network had been up and running for over a month, Satoshi wrote of Bitcoin, "It's completely decentralized, with no central server or trusted parties, because everything is based on crypto proof instead of trust . . . I think this is the first time we're trying a decentralized, non-trust-based system."[30]

On December 5, 2010, Satoshi showed an unnervingly human side, pleading that WikiLeaks not accept bitcoin as a means of payment after major credit card networks had blocked users from supporting the site. Satoshi wrote, "No, don't 'bring it on'. The project needs to grow gradually so the software can be strengthened along the way. I make this appeal to WikiLeaks not to try to use Bitcoin. Bitcoin is a small beta community in its infancy. You would not stand to get more than pocket change, and the heat you would bring would likely destroy us at this stage."[31]

Shortly thereafter, Satoshi vanished. Some speculate it was for the good of Bitcoin. After all, being the creator of a technology that has the potential to replace much of the current financial system is bound eventually to invoke the wrath of powerful government and private sector forces. By disappearing into the ether, Satoshi removed the head of Bitcoin, and with it a single point of failure. In his wake stands a network with thousands of access points and millions of users.

Wall Street, on the other hand, suffered from many points of failure. When the dust settled, the U.S. government had spent well beyond the $700 billion initially secured for TARP. In all, $2.5 trillion was injected into the system, not to mention $12.2 trillion committed to reinstall faith in the fidelity of financial institutions.[32]

While Wall Street as we knew it was experiencing an expensive death, Bitcoin's birth cost the world nothing. It was born as an open-source technology and quickly abandoned like a motherless babe in the world. Perhaps, if the global financial system had been healthier, there would have been less of a community to support Bitcoin, which ultimately allowed it to grow into the robust and cantankerous toddler that it currently is.

WELCOME TO THE WORLD THAT BITCOIN CREATED

Since Satoshi disappeared, Bitcoin has unleashed a tidal wave of disruption and rethinking of global financial and technological systems. Countless derivations of Bitcoin have been created—systems such as Ethereum, Litecoin, Monero, and Zcash—all of which rely on blockchain technology, Satoshi's gift to the world. At the same time, many financial and technological incumbents have moved to embrace the technology, creating confusion around all the innovation unfolding and what is most relevant to the innovative investor. The next chapter will involve solidifying understanding of blockchain technology, Bitcoin, bitcoin, cryptoassets, and where the investment opportunities await.

Chapter 2

The Basics of Bitcoin and Blockchain Technology

t's time to crystallize the difference between Bitcoin, Bitcoin's blockchain, bitcoin with a lowercase *b*, blockchain technology, and other related but distinct concepts. At first blush, this space appears jargon heavy, deterring many from even attempting to understand it. In reality, there are only a few foreign concepts, encapsulated in recently invented words, which unfortunately keep people out. Since these words are used frequently when people talk about different applications of Bitcoin or blockchain technology, the space appears impenetrable—but it's not. All that's required is a concerted effort to nail down the key concepts, which then become the mental scaffolding that will support understanding of the many applications of blockchain technology.

Bitcoin with an uppercase *B* refers to the software that facilitates the transfer and custody of bitcoin the currency, which starts with a lowercase *b*.

- Bitcoin equals software.
- bitcoin equals currency.

Much of this book will use Bitcoin (with a capital *B*) as the starting point. Bitcoin is the genesis of the blockchain movement. It is common to compare newly created blockchains with Bitcoin's because Bitcoin's blockchain is the longest standing point of reference. Therefore, understanding the basics of Bitcoin is critical.

However, to truly understand Bitcoin, one has to move beyond thinking of it as some digital Ponzi scheme or shadowy system used by criminals.

Those are stale stories that continue to tumble through the media mill. In July 2016, researchers from the London School of Economics and Political Science, Deutsche Bundesbank (Germany's central bank), and the University of Wisconsin at Madison released the paper "The Evolution of the Bitcoin Economy." Three reputable institutions would not waste their time, nor jeopardize their reputations, on a nefarious currency with no growth potential.

In that paper, the researchers describe an extensive analysis they performed on Bitcoin's blockchain and the transactions therein. Below is a summary of what they found:

> In this paper, we gather together the minimum units of Bitcoin identity (the individual addresses), and group them into approximations of business entities, what we call "super clusters." While these clusters can remain largely anonymous, we are able to ascribe many of them to particular business categories by analyzing some of their specific transaction patterns, as observed during the period from 2009–2015. We are then able to extract and create a map of the network of payment relationships among them, and analyze transaction behavior found in each business category. We conclude by identifying three marked regimes that have evolved as the Bitcoin economy has grown and matured: from an early prototype stage; to a second growth stage populated in large part with "sin" enterprise (i.e., gambling, black markets); to a third stage marked by a sharp progression away from "sin" and toward legitimate enterprises.[1]

Certainly, some of the earliest adopters of Bitcoin were criminals. But the same goes for most revolutionary technologies, as new technologies are often useful tools for those looking to outwit the law. We'll get into the specific risks associated with cryptoassets, including Bitcoin, in a later chapter, but it's clear that the story of bitcoin as a currency has evolved beyond being solely a means of payment for illegal goods and services. Over 100 media articles have jumped at the opportunity to declare bitcoin dead,[2] and each time they have been proven wrong.

When one considers Bitcoin neutrally in the context of a broader theme of technological evolution, it sits in the sweet spot of key technology trends. For example, the world is increasingly real-time, with people connecting in peer-to-peer manners, empowering and connecting individuals regardless of geographic or socioeconomic birth. Bitcoin fits these thematic molds. It allows a global transaction to be settled in an hour as opposed to a couple of days. It operates in a peer-to-peer manner, the same movement that has driven Uber, Airbnb, and LendingClub to be multibillion-dollar companies in their own realms. Bitcoin lets anyone be their own bank, putting control in the hands of a grassroots movement and empowering the globally unbanked.

However, Bitcoin has done something arguably more impressive than Uber, Airbnb, and LendingClub. Those companies decentralized services that were easily understandable and had precedent for being peer-to-peer. Everyone has had a friend drive them to the airport, or stayed with a relative in another country, or borrowed money from their parents. Decentralizing a currency, without a top-down authority, requires coordinated global acceptance of a shared means of payment and store of value.

Currency originally came about to facilitate trade, allowing society to move past barter and the *double coincidence of wants*. It has evolved over time to be more convenient, resulting in its present paper state. Inherently, that paper has little value other than the fact that everyone else thinks it has value and the government requires it be accepted to fulfill financial obligations. In that sense, it is a usefully shared representation of value. The libertarians in the room would say it's a *usefully shared illusion* of value, going back to the idea the paper itself is worth little. Bitcoin is a similarly shared representation of value, except it has no physical manifestation and no top-down authority to protect it. Despite these hurdles, the elegance of the mathematics that allow it to function has also allowed it to grow and store billions in value.

THE INNER WORKINGS OF BITCOIN'S BLOCKCHAIN

Part of the Bitcoin software involves the building of Bitcoin's blockchain, which can be thought of as a digital ledger that keeps track of user balances via debits and credits. In this sense, Bitcoin's blockchain is a database that records the flow of its native currency, bitcoin. What makes this digital ledger special? Bitcoin's blockchain is a distributed, cryptographic, and immutable database that uses proof-of-work to keep the ecosystem in sync. Technobabble? Sure. But impenetrable technobabble? No.

Distributed

Distributed refers to the way in which computers access and maintain Bitcoin's blockchain. Unlike most databases that rigidly control who can access the information within, any computer in the world can access Bitcoin's blockchain. This feature of Bitcoin's blockchain is integral to bitcoin as a global currency. Since anyone anywhere can tap into Bitcoin's blockchain to see the record of debits and credits between different accounts, it creates a system of global trust. Everything is transparent, so everyone is on a level playing field.

WHAT IS CRYPTOGRAPHY?

Initially a scary word, cryptography is the science of secure communication. It involves taking information and scrambling it in such a way that only the intended recipient can understand and use that information for its intended purpose. The process of scrambling the message is encryption, and unscrambling it is decryption, performed through complex mathematical techniques.

Cryptography is the battlefield on which those trying to transmit information securely combat those attempting to decrypt or manipulate the information. More recently, cryptography has evolved to include applications like proving the ownership of information to a broader set of actors—such as public key cryptography—which is a large part of how cryptography is used within Bitcoin.

Encryption techniques have been employed for centuries. Julius Caesar used a simple method of encryption during times of war to inform his generals of his plans. He would send messages using letters that were three letters after the letter they were supposed to represent. For instance, instead of using the letters ABC in his message, he would write them as DEF and his generals would decrypt them to understand his intended message. Understandably, this form of encryption did not remain secure for long.[3]

A more recent example that was the subject of the movie *The Imitation Game* was the effort during World War II of a group of English cryptographers to decode the messages of Nazi Germany, which were encrypted by a coding device called the Enigma machine. Alan Turing, a luminary in machine learning and artificial intelligence, was a major player on the team whose efforts to break the Enigma code ultimately had a debilitating impact on German war strategies and helped to end the war.

Cryptography has become a vital part of our lives. Every time we type in a password, pay with a credit card, or use WhatsApp, we are enjoying the benefits of cryptography. Without cryptography, it would be easy for bad actors to steal sensitive information and use it against us. Cryptography makes sure the information can only be used by those for whom it is intended.

Cryptographic

Every transaction recorded in Bitcoin's blockchain must be cryptographically verified to ensure that people trying to send bitcoin actually own the bitcoin they're trying to send. Cryptography also applies to how groups of transactions are added to Bitcoin's blockchain. Transactions are not added one at a time, but instead in "blocks" that are "chained" together, hence the term blockchain. We will go deeper into the specifics of the process in the proof-of-work section that follows, but for now here's the takeaway: cryptography allows the computers building Bitcoin's blockchain to collaborate in an automated system of mathematical trust. There is no subjectivity as to whether a transaction is confirmed in Bitcoin's blockchain: it's just math. For a deep dive on cryptography, we highly recommend *The Code Book: The Science of Secrecy from Ancient Egypt to Quantum Cryptography* by Simon Singh.

Immutable

The combination of globally *distributed* computers that can *cryptographically* verify transactions and the building of Bitcoin's blockchain leads to an *immutable* database, meaning the computers building Bitcoin's blockchain can only do so in an *append only* fashion. *Append only* means that information can only be added to Bitcoin's blockchain over time but cannot be deleted—an audit trail etched in digital granite. Once information is confirmed in Bitcoin's blockchain, it's permanent and cannot be erased. Immutability is a rare feature in a digital world where things can easily be erased, and it will likely become an increasingly valuable attribute for Bitcoin over time.

Proof-of-Work

While the previous three attributes are valuable, none of them is inherently new. *Proof-of-work* (PoW) ties together the concepts of a *distributed, cryptographic,* and *immutable* database, and is how the distributed computers agree on which group of transactions will be appended to Bitcoin's blockchain next. Put another way, PoW specifically deals with how transactions are grouped in blocks, and how those blocks are chained together, to make Bitcoin's blockchain.

The computers—or miners as they're called—use PoW to compete with one another to get the privilege to add blocks of transactions to Bitcoin's blockchain, which is how transactions are confirmed. Each time miners add a block, they get paid in bitcoin for doing so, which is why they choose to compete in the first place.

Competition for a financial reward is also what keeps Bitcoin's blockchain secure. If any ill-motivated actors wanted to change Bitcoin's blockchain, they would need to compete with all the other miners distributed globally who have in total invested hundreds of millions of dollars into the machinery necessary to perform PoW. The miners compete by searching for the solution to a cryptographic puzzle that will allow them to add a block of transactions to Bitcoin's blockchain.

The solution to this cryptographic puzzle involves combining four variables: the time, a summary of the proposed transactions, the identity of the previous block, and a variable called the *nonce*.

The nonce is a random number that when combined with the other three variables via what is called a cryptographic hash function results in an output that fits a difficult criteria. The difficulty of meeting this criteria is defined by a parameter that is adjusted dynamically so that one miner finds a solution to this mathematical puzzle roughly every 10 minutes. If all of this seems like drinking water out of a fire hose, that's okay—it's that way for everyone at the outset. We'll cover this process in greater detail in Chapter 4, and then go even deeper in Chapter 14.

The most important part of the PoW process is that one of the four variables is the identity of the previous block, which includes when that block was created, its set of transactions, the identity of the block before that, and the block's nonce. If innovative investors keep following this logic, they will realize that this links every single block in Bitcoin's blockchain together. As a result, no information in any past block, even if it was created years ago, can be changed without changing all of the blocks after it. Such a change would be rejected by the distributed set of miners, and this property is what makes Bitcoin's blockchain and the transactions therein immutable.

Miners are economically rewarded for creating a new block with a transaction that grants them newly minted bitcoin, called a coinbase transaction, as well as fees for each transaction. The coinbase transaction is also what slowly releases new bitcoin into the money supply, but more on that later.

A USEFUL ANALOGY FOR BITCOIN'S ECOSYSTEM

To tie everything together using an analogy that will prepare us for a discussion of the applications of blockchain technology in Chapter 3 (see Figure 2.1).

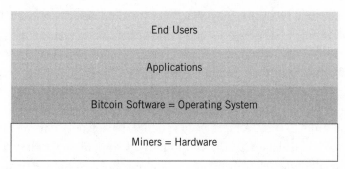

Figure 2.1 ▪ Bitcoin as a stack of hardware, OS, applications, and end users

It's helpful to think of the concepts as a stack of hardware, software, applications, and users in relation to a personal computer.

The miners that build Bitcoin's blockchain with the PoW process are the hardware, just as a MacBook Pro provides the hardware for a personal computer. That hardware runs an operating system (OS); in the case of Bitcoin, the operating system is the open-source software that facilitates everything described earlier. This software is developed by a volunteer group of developers, just as Linux, the operating system that underlies much of the cloud, is maintained by a volunteer group of developers. On top of this hardware and operating system combination are applications, just as Safari is an application that runs on an Apple operating system. The applications interface with the Bitcoin operating system, which pushes and pulls information to and from Bitcoin's blockchain as needed. Lastly, there are the end users that interface with the applications, and someday may have no concept of the hardware or software underneath because all they need to know is how to navigate the applications.

PRIVATE VERSUS PUBLIC BLOCKCHAINS

Broadly, there are two types of entities that can own the hardware supporting blockchains: public and private. The difference between public and private blockchains is similar to that between the Internet and intranets. The Internet is a public resource. Anyone can tap into it; there's no gatekeeper. Intranets, on the other hand, are walled gardens used by companies or consortiums to transmit private information. Public blockchains are analogous to the Internet, whereas private blockchains are like intranets. While both are useful today, there's little debate that the Internet has created orders of magnitude more value than intranets. This is despite vociferous proclamations by incumbents in the 1980s and 1990s that the public Internet could never be trusted. History is on the side of public networks, and while history doesn't repeat, it does often rhyme.[4]

The important distinction boils down to how the entities get access to the network. Remember, a blockchain is created by a distributed system of computers that uses cryptography and a consensus process to keep the members of the community in sync. A blockchain is useless in isolation; one might as well use a centralized database. The community of computers building a blockchain can either be public or private, commonly referred to as permissionless or permissioned.

Public systems are ones like Bitcoin, where anyone with the right hardware and software can connect to the network and access the information therein. There is no bouncer checking IDs at the door. Rather, participation in the network forms an economic equilibrium in which entities will buy more hardware to take part in building Bitcoin's blockchain if they feel they can make money doing so. Other examples of public blockchains include Ethereum, Litecoin, Monero, Zcash, and so on, which will be discussed in more detail in Chapters 4 and 5.

Private systems, on the other hand, employ a bouncer at the door. Only entities that have the proper permissions can become part of the network. These private systems came about after Bitcoin did, when enterprises and businesses realized they liked the utility of Bitcoin's blockchain, but weren't comfortable or legally allowed to be as open with the information propagated among public entities.

These private blockchains have thus far been most widely embraced by the financial services as a means to update IT architecture that hasn't had a major facelift since preparation for the Y2K bug. Within financial services, these private blockchains are largely solutions by incumbents in a fight to remain incumbents. While there is merit to many of these solutions, some claim the greatest revolution has been getting large and secretive entities to work together, sharing information and best practices, which will ultimately lower the cost of services to the end consumer.[5] We believe that over time the implementation of private blockchains will erode the position held by centralized powerhouses because of the tendency toward open networks. In other words, it's a foot in the door for further decentralization and the use of public blockchains.

The potential applications of private blockchains extend far beyond the financial services industry. Banks and other monetary intermediaries have most quickly moved to adopt the technology because the use cases are most obvious for a system that specializes in securing transactions. Beyond the financial services industry, others that are exploring the applications of blockchain technology include the music industry, real estate, insurance, healthcare, networking, polling, supply chains, charities, gun tracking, law enforcement, governments, and more.[6]

Throughout this book, we will focus on public blockchains and their native assets, or what we will define as *cryptoassets*, because we believe this is where the greatest opportunity awaits the innovative investor. Sometimes, cryptoassets have the exact same name as their parent blockchain but with different capitalization. Other times there's a slightly different name for the asset. For example, the native asset of Bitcoin's blockchain is bitcoin, the native asset of Ethereum's blockchain is ether, the native asset of Litecoin's blockchain is litecoin, etc.

Many public blockchains are markedly different from one another. Some members of the early Bitcoin community feel the definition of what makes something a blockchain should be very specific, in particular, that any blockchain must use proof-of-work as the means of consensus. We disagree with that exclusive worldview, as there are many other interesting consensus mechanisms being developed, such as proof-of-stake, proof-of-existence, proof-of-elapsed-time, and so on. Just as machine learning is not just one thing, but composed of the Symbolists, Connectionists, Evolutionaries, Bayesians, and Analogizers, so too can blockchain technology have many flavors. In *The Master Algorithm*,[7] Pedro Domingos hypothesizes that all these camps of machine learning—which at times have been bitter rivals—will one day coalesce. The same will likely be true of blockchain technology. If these distributed databases of value are to be truly transformational, they will have to interoperate and value one another.

THE MANY USES OF THE WORD *BLOCKCHAIN*

Despite increased interest in blockchain technology, confusion remains as to what it specifically means due to imprecision in the use of the term. For example, "a blockchain," "the blockchain," "blockchain," and "blockchain technology" can all refer to different things.

Typically, when people say *the blockchain*, they are referring to *the original*, or Bitcoin's blockchain. At the risk of redundancy but in pursuit of clarity, we will always use "Bitcoin's blockchain" instead of "the blockchain."

On the other hand, terms such as *a blockchain* and *blockchain technology* typically refer to derivatives of the original that now may have nothing to do with Bitcoin. Meanwhile, *blockchain* is normally used to refer to the concept itself, with no particular implementation in mind. It is the most amorphous, so our least favored of the terms.

Chapter 3

"Blockchain, Not Bitcoin?"

I n drawing a line between public and private blockchains, we have entered contentious territory that the innovative investor should understand. The difference between these two types of blockchains and the groups that support them is full of tension, because the two camps have different goals for the technology. At the risk of overgeneralizing, private blockchains are backed by incumbents in their respective industries, while public blockchains are backed by the disruptors.

To round out the context within which the innovative investor approaches cryptoassets, it's important to understand how the world evolved beyond a single blockchain—Bitcoin's blockchain—to include public and private blockchains. Otherwise, investors may be confused when they hear someone claim that Bitcoin is no longer relevant or that it's been displaced. Neither of these claims is true, but it's nonetheless helpful to understand the motivations and rationale behind those that say they are.

BITCOIN'S EARLY YEARS

We left Bitcoin in Chapter 1 with Satoshi pleading on December 5, 2010, for WikiLeaks not to accept bitcoin for donations to its site, because bitcoin was still too young and vulnerable to attack. This was about two years after the birth of Bitcoin's blockchain, during which it had lived a mostly quiet and nerdy life. That was all about to change.

A few months after Satoshi's plea, a software application was released that would make Bitcoin famous. Launched in February 2011, the Silk Road provided a rules-free decentralized marketplace for any product one could imagine, and it used bitcoin as the means of payment. You name it, the Silk Road had it. Gawker put it succinctly in a June 2011 article, "The Underground Website Where You Can Buy Any Drug Imaginable."[1] Clearly, this was one way that Bitcoin developed its dark reputation, though it's important to know that this was not endorsed by Bitcoin and its development team. The Silk Road was simply making use of this new digital and decentralized currency by building an application atop its platform.

The Gawker article led to the first Google search spike in Bitcoin's life, as shown in Figure 3.1, and would drive the price of bitcoin from about $10 to $30 in the span of a week.[2] However, the Gawker article jump paled in comparison to the global Google search volume in March to April 2013, which corresponded with a nearly eightfold increase in price, from roughly $30 to $230 in about a month. The drivers behind this bitcoin demand were more opaque than the Gawker spike, though many point to the bailout of Cyprus and the associated losses that citizens took on their bank account balances as the core driver. Bitcoin received ample interest for being outside of government control, making its holders immune to such events. Bloomberg ran a story on March 25, 2013, with the eye-catching title, "Bitcoin May Be the Global Economy's Last Safe Haven."[3]

While the spring of 2013 was notable, it was a preview for bitcoin's grand opening to global attention. This came six months later, in November 2013,

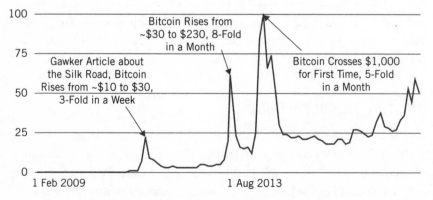

Figure 3.1 ■ Google search spikes for the term "bitcoin"
Source: Annotation of Google Search screenshot

when increased demand for bitcoin in China along with interest from the U.S. Senate on the innovation led to a stratospheric ascent through $1,000 that grabbed international headlines.[4]

THE UTILITY OF GOOGLE SEARCH TRENDS

Google search trends are a useful indicator of what is grabbing mainstream attention. The innovative investor can go to https://trends.google.com/ and explore the patterns of how people are searching for different topics. Google even provides the option to explore search trends by geographical location, giving charts of where interest is spiking, as well as showing what related topics are on the rise. For example, after typing in "bitcoin," investors can look at Google search trends for the last year, or five years, or a custom range, and investigate how Nigeria differs from India. We recommend orienting with this tool even beyond cryptoassets, as it's a fascinating window into the global mesh of minds.

At this point, bitcoin's spike captured the attention of the People's Bank of China, which promptly implemented restrictions on bitcoin's use, declaring it was "not a currency in the real meaning of the word."[5] The China ruling, combined with the FBI's capture of the creator of the Silk Road, Ross Ulbricht,[6] and soon thereafter the collapse of the biggest exchange at the time, Mt. Gox,[7] put many bitcoin investors on edge as to its long-term viability in the face of government and law enforcement crackdowns.[8] Bitcoin's subsequent price descent through all of 2014, bottoming in January 2015, was volatile, prolonged, and dispiriting for many early adopters who had been drawn to the new concept.

While bitcoin's price was declining, its developers plowed forward with improving the protocol and building applications atop it. During that time, conversations about the underlying technology gained momentum, as early Bitcoiners[9] emphasized that Bitcoin was important not only because of the decentralized currency aspect but also because of the architecture that supported it. This emphasis on the technology supporting Bitcoin came about just as a slew of developers and enterprises began to investigate Bitcoin because of the headlines that had grabbed their attention. Clearly, something was going on, and newcomers to the technology were trying to figure out what.

The trifecta of current Bitcoiners defending and explaining the disruptive potential of Bitcoin's technology, bitcoin's price descending dramatically, and newcomers investigating the technology led to a seismic shift in the Bitcoin narrative. Newcomers didn't necessarily see the need for bitcoin in the ways in which they wanted to use blockchain technology, and they felt reaffirmed in their belief by the continued descent of bitcoin's price through 2014. But to Bitcoiners it had always been "bitcoin *and* blockchain." The asset, bitcoin, was what incentivized an ecosystem of players—miners, developers, companies, and users—to secure and build upon Bitcoin's blockchain, delivering means of exchange and store of value services to the world.

Out of this examination of the technology underlying Bitcoin, two movements exploded in the blockchain technology space. One was the proliferation of new cryptoassets that supported new public blockchains, like Ethereum. These new public blockchains offered utility outside the realm of Bitcoin. For example, Ethereum's goal was to serve as a decentralized world computer, whereas Bitcoin aimed to be a decentralized world currency. This diversity has led to tension among players as some of these cryptoassets compete, but this is nothing like the tension that exists between Bitcoin and the second movement.

The second movement that exploded on the scene questioned whether bitcoin, or any cryptoasset, was necessary to get the value out of blockchain technology. It is this second movement that we will investigate further in this chapter, as it's important for the innovative investor to understand why some people will claim bitcoin and other cryptoassets aren't needed to keep their implementations secure and functioning: welcome to the world of private blockchains.

SATOSHI NEVER SAID *BLOCKCHAIN*

The word *blockchain* was not mentioned once in Satoshi's 2008 white paper. It was early Bitcoin companies that popularized the word within what was then a niche community. For example, blockchain.info, a popular Bitcoin wallet service,[10] was launched in August 2011. Satoshi, on the other hand, frequently referred to the system as a "proof-of-work chain." The closest he came to saying blockchain was with phrases such as "blocks are chained" or a "chain of blocks." Since Satoshi only places "proof-of-work" directly before "chain," many early Bitcoiners are adamant that the term blockchain should only be used if it is proof-of-work based. Remember that proof-of-work is a mechanism whereby all the computers building Bitcoin's blockchain remain in sync on how to construct it.

BLOCKCHAIN, NOT BITCOIN

Articles like one from the Bank of England in the third quarter of 2014 argued, "The key innovation of digital currencies is the 'distributed ledger,' which allows a payment system to operate in an entirely decentralized way, without intermediaries such as banks."[11] In emphasizing the technology and not the native asset, the Bank of England left an open question whether the native asset was needed.

At the Inside Bitcoins conference in April 2015,[12] many longtime Bitcoiners commented on how many Wall Street suits were in attendance. While Bitcoin was still king, there were growing whispers of "blockchain not bitcoin," which was heresy to Bitcoiners.

The term *blockchain*, independent of Bitcoin, began to be used more widely in North America in the fall of 2015 when two prominent financial magazines catalyzed awareness of the concept. First, *Bloomberg Markets* published an article titled "Blythe Masters Tells Banks the Blockchain Changes Everything: The banker who helped give the world credit-default swaps wants to upend finance again—this time with the code that powers bitcoin."[13] In emphasizing "the code that powers bitcoin," this article quietly questioned the need for the native asset, instead emphasizing the underlying technology. Masters was a well-known and respected figure in financial services, one that people associated with financial innovation. Her choice to join a little-known firm at the time called Digital Asset Holdings, after having been the head of global commodities at JPMorgan Chase, was reason to believe that blockchain technology was no longer on the fringe of the business world. In the article, a quote from Masters brought everyone to attention: "You should be taking this technology as seriously as you should have been taking the development of the Internet in the early 1990s. It's analogous to email for money."

The October 31, 2015, issue of the *Economist* featured "The Trust Machine" on its front cover, and while the article tipped its hat to Bitcoin, its focus was the more broadly applicable "technology behind bitcoin" and used the term *blockchain* throughout.[14]

The combination of Masters, Bloomberg, and the *Economist* led to a spike in interest in blockchain technology that set off a sustained climb in global Google search volumes for "blockchain" that is still in an upward trend. In the two weeks between October 18 and November 1, 2015, just after Bloomberg and the *Economist* published their articles, global Google search volumes for "blockchain" grew 70 percent (see Figure 3.2).

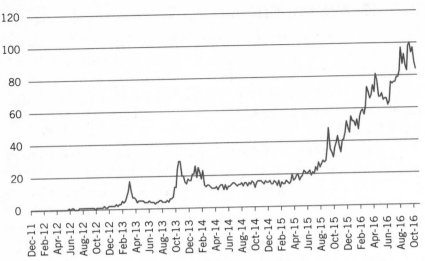

Figure 3.2 ■ The rise in Google Search trends for the term "blockchain"
Data sourced from Google Search Trends

Masters's focus for blockchain technology in financial services is on private blockchains, which are very different from Bitcoin's blockchain. Pivotal to the current conversation, private blockchains don't need native assets. Since access to the network is tightly controlled—largely maintaining security through exclusivity—the role of computers supporting the blockchain is different.[15] Since these computers don't have to worry about attack from the outside— they are operating behind a firewall and collaborating with known entities—it removes the need for a native asset that incentivizes the build-out of a robust network of miners.

A private blockchain is typically used to expedite and make existing processes more efficient, thereby rewarding the entities that have crafted the software and maintain the computers. In other words, the value creation is in the cost savings, and the entities that own the computers enjoy these savings. The entities don't need to get paid in a native asset as reward for their work, as is the case with public blockchains.

On the other hand, for Bitcoin to incentivize a self-selecting group of global volunteers, known as miners, to deploy capital into the mining machines that validate and secure bitcoin transactions, there needs to be a native asset that can be paid out to the miners for their work. The native asset builds out support for the service from the bottom up in a truly decentralized manner. Public blockchains are not so much databases as they are system architectures spawned from the bottom up to orchestrate the creation of globally decentralized digital services. Over time, miner compensation will shift from the issuance of new bitcoin to transaction fees, and if global adoption is great enough, then transaction fees will be sufficient to sustain miners.

The kernel of belief held by many avid proponents of private blockchains is that the native assets themselves (such as bitcoin) are irrelevant; they can be removed from the architecture and the best parts of the technology can remain intact. For the use cases these people are pursuing, that's true. For public blockchains, however, it's not true. Enterprises that have come to explore blockchain technology from the perspective of how they can use it to update their current technology stacks, very much in the form of a database, most often fall into the private blockchain bucket. Many financial services companies are the earliest adopters of this mindset.

Beyond questioning the need for native cryptoassets—which would naturally infuriate communities that very much value their cryptoassets—tensions also exist because public blockchain advocates believe the private blockchain movement bastardizes the ethos of blockchain technology. For example, instead of aiming to decentralize and democratize aspects of the existing financial services, Masters's Digital Asset Holdings aims to assist existing financial services companies in adopting this new technology, thereby helping the incumbents fight back the rebels who seek to disrupt the status quo.

BLOCKCHAINS AS A GENERAL PURPOSE TECHNOLOGY

While we have our beliefs about the most exciting applications of blockchain technology, we don't ascribe to an exclusive world view. Instead, we believe Bitcoin's blockchain is one of the most important blockchains in existence, and that it has given birth to a new general purpose technology that goes beyond Bitcoin.

General purpose technologies are pervasive, eventually affecting all consumers and companies. They improve over time in line with the deflationary progression of technology, and most important, they are a platform upon which future innovations are built. Some of the more famous examples include steam, electricity, internal combustion engines, and information technology.[16] We would add blockchain technology to this list. While such a claim may appear grand to some, that is the scale of the innovation before us.

As a general purpose technology, blockchain technology includes private blockchains that are going to have a profound impact on many industries *and* public blockchains beyond Bitcoin that are growing like gangbusters.

The realm of public blockchains and their native assets is most relevant to the innovative investor, as private blockchains have not yielded an entirely new asset class that is investable to the public.

WHERE IS BLOCKCHAIN TECHNOLOGY IN THE HYPE CYCLE?

By now it will be clear to the innovative investor that the blockchain technology space is still working itself out and will continue to do so for years to come. Captivating technologies have a gravitational pull that brings in new minds with varied perspectives and that will push the boundaries of the technology.

The progression of a new technology, and the way it evolves as it gains mental mindshare, is at the core of Gartner's Hype Cycle for Emerging Technologies (Gartner is a leading technology research and advisory firm),[17] which displays five common stages of technology.[18]

- Innovation Trigger
- Peak of Inflated Expectations
- Trough of Disillusionment
- Slope of Enlightenment
- Plateau of Productivity

First is the Innovation Trigger that brings the technology into the world. While not very visible, just as Bitcoin wasn't visible in the early years of its life, word spreads and expectations grow. Over time the murmurs gain momentum, building into a crescendo that is Gartner's second stage, the Peak of Inflated Expectations. The peak represents the height of confusion around the definition of the original technology, because people often apply it optimistically to everything they see. No technology is a panacea.

As companies sprout to life and attempt to transition ideas into reality, shifting from proof-of-concepts to at-scale implementations, it frequently turns out that implementing a new disruptive technology in the wild is much harder than anticipated. The new technology must integrate with many other systems, often requiring a wide-reaching redesign. It also requires retraining of employees and consumers. These difficulties slowly push the technology into the Trough of Disillusionment, as people lament that this technology will never work or is too difficult to deal with.

When enough people have given up, but the loyal keep working in dedication, the technology begins to rise again, this time not with the irrational exuberance of its early years, but instead with a sustained release of improvements and productivity. Over time the technology matures, ultimately becoming a steady platform in the Plateau of Productivity that provides a base on which to build other technologies.

While it's hard to predict where blockchain technology currently falls on Gartner's Hype Cycle (these things are always easier in retrospect), we would posit that Bitcoin is emerging from the Trough of Disillusionment. At the same time, blockchain technology stripped of native assets (private blockchain) is descending from the Peak of Inflated Expectations, which it reached in the summer of 2016 just before The DAO hack occurred (which we will discuss in detail in Chapter 5).

Cryptoassets beyond bitcoin are at different points between the Innovation Trigger and the Trough of Disillusionment. These differ because they came to life at different points after bitcoin and many are still emerging. Suffice it to say, the promise is great, the tensions are high, and opportunity awaits the innovative investor. Let's now take a tour of the various cryptoassets that currently exist.

Chapter 4

The Taxonomy of Cryptoassets

As we've seen, bitcoin ignited the cryptoasset revolution, and its success has led to the birth of numerous other permissionless (public) blockchains with their own native cryptoassets. We also refer to these as bitcoin's digital siblings. As of March 2017, there were over 800 cryptoassets with a fascinating family tree, accruing to a total network value[1] of over $24 billion.[2] At the time, bitcoin was the largest and most widely transacted of these assets by a wide margin, with a network value of $17 billion, accounting for nearly 70 percent of the total network value of cryptoassets. The next largest cryptoasset by network value was Ethereum's ether at over $4 billion. Yes, the numbers have changed a lot since. Crypto moves fast.

As the investment landscape for cryptoassets continues to grow beyond bitcoin, it's vital for the innovative investor to understand the historical context, categorization, and applicability of these digital siblings, so that potential investment opportunities can be identified. To this end, we aim to provide a historical grounding of who and what led to the creation of many notable cryptoassets. Through this process, we will also introduce more detailed concepts that will go into the innovative investor's toolset when investigating future cryptoassets.

CRYPTOCURRENCIES, CRYPTOCOMMODITIES, AND CRYPTOTOKENS

Historically, cryptoassets have most commonly been referred to as *cryptocurrencies*, which we think confuses new users and constrains the conversation on the future of these assets. We would not classify the majority of cryptoassets as currencies, but rather most are either digital commodities (*cryptocommodities*), provisioning raw digital resources, or digital tokens (*cryptotokens*), provisioning finished digital goods and services.

A currency fulfills three well-defined purposes: to serve as a means of exchange, store of value, and unit of account. However, the form of currency itself often has little inherent value. For example, the paper bills in people's wallets have about as little value as the paper in their printer. Instead, they have the illusion of value, which if shared widely enough by society and endorsed by the government, allows these monetary bills to be used to buy goods and services, to store value for later purchases, and to serve as a metric to price the value of other things.

Meanwhile, commodities are wide-ranging and most commonly thought of as raw material building blocks that serve as inputs into finished products. For example, oil, wheat, and copper are all common commodities. However, to assume that a commodity must be physical ignores the overarching "offline to online" transition occurring in every sector of the economy. In an increasingly digital world, it only makes sense that we have digital commodities, such as compute power, storage capacity, and network bandwidth.

While compute, storage, and bandwidth are not yet widely referred to as commodities, they are building blocks that are arguably just as important as our physical commodities, and when provisioned via a blockchain network, they are most clearly defined as *cryptocommodities*.

Beyond cryptocurrencies and cryptocommodities—and also provisioned via blockchain networks—are "finished-product" digital goods and services like media, social networks, games, and more, which are orchestrated by *cryptotokens*. Just as in the physical world, where currencies and commodities fuel an economy to create finished goods and services, so too in the digital world the infrastructures provided by cryptocurrencies and cryptocommodities are coming together to support the aforementioned finished-product digital goods and services. Cryptotokens are in the earliest stage of development, and will likely be the last to gain traction as they require a robust cryptocurrency and cryptocommodity infrastructure to be built before they can reliably function.

In summation, we believe that a clearer view of this brave new world of blockchain architecture includes *cryptocurrencies, cryptocommodities,* and *cryptotokens,* just as we have had currencies, commodities, and finished goods and services in the preceding centuries. Be it a currency, commodity, or service, blockchain architectures help provision these digital resources in a distributed and market-based manner.

In this chapter, we focus on the most important cryptocurrencies today, including bitcoin, litecoin, ripple, monero, dash, and zcash. The next chapter covers the world of cryptocommodities and cryptotokens, the development of which has been accelerated by the launch of Ethereum and its value proposition as a decentralized world computer. Besides its status as the number two cryptoasset by network value, Ethereum has also spawned many other cryptoassets that creatively utilize its network.

While we cannot possibly cover all the cryptoassets, we will focus on those we believe will help the innovative investor gain the broadest perspective. To those entrepreneurs and developers who've created assets that we're unable to cover here, we apologize. Many amazing projects were created in the process of writing the book, and if we tried to incorporate them all the book would never have been finished. To that end, we've included a listing in the resources section to enable access to information on other cryptoassets.

WHY *CRYPTO*?

Sometimes the word *crypto* makes people shudder, perhaps because they associate it with illicit activity, but that's a mental bias that is important to overcome. Crypto is simply a tip of the hat to and a shortening of the key technology underlying these systems: cryptography. As discussed in Chapter 2, cryptography is the science of securely transmitting data so that only intended recipients can make use of it. Cryptography is used to ensure that cryptoassets are transferred to the intended recipients securely. Given our digital world and the increasing prevalence of hacks, the secure transmission of resources is paramount, and cryptoassets have such security in spades.

THE EVER-EVOLVING NATURE OF CURRENCIES

The pursuit of a decentralized, private, and digital currency predates bitcoin by decades. Bitcoin and its digital siblings are just part of a broader evolution of currencies that has taken place over centuries. At their inception, currencies were a solution to ease the impreciseness of barter trade, and for centuries metal coins with material value served as the currencies of choice. Fiat currency was an innovation beyond metal coins, as it was much easier to transport, but the entirety of its value relied upon the government's stamp of approval and mandate of legal tender. We believe that currency void of any physical representation is the next phase of the evolution, and in our Internet-tethered world an inevitable one.

As innovations underlying the Internet gained steam, so too did the realization that we would need a secure form of digital payment. One of Bitcoin's most famous ancestors was pioneered by a company called DigiCash, led by David Chaum, who remains one of the most famous cryptographers in crypto-asset history. In 1993, prior to Marc Andressen founding Netscape, Chaum invented the digital payment system called ecash. This allowed secure and anonymous payments across the Internet, no matter the amount.[3]

Clearly, Chaum's timing could not have been better given the tech boom that followed through the mid- to late-1990s, and his company, DigiCash, had several opportunities for growth, any of which might have made it a household name. However, while Chaum was widely regarded as a technical genius, as a businessperson he left much to be desired. Bill Gates approached Chaum about integrating ecash into Windows 95, which would have immediately given it global distribution, but Chaum refused what was rumored to be a $100 million offer. Similarly, Netscape made initial inquiries about a relationship, but management was quickly turned off by Chaum's attitude. In 1996, Visa wanted to invest $40 million into the company but were dissuaded when Chaum demanded $75 million (if these reports are correct, it's clear that the potential price for Chaum's creation was dropping).[4]

If all had gone well, DigiCash's ecash would have been integrated into all our web browsers at the ground floor, serving as the global Internet payment mechanism and potentially removing the need for credit cards in online payments. Sadly, mismanagement ultimately ran DigiCash into the ground, and in 1998 it declared bankruptcy. While DigiCash failed to become a household name, some players will resurface in our story, such as Nick Szabo, the father of "smart contracts," and Zooko Wilcox, the founder of Zcash, both of whom worked at DigiCash for a time.[5]

Other attempts were made at digital currencies, payment systems, or stores of value after ecash, like e-gold and Karma. The former ran into trouble with the FBI for serving a criminal element,[6] while the latter never gained mainstream adoption.[7] The pursuit of a new form of Internet money drew the attention of present day tech-titans such as Peter Thiel and Elon Musk, both of whom had a hand in founding PayPal. Except for Karma, the problem with all these attempts at digital money was that they weren't purely decentralized— one way or another they relied on a centralized entity, and that presented the opportunity for corruption and weak points for attack.

THE MIRACLE OF BITCOIN

One of the most miraculous aspects of bitcoin is how it bootstrapped support in a decentralized manner. The importance, and difficulty, of being the first currency to do so cannot be emphasized enough. Until people understand how bitcoin works, they often argue that it has no value as currency because, unlike what they're used to, you can't see it, touch it, or smell it.

Paper currency has value because it is mutually agreed upon by members of society that it has value. It's much easier for society to agree to this with a government involved. Getting a global society to agree that something has value and can be used as a currency without government support and without a physical form is one of the most significant accomplishments in monetary history.

When bitcoin was launched, it had zero value in the sense that it could be used to purchase nothing. The earliest adopters and supporters subjectively valued bitcoin because it was a fascinating computer science and game theory experiment. As the utility of Bitcoin's blockchain proved itself a reliable facilitator of Money-over-Internet-Protocol (MoIP),[8] use cases began to be built using bitcoin, some of which now include facilitating e-commerce, remittances, and international business-to-business payments.

Concurrent with the early development of use cases, investors started to speculate on what future use cases would look like and how much bitcoin those use cases would require. Together, the combination of current use cases and investors buying bitcoin based on the expectation for even greater future use cases creates market demand for bitcoin. How much is a buyer willing to pay for something (the bid), and how much is a seller willing to receive to part with that item (the ask)? As with any market, where the bid and ask meet is where the price is set.

Mathematically Metered Supply

One of the keys to supporting bitcoin's value was its issuance model. Recall from Chapter 2 that miners—the people running the computers building Bitcoin's blockchain—are paid each time they append a block of transactions. They are paid in new bitcoin created by a *coinbase transaction* that is included in each block.[9] For the first four years of Bitcoin's life, a coinbase transaction would issue 50 bitcoin to the lucky miner. The difficulty of this proof-of-work process was recalibrated automatically every two weeks with the goal of keeping the amount of time between blocks at an average of 10 minutes.[10] In other words, 50 new bitcoin were released every 10 minutes, and the degree of difficulty was increased or decreased by the Bitcoin software to keep that output time frame intact.

In the first year of bitcoin running, 300 bitcoin were released per hour (60 minutes, 10 minutes per block, 50 bitcoin released per block), 7,200 bitcoin per day, and 2.6 million bitcoin per year.

Based on our evolutionary past, a key driver for humans to recognize something as valuable is its scarcity. Satoshi knew that he couldn't issue bitcoin at a rate of 2.6 million per year forever, because it would end up with no scarcity value. Therefore, he decided that every 210,000 blocks—which at one block per 10 minutes takes four years—his program would cut in half the amount of bitcoin issued in coinbase transactions.[11] This event is known as a "block reward halving" or "halving" for short.

On November 28, 2012, the first halving of the block reward from 50 bitcoin to 25 bitcoin happened, and the second halving from 25 bitcoin to 12.5 bitcoin occurred on July 9, 2016. The third will happen four years from that date, in July 2020.[12] Thus far, this has made bitcoin's supply schedule look somewhat linear, as shown in Figure 4.1.

However, when we step back and take a longer-term perspective, bitcoin's supply trajectory looks anything but linear (see Figure 4.2). In fact, by the end of the 2020s it will approach a horizontal asymptote, with annual supply inflation less than 0.5 percent. In other words, Satoshi rewarded early adopters with the most new bitcoin to get sufficient support, and in so doing created a big enough base of monetary liquidity for the network to use. He understood that if bitcoin was a success over time its dollar value would increase, and therefore he could decrease the rate of issuance while still rewarding its supporters.

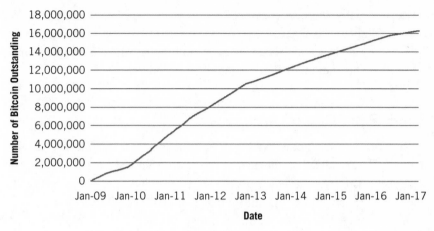

Figure 4.1 ■ Bitcoin's supply schedule (short-term view)
Data sourced from Blockchain.info

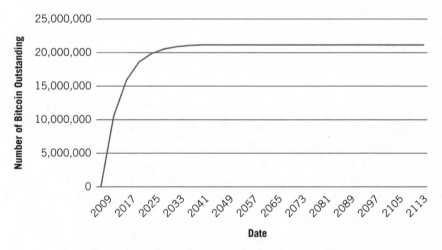

Figure 4.2 ■ Bitcoin's supply schedule (long-term view)

Long term, the thinking is that bitcoin will become so entrenched within the global economy that new bitcoin will not need to be issued to continue to gain support. At that point, miners will be compensated for processing transactions and securing the network through fees on high transaction volumes.

It's common to hear that bitcoin supply will max out at 21 million units by 2140. This is a function of continuing to divide the units of supply released by a factor of two every four years. As of January 1, 2017, already 76.6 percent of bitcoin's supply had been brought into existence,[13] and by the time the next block reward halving happens in 2020, 87.5 percent of the bitcoin ever to be minted will be in existence. A few years after 2100, we will reach a supply of 20,999,999 bitcoin, which is effectively 21 million. It is bitcoin's scarce supply schedule that makes many think of it as digital gold.[14]

THE BIRTH OF ALTCOINS

Within a couple years of launching, it had become clear that bitcoin was the first fully decentralized cryptocurrency to gain significant adoption, but there were some aspects with which people were not fully satisfied. For example, bitcoin's 10-minute block time meant that, depending on when a consumer hit send, it could take up to 10 minutes, sometimes more, for the transaction to be appended to Bitcoin's blockchain.

Often this delay was more of an issue for the merchant than the consumer, as the merchants needed to know they were getting paid before they could release a good or service. Others worried about bitcoin's hash function in the proof-of-work process, because hardware was being created that specialized in this hash function and would lead to increased centralization of the mining network. For a decentralized currency, increased centralization of the machines that processed its transactions was concerning. Fortunately, Bitcoin's protocol is open-source software, which meant developers could download the entirety of its source code and tweak the aspects they felt most needed fixing. When the updated software was ready, the developers released it in a manner similar to how Bitcoin was originally released. The new software operated similarly to Bitcoin, but required its own set of developers to maintain it, miners to provide the hardware, and a separate blockchain to keep track of the debits and credits of the new native asset.

Through this combination of open-source software and ingenious programmers, many other cryptocurrencies have been brought into existence. Those that are only slight modifications of Bitcoin are often referred to as *altcoins*.

BITCOIN'S FIRST DIGITAL SIBLING

Namecoin[15] was the first significant fork away from Bitcoin. Interestingly, it was less about creating a new currency and more about utilizing the immutable nature of the blockchain, a use case we'll address more in the next chapter. A website created with Namecoin comes with the .bit domain (as opposed to the .com domain) and provides security and censorship resistance to those sites registered with it.[16]

Namecoin grew out of an idea on the Bitcointalk forum in 2010 that focused on BitDNS (DNS stands for domain naming service, which handles all web addresses).[17] In 2013, a service called NameID was released that uses the Namecoin blockchain to enable the creation of and access to websites that have a Namecoin identity.

Namecoin acts as its own DNS service, and provides users with more control and privacy. As opposed to the typical way in which websites are registered through a government controlled service such as ICANN, a Namecoin site is registered through a service that exists on each computer on the Namecoin network. This improves security, privacy, and speed. To gain a .bit site, one must have namecoin to do so, thus the need for the native asset.

Litecoin

While a handful of altcoins were released through 2011, Litecoin was the first that would retain significant value to this day. The cryptocurrency was developed by Charlie Lee, an MIT graduate who was a software engineer at Google. When Lee learned of Bitcoin he quickly understood its power, leading him to mine bitcoin before trying to create his own variants. After the unsuccessful launch of Fairbrix in September 2011, Lee tried again with Litecoin in October.[18]

Litecoin aimed to improve upon Bitcoin in two ways. For one, Litecoin's block times were 2.5 minutes, four times faster than Bitcoin's, which would be important for merchants needing faster confirmation of consumer's payments.

Second, Litecoin used a different hash function in the proof-of-work process—also known as a block hashing algorithm—which tried to make the mining process more accessible to hobbyists. To put it into perspective, in the early years of Bitcoin mining, people used central processing units (CPUs), which are the core chips in personal computers, effectively forcing the computers to be used solely for mining purposes. In 2010, people after greater efficiency began using the graphic card (GPU) of an existing computer for the mining process.

Many, including Lee, anticipated a shift to yet more dedicated and specialized mining devices called ASICs (application-specific integrated circuits). ASICs required custom manufacturing and specifically designed computers.

As a result, Lee correctly foresaw that bitcoin mining would ramp beyond the reach of hobbyist miners and their homegrown PCs.

Lee wanted a coin that retained its peer-to-peer roots and allowed users to be miners without the need for specialized and expensive mining units. Litecoin accomplished this by using a block hashing algorithm called *scrypt*, which is memory intensive and harder for specialized chips like ASICs to gain a significant edge upon.

Other than these two tweaks, much of Litecoin remained similar to Bitcoin.

The innovative investor will have realized, however, that if blocks are issued four times as fast as bitcoin, then the total amount of litecoin released will be four times greater than that of bitcoin. This is exactly the case, as litecoin will converge upon a fixed 84 million units, whereas bitcoin will converge upon a quarter of that, at 21 million units.[19] Lee tweaked the halving characteristics, too, so that a halving occurs at 840,000 blocks, as opposed to bitcoin's 210,000. As Figure 4.3 shows, this puts litecoin on a similar yet larger supply trajectory than bitcoin. Notably, the annual rates of supply inflation are exactly the same for the number of years the cryptocurrency is from launch.

It's important to realize that if bitcoin and litecoin are both being used in similar size markets and therefore have the same size network values, a unit of litecoin will be one-fourth as valuable as a unit of bitcoin because there are four times as many units outstanding. This is an important lesson, because all cryptocurrencies differ in their supply schedules, and thus the direct price of each cryptoasset should not be compared if trying to ascertain the appreciation potential of the asset.

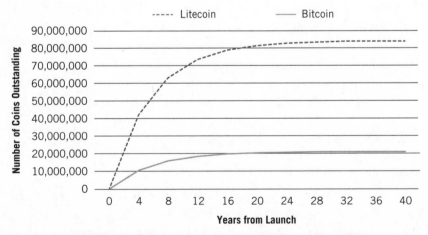

Figure 4.3 ■ The comparative supply schedules of Litecoin and Bitcoin

Litecoin's network is often used as a testing ground for Bitcoin software updates, given that Litecoin is nimbler than Bitcoin because it stores a fraction of the monetary value. It has also been used as the basis for other cryptoassets. At the start of 2017, litecoin was the fourth largest cryptoasset in terms of network value.[20]

Ripple

Ripple is a cryptocurrency created in 2004 by Ryan Fugger, a web developer from Vancouver, British Columbia. Work on the project actually began before Satoshi and Bitcoin,[21] when Fugger was searching for a way to allow communities to create a system of money out of chains of trust. For example, if Alice trusts Bob, and Bob trusts Candace, and Candace trusts Dave, then Alice can send money to Dave (whom she doesn't know) by first transferring value to Bob, who transfers that same value to Candace, who takes that value and deposits it in Dave's account. Using this concept, payments can "ripple" through the network via these chains of trust. Fugger called this concept RipplePay.com.

While Fugger's RipplePay did grow to 4,000 users,[22] it did not catch fire the way bitcoin did. In August 2012, Fugger was approached by the notable financial innovators Chris Larsen and Jed McCaleb. Larsen had founded E-Loan—one of the first companies to provide access to mortgage loans online—and Prosper, a leader in the peer-to-peer lending space.[23] McCaleb was the founder of Mt. Gox, the biggest bitcoin and cryptocurrency exchange in the world at that time.

Fugger announced the partnership: "I believe if anyone can develop the Ripple concept on a global scale, they can. Their system is based on a Bitcoin-style blockchain, much as we have discussed here over the last few years as an interesting possibility, but with a novel miner-less consensus mechanism that allows transactions to be confirmed near instantaneously."

Interestingly, in November 2012, this statement from Fugger appeared on Bitcoin's dedicated communication channel, a Reddit-style site called bitcoin-talk, under the heading, "Is Ripple a Bitcoin Killer or Complementer? Founder of Mt. Gox will launch Ripple."[24] This would not be the last time someone asked if a new upstart would be a Bitcoin-killer.

Not long after, in the spring of 2013, it was announced that Larsen and McCaleb's company that developed the Ripple protocol, then called OpenCoin, had secured funding from prestigious venture capitalists, including Andreessen Horowitz.[25] This was a notable development—a sign of approval of the viability of cryptocurrency from one of the most revered venture capital firms in the world. OpenCoin would later rebrand as Ripple Labs.

Ripple's technology did several new things. It didn't have miners. Instead it utilized a consensus algorithm that relied on trusted subnetworks to keep a broader decentralized network of validators in sync. That's enough to confuse any innovative investor. What's important to recognize is that Ripple's consensus algorithm relied on trust of some sort, which was vastly different from Bitcoin's proof-of-work design that assumed anyone could be a bad actor.

Ripple also used trusted gateways as endpoints for users, and these gateways could take deposits and redeem debts in all kinds of asset pairs, including traditional fiat currency. This built off Fugger's original chains of trust but on a global multi-asset scale. Routing a transaction through Ripple's network was like sending a packet of information through the Internet, pinging amid connected servers.

If users didn't want to rely on these gateways, Ripple also had its own native cryptocurrency, called ripples, and commonly referred to as XRP. XRP could be used to connect two endpoints in the Ripple network that didn't have a connection of trust.

But this is where the Ripple team ran into contentious territory, even if the concept was born of good intentions. Since there was no mining process, there was no means to distribute XRP. Instead, 100 billion units of XRP were created and initially held by Ripple Labs (at that time, OpenCoin). While there was, and still is, intent to distribute all this XRP to seed use, as of writing the majority of XRP is still under the control of Ripple Labs.

This has led to mistrust of the Ripple protocol from much of the cryptocurrency community. Vitalik Buterin, who would later go on to create Ethereum, wrote in February 2013 for *Bitcoin Magazine*: "Because of the monetary distribution, OpenCoin may well face an uphill battle convincing the community that they can be trusted."[26]

Pricing services like CoinCap don't list XRP's total available supply as the 100 billion that Ripple lists[27] but only include the ripple that has thus far been distributed to the public, which is just north of 37 billion units.[28] A word to the wise for the innovative investor: with a new cryptocurrency, it's always important to understand how it's being distributed and to whom (we'll discuss this further in Chapter 12). If the core community feels the distribution is unfair, that may forever plague the growth of the cryptocurrency.

Ripple has since pivoted away from being a transaction mechanism for the common person and instead now "enables banks to send real-time international payments across networks."[29] This focus plays to Ripple's strengths, as it aims to be a speedy payment system that rethinks correspondent banking but still requires some trust, for which banks are well suited.

Dogecoin

A somewhat comic cryptocurrency addition arrived on December 8, 2013 (less than two weeks after bitcoin hit a notable high of $1,242) in the form of dogecoin.[30] Dogecoin was launched as a riff off Doge the dog, which *Wired* magazine had pegged as 2013's meme[31] of the year.[32] Doge was a Shiba Inu dog whose image with captions of an internal monologue went viral.

Dogecoin was initially floated as a joke. Jackson Palmer, who worked in the marketing department of Adobe's Sydney offices and was a cryptocurrency enthusiast, sent the tweet: "Investing in Dogecoin, pretty sure it's the next big thing."[33] After a positive reception to what was intended as a joke, he bought the domain, Dogecoin.com. Jackson's activity caught the attention of Billy Markus, a Portland, Oregon-based developer who aspired to launch a new cryptoasset. In Markus's own words: "The first thing I said was, 'This is so funny.' Then I said, 'I should just make this coin.'"[34]

Markus used Litecoin's code to derive Dogecoin, thereby making it one more degree of separation removed from Bitcoin. If Litecoin was a child of Bitcoin, then Dogecoin was a grandchild of Bitcoin. A notable variation was that Dogecoin planned to issue a much larger amount of dogecoin than bitcoin or even litecoin. The plan was to have 100 billion dogecoin in circulation after 1.5 years.[35] That would equal nearly 5,000 times more coins than bitcoin when it reaches its maximum supply.

Markus's team later chose to issue roughly 5 billion coins each year, and this created a vastly different supply schedule from those of the deflationary bitcoin and litecoin. Dogecoin mostly gained traction amongst Internet tippers. The supply schedule has kept the value of a single dogecoin to a fraction of a cent, which is suited to its intended use case. As Palmer stated in an early interview:

> It's not taking itself as seriously, it's not being used by people worrying about whether they'll become rich . . . It's something to share for thanks or kudos.[36]

Palmer's marketing expertise was another feature that differentiated Dogecoin from other cryptocurrencies at the time. The Dogecoin community raised $50,000 via Dogecoin to send the Jamaican bobsled team to the Olympics; raised another $55,000 via Dogecoin to sponsor a NASCAR driver who raced with the Dogecoin logo at the Talladega Speedway; and raised money to support clean water projects in Kenya via Doge4Water, making the donation via a Twitter-based tip service.[37]

While Dogecoin may have been launched as a joke, its association with a wildly popular Internet meme, its lighthearted origins, and its savvy focus on slick marketing led to a quick rise, and its network value grew to $70 million only seven weeks after launch.[38] But that did not last long. As of March 2017, its network value had dipped to slightly above $20 million.

This bizarre merger of a cryptoasset and pop culture is not surprising considering 2013 was the year that the price of bitcoin ranged from $13 in January to over $1,000 in early December.[39] The power and enthusiasm of Dogecoin's user community shouldn't be dismissed, even if we encourage the innovative investor to do ample due diligence on it as an investment. While Dogecoin had its flaws, it continues to exist and has taught the cryptocurrency space valuable lessons about gathering community support in an Internet era.

AURORACOIN: ICELAND'S NATIONAL CRYPTOCURRENCY?

Much like the anonymous Satoshi, Auroracoin's creator also had a fictitious name: Baldur Friggjar Óðinsson. Baldur created Auroracoin based on Litecoin's code and decided to "air-drop" the cryptocurrency to Icelanders with the intent of providing 50 percent of all auroracoin in existence to residents. The hope was that such a distribution would jump-start national use of the cryptocurrency.

A key to Baldur's plan was his access to the government's national identification system, which led speculators to believe mistakenly that Auroracoin was sponsored by the Icelandic government. In anticipation of the airdrop, speculators bid Auroracoin's network value over $1 billion.[40]

By the time the airdrop began on March 25, 2014, speculators had sobered somewhat, and Auroracoin was hovering just over a $100 million network value. By the end of the month, it would be below $20 million, as citizens receiving Auroracoin moved to sell it on exchanges to turn a profit.[41] Along with the drop in price was a loss of confidence and enthusiasm for the new cryptocurrency. Few, if any, retailers were willing to accept auroracoin, and it was soon considered a "failed experiment."[42] Some also saw it as a scam perpetrated by its creator. To this day, auroracoin takes the cake as the crypto-currency with the grandest plan for widespread usage throughout one country. It continues to exist, with a handful of Icelandic developers working to revive the concept and the technology. In 2016, ads began to appear through-out Iceland's capital city of Reykjavik heralding the return of Auroracoin. As a result, beers in Iceland were being purchased for auroracoin,[43] and many other retail establishments began to utilize the cryptocurrency. Then a scandal hit and the prime minister was forced to resign because of his involvement with the Panama Papers.[44] This led to the growth in popularity of a political party known as the Pirate Party, which had a favorable view on cryptocurrencies.[45] Suddenly there was speculation[46] that Iceland could revisit the potential for Auroracoin and its role as a national cryptocurrency.[47] As acceptance grows and politics change, it will be interesting to watch what happens next for the Icelandic cryptocurrency.

Auroracoin is a cautionary tale for both investors and developers. What began as a seemingly powerful and compelling use case for a cryptoasset suf-fered from its inability to provide value to the audience it sought to impact. Icelanders were given a cryptocurrency with little education and means to use it. Unsurprisingly, the value of the asset collapsed and most considered it dead. Nevertheless, cryptocurrencies rarely die entirely, and Auroracoin may have interesting times ahead if its developer team can figure out a way forward.

THE RACE FOR PRIVACY: DASH, MONERO, AND ZCASH

While Litecoin, Ripple, and Dogecoin all added elements to the mix of what it meant to be a cryptocurrency, they did not provide the privacy that many early Bitcoin advocates yearned for. It is a common misconception, even for Bitcoin, that it is an anonymous payment network. Bitcoin transactions are *pseudony-mous*, and since every transaction can be seen by any third party, there is a wealth of information for anyone who would like to pinpoint who the partici-pants are. Inarguably, someone who wants to use a currency for illegal activity is better off using cash than bitcoin. With every transaction, bitcoin leaves an indelible digital mark in Bitcoin's blockchain.

Currently, three notable cryptocurrencies put privacy and anonymity first. In order of launch, they are Dash, Monero, and Zcash. All three pursue this value proposition differently. Monero is likely the most relevant to the innovative investor, with a sustained record of operations, solid cryptography, and a sound issuance model. While Dash has merits, it has contested origins. Meanwhile, Zcash uses some of the most bleeding-edge cryptography in the world, but it is one of the youngest cryptoassets in the book and suitable only for the most experienced cryptoasset investors.

Monero and Its Predecessor, Bytecoin

Monero is a descendent of a lesser-known cryptocurrency called Bytecoin. Bytecoin was crafted quite differently from Bitcoin, using technology known as CryptoNote. Similar to Litecoin's scrypt, CryptoNote's block hashing algorithm aims to avoid the specialization and therefore centralization of the miners supporting the network by requiring an order of operations that favors general purpose chips like the CPUs found in PCs.[48] Beyond a focus on more egalitarian proof-of-work, CryptoNote provided untraceable payments, unlinkable transactions, and blockchain analysis resistance.[49] Adam Back is considered the inspiration for Satoshi's proof-of-work algorithm and is president of Blockstream, one of the most important companies in the Bitcoin space. In March 2014, he tweeted about CryptoNote, saying it was one of the few ideas in the cryptocurrency space outside of Bitcoin that held a "defensible rationale for existence."[50]

Some may ask why Monero stole the show from Bytecoin. Bytecoin's blockchain and the issuance of its currency, bytecoin, started on July 4, 2012, but it did not become widely known until almost two years later when an announcement for it appeared on bitcointalk.org on March 12, 2014.[51] People were intrigued but confused about why the Bytecoin team had taken two years to make it public. Some argued that it was because the developers wanted to make sure the technology was soundly running before drawing more attention. Others argued that something more insidious was at play, called a *premine* (pronounced "pre-mine").

Bytecoin planned to issue 184.46 billion bytecoin via the mining process, but by the time it was made publicly known, 150 billion bytecoin were already in existence, more than 80 percent of the total supply.[52] A classic premine, Bytecoin had quietly released a large amount of the coins in a manner that disadvantaged the broader community. Bitcoin and the permissionless blockchain movement was founded on principles of egalitarian transparency, so premines are widely frowned upon. While they still occur, many are scams that the innovative investor should be wary of. A key differentiator between a scam and good intent is the communication and rationale of the developer team behind the issuance model.

On April 8, 2014, the bitcointalk.org user named "eizh," who would later become a Monero developer, made the comment, "I'm surprised someone hasn't started a clone for a fairer distribution and active development."[53] On April 9, 2014, only a month after the public announcement of Bytecoin, an involved user known as "thankful_for_today," made a post to bitcointalk.org titled "Bitmonero—a new coin based on CryptoNote technology—launched," with the intent to launch mining in nine days.[54] BitMonero was quickly renamed Monero and often referred to as XMR.

The most defining feature of Monero is its use of *ring signatures*, a cryptographic technology that had been evolving since 1991.[55] Monero's ring signatures are best explained in the context of Bitcoin. In Bitcoin, to create a transaction, a known individual signs off on the balance of bitcoin he or she is trying to send. In Monero, a group of individuals signs off on a transaction creating a ring signature, but only one in the group owns that monero. The CryptoNote website puts it succinctly:

> In the case of ring signatures, we have a group of individuals, each with their own secret and public key. The statement proved by ring signatures is that the signer of a given message is a member of the group. The main distinction with the ordinary digital signature schemes is that the signer needs a single secret key, but a verifier cannot establish the exact identity of the signer. Therefore, if you encounter a ring signature with the public keys of Alice, Bob and Carol, you can only claim that one of these individuals was the signer but you will not be able to pinpoint him or her.[56]

While many are suspicious of such privacy, it should be noted that it has tremendous benefits for fungibility. Fungibility refers to the fact that any unit of currency is as valuable as another unit of equal denomination. A danger for bitcoin, especially for balances known to have been used for illegal activity, is that if an exchange or other service blacklists that balance, then that balance becomes illiquid and arguably less valuable than other balances of bitcoin. While subtle, losing fungibility could be the demise of a digital and distributed currency, hurting the value of all units, not just the ones used for illegal activity. Fortunately, this is one problem that Monero does not have to deal with.

Monero's supply schedule is a hybrid of Litecoin and Dogecoin. For monero, a new block is appended to its blockchain every 2 minutes, similar to Litecoin's 2.5 minutes. Like Dogecoin, however, it will have a small degree of inflation for its entire life beginning in May 2022, when 0.3 monero will be released every minute, totaling 157,680 monero every year. At that time, there will be 18.1 million units of monero outstanding, so inflation in that first year will be only 0.87 percent.[57] As we head further into the future, that inflation decreases as the base of monero outstanding increases. Interestingly, in 2040 there will be nearly equivalent units of bitcoin and monero outstanding, and in the period of 2019 to 2027, Monero's rate of supply inflation will be lower than Bitcoin's, but in all other periods the opposite is true.[58]

Expectedly, Monero's ability to create privacy in transactions was a technological breakthrough that was recognized within the cryptoasset community and the markets. By the end of 2016, Monero had the fifth largest network value of any cryptocurrency and was the top performing digital currency in 2016, with a price increase over the year of 2,760 percent. This clearly demonstrates the level of interest in privacy protecting cryptocurrency. Some of that interest, no doubt, comes from less than savory sources.

Dash

Another cryptocurrency targeting privacy and fungibility is Dash. It launched its blockchain a few months before Monero, on January 19, 2014. Its lead developer, Evan Duffield, created Dash by forking the Bitcoin protocol and implementing a coin focused on privacy and speedy settlement of transactions. The Dash white paper that Duffield coauthored outlined his intent:

> A crypto-currency based on Bitcoin, the work of Satoshi Nakamoto, with various improvements such as a two-tier incentivized network, known as the Masternode network. Included are other improvements such as Darksend, for increasing fungibility and InstantX which allows instant transaction confirmation without a centralized authority.[59]

Dash, however, got off to a rocky start. Instead of a premine, it had what is called an *instamine*, where 1.9 million coins were created in the first 24 hours. Considering that three years later, in January 2017, there were just north of 7 million coins, this was a significant error that drastically benefited the computers that supported the Dash network in the first 24 hours, notably Duffield himself.

Duffield reasonably pleaded best intentions, arguing that, "I was working a very challenging day job while working on Dash in the first couple weeks. So I was putting out fires every night, keeping tabs on Dash during the day (while getting yelled at by my boss when he caught me a couple times)."[60]

From our perspective, if there is a major disruption or error in the launch of a cryptocurrency that significantly skews its distribution, then that cryptocurrency should be relaunched. In fact, Duffield easily could have relaunched Dash, especially considering the network was only days old when the instamine began to be widely talked about, but he chose not to. It wouldn't have been unusual to relaunch, given that other cryptocurrencies have done so via the forking of original code. The creators of Monero, for example, specifically chose not to continue building off Bytecoin because the premine distribution had been perceived as unfair.

Zcash

The most interest in a cryptocurrency in 2016 was generated by a new cryptoasset called Zcash. The Bitcoin and blockchain community has always been excited by new developments in anonymity and privacy, but Zcash took that excitement to a new level, which upon issuance drove the price through the roof. Like bitcoin's, zcash's issuance model was ethical. However, when bitcoin launched from zero units outstanding, next to no one knew about it. When zcash launched from zero units outstanding, it seemed like the entire cryptouniverse knew about it, and everyone wanted some.

The scarcity in initial supply combined with the hype pushed the price of zcash to astronomical levels. It quickly reached $1,000 per coin, which at the time was even higher than the price of bitcoin. At one point on Poloniex, a popular cryptoasset exchange, the price reached 1 zcash for 3,299 bitcoin, or almost $2 million at the time.[61] However, by the end of 2016, the hysteria had dissipated and zcash was trading in a stable range of $45 to $50.

The Zcash team is led by Zooko Wilcox, whom we have mentioned prior as an early employee at David Chaum's DigiCash. Through his time at DigiCash and longstanding involvement in cryptography and cryptoassets, Zooko has become one of the most respected members in the community. A key innovation of Zcash is the use of a type of zero-knowledge proof, referred to as zk-SNARKs, which allow transactions to be sent between parties without any information being revealed other than the validity of the transaction. While it is still early days for Zcash, we are of the belief that the ethics and technology chops of Zooko and his team are top-tier, implying that good things lie in wait for this budding cryptocurrency.

• • •

By the end of 2016, the price of bitcoin had reached a level just below $1,000 (which it broke in January 2017), and there were over 800 cryptoassets in a market that totaled over $17 billion. At that time, the top assets in order of network value were: Bitcoin, Ethereum, Ripple, Litecoin, Monero, Ethereum Classic, and Dash.

The innovative investor may note from this list that Ethereum follows Bitcoin. Its story is one that includes brilliant developers, a wider definition of blockchain technology, and one of the largest hacks on a cryptoasset ecosystem to date. In the next chapter, we'll look at the creation of Ethereum and the significant impact it has and will have on the future of cryptoassets.

Chapter 5

Cryptocommodities and Cryptotokens

ryptocurrencies are a powerful vertical of cryptoassets, but as we laid
out in the start of the last chapter, only one of three. The other two,
cryptocommodities and cryptotokens, are a rapidly growing segment
of this budding new asset class. First, let's look at cryptocommodities.

In some ways, cryptocommodities are more tangible in value than cryptocurrencies. For example, the largest cryptocommodity, Ethereum, is a decentralized world computer upon which globally accessible and uncensored
applications can be built. It's easy to appreciate the value of using such a computer, and therefore Ethereum provides a digitally tangible resource. Paying
to use Ethereum's world computer—also known as the Ethereum Virtual
Machine (EVM)—is reminiscent of when schools and libraries had shared
computers that students could use. One person could sit down and use a computer for a while before moving on, and then another person would come and
use it.

The Ethereum Virtual Machine operates somewhat similarly to a shared
computer, except it is global in scale and more than one user can operate it
at a time. Just as everyone can see Bitcoin transactions from anywhere in the
world, anyone can see Ethereum's programs running from anywhere in the
world. While this chapter will dive deep into Ethereum as a cryptocommodity,
there are many other budding cryptocommodities, provisioning decentralized

resources like cloud storage, bandwidth, transcoding, proxy re-encryption, and so on.

THE IDEA BEHIND ETHEREUM'S WORLD COMPUTER

The founding team of Ethereum and its native asset, ether, weren't the first to dream of globally distributed computer programs, or what are commonly referred to as smart contracts. For example, Nick Szabo, who was also one of Chaum's disciples at DigiCash (Chapter 4), had been talking about smart contracts and digital property since the early 1990s. In 1996, he published an article in the magazine *Extropy* on the topic entitled "Smart Contracts."[1]

Smart contracts are critical to understand but have a misleading name. The first thing people think of when they hear smart contracts is legal documents that think for themselves, which misses the mark by a wide margin. We believe smart contracts are better thought of as *conditional transactions* because they refer to logic written in code that has "IF this, THEN that" conditions. For example, it can easily be programmed in a smart contract that "IF Jack misses his flight and IF it was the airline's fault, THEN the airline pays him the cost of the flight." A vending machine is another commonly used example of a smart contract: "IF the user puts in enough money and IF the user types in the right code, THEN the user gets Doritos." These conditions can become much more complex, creating conditional waterfalls depending on the process being programmed and the variables that need to be met.

While Szabo had the early vision for smart contracts, the Ethereum team would be the first to create a mainstream and attention-grabbing platform to execute smart contracts in a decentralized manner. At the core of the team is Vitalik Buterin, who many regard as Ethereum's Satoshi.

Buterin was born in Russia but grew up in Canada. He had the good fortune of a freethinking father,[2] who in February 2011 introduced 17-year-old Buterin to Satoshi's work and Bitcoin.[3] Bitcoin had only been functioning for two years at that point, and no major alternative was in existence. It would not be until October of that year that Charlie Lee would release Litecoin.

It wasn't long before Buterin fell down the Bitcoin rabbit hole. He quickly became one of the first well-known journalists pioneering the world of cryptoassets, even cofounding *Bitcoin Magazine*, which remains one of the best deep dive sites for technical analysis of blockchain architectures. While writing articles that merged sophisticated technical information with an enthusiastic and optimistic style, he used his mathematical prowess to consider how to improve on the technology. He was, after all, a Bronze medal winner at the International Olympiad in Informatics[4] at the age of 18 and could reportedly add three-digit numbers in his head at twice the speed of the average human being.[5]

To that end, Buterin tinkered with a number of Bitcoin projects that would inform his future work on Ethereum. In a blog post titled "Ethereum: Now Going Public," he started with a tip of the hat to Bitcoin:

> I first wrote the initial draft of the Ethereum whitepaper on a cold day in San Francisco in November, as a culmination of months of thought and often frustrating work into an area that we have come to call "cryptocurrency 2.0"—in short, using the Bitcoin blockchain for more than just money. In the months leading up to the development of Ethereum, I had the privilege to work closely with several projects attempting to implement colored coins, smart property, and various types of decentralized exchange.[6]

The projects Buterin references in the last sentence approached the transaction of bitcoin using Bitcoin's blockchain more abstractly. As we have already learned, transacting bitcoin involves the transmission of information that results in a debit or credit of a balance of bitcoin in a user's address.

In his blog post, Buterin mentions *colored coins*. These involve the marking of an address in Bitcoin with information beyond just the balance of bitcoin in that address. Further identifiers could also be appended to the address, such as information that represented ownership of a house. In transferring that bitcoin in that address to another address, so too went the marker of information about house ownership.

In this sense, by sending bitcoin, the transaction also signified the transaction of property rights to a house. There are several regulatory authorities that need to recognize that transfer for this example to become an everyday reality, but the point is to show how all kinds of value can be transmitted through Bitcoin's blockchain.

COUNTERPARTY: SMART CONTRACTS ON BITCOIN

Counterparty is a cryptocommodity that runs atop Bitcoin, and was launched in January 2014 with a similar intent as Ethereum. It has a fixed supply of

2.6 million units of its native asset, XCP, which were all created upon launch. As described on Counterparty's website, "Counterparty enables anyone to write specific digital agreements, or programs known as Smart Contracts, and execute them on the Bitcoin blockchain."[7] Since Bitcoin allows for small amounts of data to be transmitted in transactions and stored on Bitcoin's blockchain, it becomes the system of record for Counterparty's more flexible functionality. Since Counterparty relies upon Bitcoin, it does not have its own mining ecosystem.

The reason Bitcoin developers haven't added extra functionality and flexibility directly into its software is that they have prioritized security over complexity. The more complex transactions become, the more vectors there are to exploit and attack these transactions, which can affect the network as a whole. With a focus on being a decentralized global currency, Bitcoin developers have decided bitcoin transactions don't need all the bells and whistles. Instead, other developers can either find ways to build atop Bitcoin's limited functionality, turning to Bitcoin's blockchain as a system of record and means of security (e.g., Counterparty), or build an entirely different blockchain system (e.g., Ethereum).

Many were working on building this decentralized future on top of Bitcoin, but it wasn't easy. The flexibility in adding identifiers to addresses and creating different kinds of transactions was purposefully restricted in Bitcoin for the sake of scalability and security. Bitcoin, after all, was still an experiment. A decentralized currency was enough of a holy grail for Satoshi, and he didn't have to swallow the whole world in one bite. But Buterin wasn't satisfied with Bitcoin as it was and had wide-ranging aspirations for improvements. He wanted a system that was more flexible and that behaved more like a computer and less like a calculator for debits and credits of bitcoin balances.

Although he invented Ethereum in 2013, Buterin formally announced it in January 2014 at the North American Bitcoin Conference,[8] where he was surrounded by eager reporters, many of whom had been his colleagues in months past. By that time, he had already garnered the support of over 15 developers and dozens in the community outreach team.[9]

In Ethereum's white paper that initially described its inner workings, Buterin's team made no qualms about their aspirations:

What is more interesting about Ethereum, however, is that the Ethereum protocol moves far beyond just currency. Protocols around decentralized file storage, decentralized computation and decentralized prediction markets, among dozens of other such concepts, have the potential to substantially increase the efficiency of the computational industry, and provide a massive boost to other peer-to-peer protocols by adding for the first time an economic layer.[10]

Importantly, Buterin did not intend for Ethereum and its native asset, ether, to be a minor variation on Bitcoin's codebase. This distinguished Ethereum from many of the altcoins that came before it.

By having no affiliation with "coin" in its name, Ethereum was moving beyond the idea of currency into the realm of *cryptocommodities*. While Bitcoin is mostly used to send monetary value between people, Ethereum could be used to send information between programs. It would do so by building a decentralized world computer with a *Turing complete programming language*.[11] Developers could write programs, or applications, that would run on top of this decentralized world computer. Just as Apple builds the hardware and operating system that allows developers to build applications on top, Ethereum was promising to do the same in a distributed and global system. Ether, the native unit, would come into play as follows:

Ether is a necessary element—a fuel—for operating the distributed application platform Ethereum. It is a form of payment made by the clients of the platform to the machines executing the requested operations. To put it another way, ether is the incentive ensuring that developers write quality applications (wasteful code costs more), and that the network remains healthy (people are compensated for their contributed resources).[12]

Miners of Ethereum would be processing transactions that could transfer not just ether but also information among programs. Just as Bitcoin miners were compensated for supporting the network by earning bitcoin, so too would Ethereum miners by earning ether, and the process would be supported by a similar proof-of-work consensus mechanism.

GETTING ETHEREUM OFF THE GROUND

Buterin understood that building a system from the ground up required a significant amount of work, and his announcement in January 2014 involved the collaboration of a community of more than 15 developers and dozens of community members that had already bought into the idea. Satoshi's announcement of Bitcoin, in contrast, had involved a quiet mailing of the white paper to a relatively unknown mailing list composed mainly of academics and hardcore cryptographers. The ensuing development of the Bitcoin software before launch mostly involved just two people, Satoshi and Hal Finney.[13]

Buterin also knew that while Ethereum could run on ether, the people who designed it couldn't, and Ethereum was still over a year away from being ready for release. So he found funding through the prestigious Thiel Fellowship. Billionaire Peter Thiel, who cofounded PayPal and was Facebook's first outside investor, created the Thiel Fellowship to reward talented individuals who leave the traditional path of college and pursue immediate ways to make an impact in the world. Winners might conduct scientific research, create a startup, or find other ways to improve society and the world. Thiel Fellowship's carefully chosen visionaries receive $100,000 over the course of two years, and the award has been considered more competitive than gaining acceptance to the world's best universities. In June 2014, Buterin received the Thiel Fellowship[14] as a 20-year-old dropping out of the University of Waterloo to pursue his interest in Ethereum on a full-time basis.

While Buterin may go down as one of Thiel's greatest investments, Thiel wasn't alone in recognizing the potential of Ethereum. In 2014, Buterin was given the World Technology Award in Information Technology Software,[15] alongside influential names such as Elon Musk in the Energy category and Walter Isaacson in Media & Journalism.

While the Thiel Fellowship was an indication of what was to come for Buterin, $100,000 wasn't enough to sustain his team. To that end, from July 23, 2014, to September 2, 2014, they staged a 42-day presale of ether, the cryptocommodity underlying the Ethereum network.[16]

Ether was sold at a range of 1,337 to 2,000 ether per bitcoin, with 2,000 ether per bitcoin on offer for the first two weeks of the presale and then declining linearly toward 1,337 ether per bitcoin in the latter half of the sale, creating momentum by incentivizing people to buy in at the beginning. Overseeing the legal and financial nuances around this sale was the newly created Ethereum Foundation headquartered in Zug, Switzerland.[17]

Ethereum's fund-raising effort was not only innovative and timely, it was also record-breaking. The public invested 31,591 bitcoin, worth $18,439,086, for a total of 60,102,216 ether—an implied rate of $0.31 per ether. At the time, it was the largest single crowdfunding effort.[18] Some thought it outrageous that the team supporting a blockchain architecture could raise $18 million without a functioning product, as this was clearly different from Bitcoin's process.

Venture capital investors (VCs) often invest in ideas and development teams, having faith they will work their way toward success. Ethereum democratized that process beyond VCs. For perspective on the price of ether in this crowdsale, consider that at the start of April 2017, ether was worth $50 per unit, implying returns over 160x in under three years.[19] Just over 9,000 people bought ether during the presale, placing the average initial investment at $2,000, which has since grown to over $320,000.[20]

According to the Ethereum white paper, the profits from this sale would be "used entirely to pay salaries and bounties to developers, and invested into various for-profit and non-profit projects in the Ethereum and cryptocurrency ecosystem." In addition to the 60 million ether sold to the public, roughly 6 million was created to compensate early contributors to Ethereum, and another 6 million for long-term reserves of the Ethereum Foundation.

The extra allocation of 12 million ether for the early contributors and Ethereum Foundation has proved problematic for Ethereum over time, as some feel it represented double dipping. In our view, with 15 talented developers involved prior to the public sale, 6 million ether translated to just north of $100,000 per developer at the presale rate, which is reasonable given the market rate of such software developers.

That said, the allocation of capital into founders' pockets is an important aspect of crowdsales. Called a "founder's reward," the key distinction between understandable and a red flag is that the founders should be focused on building and growing the network, not fattening their pockets at the expense of investors. In our opinion, the Ethereum developers were not fattening their pockets, they were putting food on the table. Their modest allocation is a far cry from the antics that some cryptoasset creators have attempted since.

Following the presale, it was a year of development before the Ethereum network went live. During this time, the Ethereum team stayed in close touch with its burgeoning community, releasing proof-of-concepts for the community to evaluate, organizing conferences, funding projects based on Ethereum, and writing frequent blog updates.[21] Perhaps taking note from Dogecoin, the Ethereum team understood the importance of the community in bootstrapping support for its decentralized system. Although blockchain architectures are cold code, they are warm social networks.

With the money they raised, the Ethereum team was also able to test the network before launch in a way that Satoshi and his small group of supporters were not able to. Starting at the end of 2014 and for the first half of 2015, the Ethereum Foundation encouraged battle testing of its network, both in a grassroots bug bounty program and in formal security audits that involved professional third-party software security firms.[22] The innovative investor should take note of this battle-testing practice, which we also saw with Zcash, as it is an indicator of how seriously core developers take security in their decentralized architectures.

ETHEREUM AS A PLATFORM FOR dAPPS

Ethereum's network with its underlying blockchain went live on July 30, 2015. While much development energy had gone into creating the Ethereum software, this was the first time that miners could get involved because there was finally a blockchain for them to support. Prior to this launch, Ethereum was quite literally suspended in the ether. Now, Ethereum's decentralization platform was open for business, serving as the hardware and software base for decentralized applications (dApps). These dApps can be thought of as complex smart contracts, and could be created by developers independent of the core Ethereum team, providing leverage to the reach of the technology.

To explain how a dApp works, we'll use an example from the company Etherisc, which created a dApp for flight insurance to a well-known Ethereum conference. This flight insurance was purchased by 31 of the attendees.[23] Figure 5.1 shows a simplified diagram. Using Ethereum, developers can mimic insurance pools with strings of conditional transactions. Open sourcing this process and running it on top of Ethereum's world computer allows everyday investors to put their capital in an insurance pool to earn returns from the purchasers of insurance premiums that are looking for coverage from certain events. Everyone trusts the system because it runs in the open and is automated by code.

WELCOME TO THE AGE OF dAPPS AND CRYPTOTOKENS

Since the launch of Ethereum, a near endless stream of dApps have been released to run on it, many of which have their own native unit. We refer to

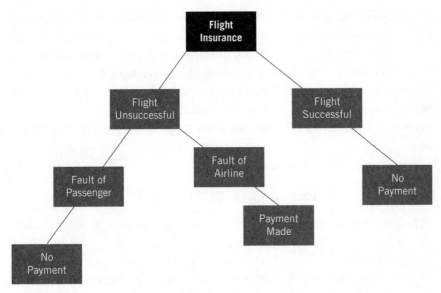

Figure 5.1 ■ Hypothetical dApp-based flight insurance

many of these dApp native units as cryptotokens, while others refer to them as *appcoins*. A dApp with its own native cryptotoken will use ether as a crypto-commodity to pay the Ethereum network to process certain dApp transactions. While many dApps use a cryptotoken, the native units of some dApps should be classified as a cryptocommodity layered on top of Ethereum, like Golem, which aims to be a supercomputer for compute intensive problems. The difference boils down to whether a raw digital resource is being provisioned (cryptocommodity) or if the dApp is providing a consumer-facing finished digital good or service (cryptotoken).

Most cryptotokens are not supported by their own blockchain. Often these cryptotokens operate within applications that are built on a cryptocommodity's blockchain, such as Ethereum. To continue with the Apple analogy: applications in Apple's App Store don't have to build their own operating systems, they run on Apple's operating system. Due to Ethereum's wild success, other decentralized world computers have popped up, such as Dfinity, Lisk, Rootstock, Tezos, Waves, and more that can support their own dApps. Just as many altcoins tried to improve upon Bitcoin, these platforms are cryptocommodities that aim to improve upon Ethereum's design, thereby attracting their own dApps and associated cryptotokens.

A full list of Ethereum dApps can be seen and explored here: http://dapps .ethercasts.com/. The code of many can be investigated in full here: https://live

.ether.camp/contracts. We will look at the most (in)famous of the dApps thus far, as it will inform the innovative investor on all future dApps and potential cryptotoken investments. We should note that dApp development and the associated native units has been one of the fastest moving areas in the cryptoasset space, as we watched new ones come out each week during the writing of this book. Thus, the curious reader should take time after this chapter to further explore them as we are only scratching the tip of the iceberg in this section.

THE RISE AND (HARD) FALL OF THE DAO

Standing for decentralized autonomous organization, The DAO was a complex dApp that programmed a decentralized venture capital fund to run on Ethereum. Holders of The DAO would be able to vote on what projects they wanted to support, and if developers raised enough funding from The DAO holders, they would receive the funds necessary to build their projects. Over time, investors in these projects would be rewarded through dividends or appreciation of the service provided.

The vision of a decentralized autonomous organization like The DAO is somewhat like autonomous vehicles—whereas humans used to have to drive cars, the cars increasingly can drive themselves. Similarly, whereas humans used to be needed for all aspects of business processes, often in manual paper pushing, approval, orchestration, and so on, a decentralized autonomous organization can codify much of those processes so that the company better drives itself. As exciting as the concept was, The DAO was nearly Ethereum's undoing.

The creators of The DAO implemented a crowdfunding effort. Theirs surpassed the amount raised by Ethereum by nearly an order of magnitude, setting the record for the largest amount ever raised in this manner: over $168 million.[24] The crowdfunding required that investments be made with ether, and because of this, by the end of the crowdfunding period The DAO team held 11.5 million ether, or 15 percent of all the ether created to that point.

While enthusiasm and interest in The DAO was clear, some developers were concerned it was not ready for prime time. A paper published by a group of computer scientists who examined the workings of The DAO expressed concern that there were major security vulnerabilities that threatened its pending release on Ethereum's network. "The current implementation can enable attacks with severe consequences," explained Dino Mark, Vlad Zamfir, and Emin Gün Sirer.[25]

Subsequently, there was a call for a moratorium on activity around The DAO until the issues were satisfactorily addressed.[26] However, the call went unheeded and on May 28, 2016, the day after the crowdsale was completed, tokens in The DAO (DAOs)—which were received in exchange for the ether invested at the crowdfunding—began trading on exchanges.

Less than three weeks later, on June 17, 2016, a major hack on The DAO was conducted that gained control of 3.6 million ether, one-third of the amount that had been committed to the project. The hack had nothing to do with an exchange, as had been the case with Mt. Gox and other widely publicized Bitcoin-related hacks. Instead, the flaw existed in the software of The DAO. This software was hosted on Ethereum's blockchain, for all eyes to see, and it needed to be flawless.[27] However, as critics had pointed out, the code was far from perfect. Given the scale of assets The DAO had raised, there was significant incentive for a hacker to break in. As a result, the world's largest crowdfunding effort and a major showcase for the capabilities of Ethereum became a bust.

Buterin and those involved with The DAO and Ethereum immediately began to address the hack. The situation was problematic, however, because Ethereum was a decentralized world computer that provided the platform for dApps to run on. However, it did not promise to audit and endorse each application. Similarly, while Apple may screen the apps that go into its App Store, it doesn't claim responsibility for their inner workings. Core Ethereum developers were helping The DAO team. This was analogous to Apple engineers helping to fix a flailing app.

None of the options to correct the situation were particularly palatable. The primary solution was to release a software update to Ethereum that would remove the funds from the hacker's account within The DAO, returning them to the rightful shareholders. Known as a "hard fork," Ethereum's blockchain would be slightly modified to allow for the investors in the project to have their funds returned. Stephen Tual, founder and COO of Slock.it, the main company behind The DAO, explained the fix as follows, "In summary, a hard fork will retrieve all stolen funds from the attacker. If you have purchased DAO tokens, you will be transferred to a smart contract where you can only retrieve funds. Since no money in The DAO was ever spent, nothing was lost."[28]

However, a hard fork would run counter to what many in the Bitcoin and Ethereum communities felt was the power of a decentralized ledger. Forcefully removing funds from an account violated the concept of immutability. This was exacerbated by the fact that a centralized set of players was making the decision. Many complained of moral hazard, and that this would set a precedent for the U.S. government or other powerful entities to come in someday and demand the same of Ethereum for their own interests. It was a tough decision for all involved, including Buterin, who while not directly on The DAO developer team, was an administrator.

With an understanding of both sides of the debate, Buterin supported the decision to hard fork because of his view that Ethereum was still in a development stage and that a lesson such as this would help shape the technology going forward. "I don't think the way things are done right now are precedent-setting," he said.[29] In the end, Buterin and much of the Ethereum team used their own technical skills to aggressively correct the situation that The DAO had created.[30]

A hard fork doesn't come without risks, and unfortunately, Ethereum would pay a dear price for its decision to help The DAO. While hard forks are often used to upgrade a blockchain architecture, they are typically employed in situations where the community agrees entirely on the beneficial updates to the architecture. Ethereum's situation was different, as many in the community opposed a hard fork. Contentious hard forks are dangerous, because when new software updates are released for a blockchain in the form of a hard fork, there are then two different operating systems. While the two operating systems share a common ancestor, and therein a common record of transactions, once the hard fork occurs, the two operating systems split, and so too do their blockchains, each with separate native units. While some people think, "Great, I've just doubled my money," a hard fork can often crash the value of the native units on the two separate blockchains, as people worry about an ongoing schism within a divided community (see Figure 5.2). With two separate blockchains, miners, developers, and companies building applications, users must decide which blockchain and its inherent operating system to support. While many initially claimed the hard fork a success for Ethereum, a few big traders started to buy up as much of the native asset on the lesser supported chain as possible.

On July 23, 2016, cryptoasset exchange Poloniex listed this newly branded network, called Ethereum Classic, with its own native ether classic (ETC).[31] Once a widely used exchange like Poloniex listed ETC, an open market was created for the asset, and people quickly started to speculate on its value. This drew more miners to support Ethereum Classic's blockchain, which continues to exist to this day and as of writing tends to stick near 5 percent the network value of Ethereum.[32]

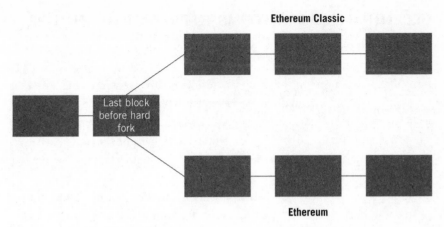

Figure 5.2 ■ The forking of Ethereum as a result of The DAO's bug

The site for Ethereum Classic defines the cryptoasset as "a continuation of the original Ethereum blockchain—the classic version preserving untampered history; free from external interference and subjective tampering of transactions."[33]

While The DAO may have been a disaster, the concept of a decentralized autonomous organization is generalizable past this single instance. The innovative investor should expect to see similar concepts coming to market over the years with their own cryptotokens and should know that not all DAOs or dApps with cryptotokens are similarly shaky.

For example, a fully functional decentralized insurance company, Airbnb, or Uber all hold great promise, and developer teams are working on similar use cases. One can think of an Airbnb or Uber as a middleman, connecting the consumer and provider of a service, and then taking a 20 to 30 percent fee for doing so. While many merchants understandably complain about credit card fees of 2 to 3 percent, the "platform fees" of Airbnb, Uber, and similar platform services are borderline egregious. Many of the cryptotoken systems that are imitating such platforms plan to take a fee that is an order of magnitude less, using underlying blockchain architectures to facilitate the decentralized transfer of value and services. Many of these systems have their own cryptotokens and will run on Ethereum or a similar platform. However, some will be much better constructed than others, and it is unlikely that Ethereum, or platforms like it, will help dApps in future debacles.

DECENTRALIZED PLATFORMS TO PREDICT THE FUTURE

One of the more interesting dApps in development uses Ethereum's blockchain to facilitate prediction markets. The company Augur seeks to provide a platform that allows users to wager on the results of any event, creating a market for people to test their predictions.[34] Hence the term "prediction market." For instance, if someone had sought to predict whether Donald Trump or Hillary Clinton would win the 2016 U.S. presidential election, he or she could have used Augur to create a prediction market and wager against others on the outcome (if the service had been up and running at the time).

Augur uses a cryptotoken, which it calls Reputation (REP), to incentivize people to report on the outcomes of events truthfully. These reporters are different from the people wagering on the outcome of events. The problem with a decentralized prediction market is that there's no centralized authority on the outcome of events. Augur uses REP to reward people who report truthfully and penalize those who lie. Augur explains it as follows:

> Those who hold Reputation are expected to report accurately on the outcome of randomly selected events within Augur every few weeks. If holders fail to report accurately on the outcome of an event, or attempt to be dishonest—the Augur system redistributes the bad reporter's Reputation to those who have reported accurately during the same reporting cycle.[35]

Augur conducted its own crowdfunding effort in 2015, selling 80 percent of a fixed supply of 11 million REP. In so doing, it raised over $5 million to fund the creation of the platform. Brian Armstrong, CEO of Coinbase, which is one of the largest companies in the cryptoasset sector, has called it an "awesome project with huge potential."[36] Even Vitalik Buterin acknowledged its potential when he called it an "Uber for knowledge."[37]

Augur is one of the clearest uses of cryptotokens, and its potential success could set the stage for even more implementations of crypotokens in the future. A similar prediction market system, Gnosis, held a crowdsale in April 2017 raising money at an implied valuation north of $300 million.

A GROWING WEB OF CRYPTOCOMMODITIES AND CRYPTOTOKENS

While Ethereum has a robust community building on it, several similar platforms have taken note of its success. The aforementioned Dfinity, Lisk,

Rootstock, Tezos, and Waves as of writing all are at different stages of development, between pre-crowdsale to already operating in the wild, and offer their own variations of a decentralized world computer.

Rootstock, similar to Counterparty, intends to run on Bitcoin. Rootstock is led by Sergio Lerner, who specialized in IT security for much of his life, and when he first came to Bitcoin audited many aspects of the code. He now leads a team that is basically building Ethereum on Bitcoin, and the system will be compatible with all dApps that run on Ethereum. Just as Ethereum has ether, Rootstock will have its own native currency called RSK.

While some posit that Rootstock will be a significant competitor to Ethereum,[38] we think the two will coexist and provide healthy redundancy. Having two or more widely recognized decentralized world computers to run on will make dApps more resilient to disruptions. If one network is experiencing severe trouble, then a dApp can replicate its state on another similar platform, and from then on process all transactions through that platform. While the transition would likely induce harrowing market volatility, such optionality means that dApps are not beholden to the platforms they build upon.

Lastly, at the risk of confusing the innovative investor, we should add that a dApp may use many cryptocommodities simultaneously, but for different infrastructural purposes. For example, a dApp may use a decentralized cloud storage system like Filecoin to store large amounts of data, and another cryptocommodity for anonymized bandwidth, in addition to using Ethereum to process certain operations.

For such bleeding-edge platforms, it is most important for the innovative investor to keep track of developer mindshare and miner support. Both are vital to the long-term growth and survival of these platforms. Developers will quickly iterate and fix bugs, while miners will provide the hardware and resources necessary to computationally secure the platform. Since these are decentralized systems operating in the wild, they need to move fast and be properly secured. Only then will other developers build dApps on them.

Now that the innovative investor has an understanding of *what* these assets are, we want to move into *why* that investor should consider placing them in his or her investment portfolio. Although cryptoassets are creating a rapidly evolving and somewhat complex future, investment tenets that have stood the test of time still apply. Returning to the fundamentals of investment theory will allow innovative investors to properly position their overarching portfolio to take advantage of the growth of cryptoassets responsibly.

Part II

WHY

Chapter 6

The Importance of Portfolio Management and Alternative Assets

(Jack) was a columnist at MarketWatch.com in August 2013, when I made the logical leap to add bitcoin to my portfolio. While initially born of curiosity, my interest in bitcoin had grown more mature and serious with each passing month. As a writer focused on retirement, I decided that I could only recommend the asset to others if I had the courage to put it in my own retirement portfolio.

Not only did I decide to invest in bitcoin, I decided to place the entirety of that year's allocation for my Simplified Employee Pension (SEP) plan into bitcoin. When I announced what I had done in my article "Do Bitcoins Belong in your Retirement Portfolio?,"[1] it created a stir online and in the financial planning community. My writing over the years had consistently discussed the need to remain prudent when making investment decisions, rationally building portfolios that balanced risks and returns.

A balanced approach to investing grew from my experience as a financial consultant. I come from a background of not only working within companies in the financial community, but also from nearly a decade of working directly with regular investors who are trying to accomplish their financial goals and objectives. I have sat around hundreds of kitchen tables with my clients and near-clients, explaining my belief that their personal dreams of retirement or sending their children to college could be accomplished by following a discipline of saving and proper asset allocation. I believe in the power of building a prudent portfolio based upon the needs and risks of each individual client.

To some, my decision to invest in bitcoin flew in the face of my own advice. I may have managed portfolios in a prudent manner for myself and others, but my interest in new technologies in the past made me no stranger to criticism. During the dot-com days, I made (and lost) a sizeable amount of money investing in companies that flew high in terms of valuation only to crash on the shores of reality as they were little more than business facades. Was I chasing a similar crash-and-burn scenario with bitcoin? Even my technologically and investment savvy son, Eric, initially criticized me about bitcoin. "They have these things called dollar bills, Dad. Stick to using those."[2]

However, I saw real potential in the virtual currency. Over the months I spent evaluating it, I analyzed bitcoin the same way I analyzed every other asset I added to my own or a client's portfolio, just as I had done over the last 30 years. I carefully considered and quantified bitcoin's market behavior (using the tools that follow), so I knew what beast I was dealing with. I ruminated on the percentage of my portfolio I could responsibly allocate to it, with the overarching goal of sensible asset allocation among stocks, bonds, and alternative assets. Then, I investigated the mechanics of putting bitcoin into a retirement account. The overall process of analyzing an asset was the same; I'd done it countless times before. The only difference this time was that it was bitcoin.

MODERN PORTFOLIO THEORY

When evaluating any investment decision, the starting point is always an individual's financial goals, time horizon, and risk tolerance. Goals are what the funds will be used for, and the time horizon reveals when they will be used. Risk tolerance takes a bit more analysis. Each investor has a unique tolerance for the ongoing gyrations of the value of his or her portfolio. For example, do people lose sleep when their portfolio fluctuates, or do they slumber through ups and downs, dreaming of long-term gains? Once goals, time horizon, and risk tolerance are determined, one can proceed to developing an investment portfolio that maximizes returns while staying within the bounds of these parameters.

Nobel Prize winner Harry Max Markowitz defined an approach to constructing portfolios in 1952 that has been the model that most advisors and investors have followed since. His Nobel Prize winning effort created *modern portfolio theory* (MPT), which provides for the construction of investment portfolios that maximize expected returns based upon a targeted level of risk.

His efforts showed that higher returns are achieved by taking on higher risk, while also recognizing what he called an *efficient frontier*, which defines the maximum possible expected return for a given level of risk.

The key for any investor employing MPT is to explicitly consider risk. While risk is not a palatable thought for retail investors—many of whom prefer to dream of risk-free million-dollar returns—there can be no reward without risk. The Securities and Exchange Commission, which regulates securities markets in the United States, has this advice about risk for investors:

> When it comes to investing, risk and reward are inextricably entwined. You've probably heard the phrase "no pain, no gain." Those words come close to summing up the relationship between risk and reward. Don't let anyone tell you otherwise. All investments involve some degree of risk. If you intend to purchase securities—such as stocks, bonds, or mutual funds—it's important that you understand before you invest that you could lose some or all of your money. The reward for taking on risk is the potential for a greater investment return.[3]

We'll tackle the specifics of quantifying risk shortly, mainly through a discussion of volatility. Similarly, we will dive into how to approach absolute returns and the returns per unit of volatility, or risk-reward ratio.

While it's vital to understand the individual attributes of each asset in a portfolio, MPT goes beyond single assets to emphasize a holistic approach to the risks and returns of the overall portfolio. The same can be said of how a coach approaches any team. Understanding the strengths and weaknesses of each team member is important, but it's more important to understand how the team members play together. Great teams can be composed of average players, while a disjointed combination of great players can make average teams.

Markowitz's efficient frontier, which maximizes returns for a given level of risk, is reached by smartly combining assets in a portfolio. A savvy combination of assets can actually decrease the risk of the portfolio to a lower level than any single asset in the portfolio (other than risk-free issues), which is one of the areas in which cryptoassets become particularly noteworthy. We will return to how an investor can craft such a portfolio after we outline the three core characteristics of individual assets.

Standard Deviation

Standard deviation of returns, or the range that an asset's price will vary from its mean value, is one of the most common measures of risk. While Markowitz's approach makes clear the need for risk in a portfolio, most investors are risk-averse to one degree or another, and so they must be compelled by the potential for increased reward if they are to increase their risk. To help with the anxiety of risk, MPT defines it quantitatively, removing much of the uncertainty. Typically, simply being well informed lets investors sleep better at night.

The standard deviation of returns draws from the statistics of normal bell curves. If the average value, or mean, of a bell curve is 10 and its standard deviation is 5, then 68 percent of the time a randomly chosen entity from the sample will fall between 5 and 15. Five is one standard deviation to the left of 10, and 15 is one standard deviation to the right of 10. Due to the way normal curves work, 95 percent of the time a random sample will fall within 2 standard deviations of the mean, so between 0 and 20 for our example. This is illustrated in Figure 6.1.

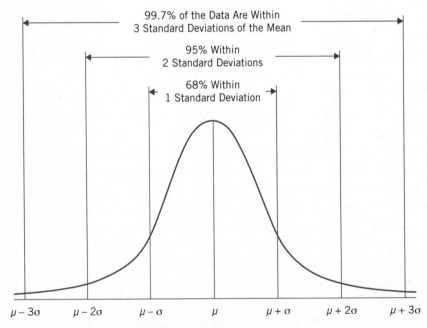

Figure 6.1 ■ A standard deviation bell curve

Source: https://www.spcforexcel.com/files/images/nd.gif

For example, take a stock that has an expected return (mean) of 7 percent and a 5 percent standard deviation of expected returns. There is a 68 percent probability that this stock will yield returns between 2 and 12 percent in the upcoming year. With a less aggressive asset, say a bond that has an expected return of 4 percent and standard deviation of 1 percent, then 68 percent of the time it can be expected to yield between 3 and 5 percent in the coming year. There is less potential for both upside and downside with the bond, whereas the stock has much more potential for some great years, but also the potential risk of seriously dreary years. Hence, the standard deviation of expected returns informs investors of the amount of risk they're taking if they were to hold only that asset.

For a more holistic view, compare a portfolio with a standard deviation of returns of 4 percent to one that has a standard deviation of 8 percent. If both portfolios have the same expected return of 7 percent, it wouldn't be a prudent decision to invest in the portfolio with more volatility, as they both have the same expected return. Taking on a higher level of risk has no benefit in this light, and if a portfolio is unwisely constructed, investors can end up taking on more risk than they're compensated for.

Sharpe Ratio

Similar to the concepts behind MPT, the Sharpe ratio was also created by a Nobel Prize winner, William F. Sharpe. The Sharpe ratio differs from the standard deviation of returns in that it calibrates returns per the unit of risk taken. The ratio divides the average expected return of an asset (minus the risk-free rate) by its standard deviation of returns. For example, if the expected return is 8 percent, and the standard deviation of returns is 5 percent, then its Sharpe ratio is 1.6. The higher the Sharpe ratio, the better an asset is compensating an investor for the associated risk. An asset with a negative Sharpe ratio is punishing the investor with negative returns and volatility.

Importantly, absolute returns are only half the story for the Sharpe ratio. An asset with lower absolute returns can have a higher Sharpe ratio than a high-flying asset that experiences extreme volatility. For example, consider an equity asset that has an expected return of 12 percent with a volatility of 10 percent, versus a bond with an expected return of 5 percent but volatility of 3 percent. The former has a Sharpe ratio of 1.2 while the latter of 1.67 (assuming a risk-free rate of 0 percent). The ratio provides a mathematical method to compare how different assets compensate the investor for the risk taken, making bonds and equities, or apples and oranges, more comparable.

Correlation of Returns and the Efficient Frontier

One of the key breakthroughs of modern portfolio theory was to show that a riskier asset can be added to a portfolio, and if its behavior differs significantly from the preexisting assets in that portfolio, it can actually decrease the overall risk of the portfolio. How can a risky asset make a portfolio less risky? The key is *correlation of returns*.

Correlation simply measures how assets move in relation to one another. The measurement ranges from a value of +1 to −1. If assets are perfectly positively correlated, then they move in tandem: if one is up 10 percent, the other is up 10 percent as well, for a score of +1. Similarly, if they are perfectly negatively correlated at −1, then when one is up 10 percent the other will be down 10 percent. If there is zero correlation, then the assets are completely independent, and how one asset is behaving in the market has no bearing on the other.

Stocks and bonds are often the major tools advisors and investors use to reduce risk as they try to build portfolios made up of assets with low correlations. Historically, stocks and bonds have moved differently from each other. When the economy is strong and stocks are generally rising, money flows out of bonds as investors fear they're missing out, causing bond prices to slump and stocks to go higher. Investors are alive and well, with *risk-on* attitudes. When stock prices falter, investors become concerned by the potential losses, and money flows from stocks into the relative safety of bonds, known as a *flight to safety*. Such *risk-off* markets depress the price of stocks and float the price of bonds.

The two assets move in different directions based on the same news. They act almost like two people on a seesaw. This historical balancing of risk between stocks and bonds should be done as precisely as possible, otherwise wild market swings one way or the other will have a painful impact on the innovative investor's portfolio.

Combining assets that have a variety of correlations makes it possible to create a portfolio that can perform in both bull and bear markets. Just because a few players are feeling sick doesn't mean the whole team has to fail. One of the crown jewels of Markowitz's MPT was his concept of the efficient frontier, which indicates where a portfolio can provide the best expectation of return for its level of risk (see Figure 6.2). The use of this concept is valuable for building portfolios because it helps to visualize how some groups of assets won't provide enough return for the risk taken.

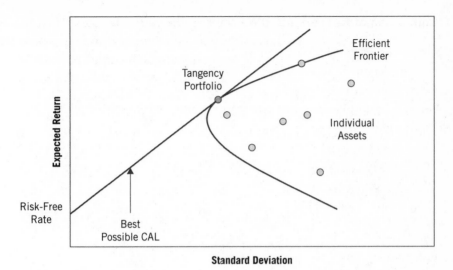

Figure 6.2 ■ The efficient frontier of modern portfolio theory

Source: https://www.ways2wealth.com/Portals/0/Images/Efficient%20Frontier.jpg?ver=2016-03-14-220603-923

Within the financial services industry, people talk about risk in two ways: systematic and unsystematic. *Systematic risk* is the risk inherent to investing in assets subject to the effects of macroeconomic events—like global gross domestic product (GDP) growth, trade relations, warfare, and so on. It is also known as undiversifiable risk because all assets are affected by it. *Unsystematic risk*, on the other hand, is the risk specific to each individual investment, such as market sector, management, product expansion, geographic exposure, and so on. It is also known as *firm-specific risk* and can be neutralized with a smartly constructed portfolio.

Unsystematic risk can be mitigated by constructing a portfolio of assets that neutralizes different firm-specific risks that could impact a portfolio. Ideally, the portfolio is crafted so that when one investment is negatively hurt by a specific event, another asset potentially could benefit by that very same event. For example, if a carbon tax is put on industry in the United States, then companies that are purely involved in oil and coal procurement may be adversely hit, while solar companies may jump. This carbon tax is not a systematic risk if it doesn't affect the market as a whole. Instead, it is an unsystematic risk that influences specific companies within the markets. In this case, the stocks of the oil company and the solar company would be examples of assets that experience negative correlation of returns to this event.

What holds true for specific assets within the same asset class also holds true between the asset classes themselves. If unsystematic risk is fully neutralized by constructing a portfolio of assets and asset classes that have low to negative correlation of returns, then that portfolio will be exposed only to systematic risk. Modern portfolio theory takes it a step further by saying over the long term, investors are rewarded *only* for the systematic risk they take on and will be adversely affected over the long run if they leave themselves exposed to unsystematic risk.

With the tools of MPT it's possible to construct a portfolio that stays within an investor's risk profile while still generating returns sufficient to meet long-term financial goals and objectives. The innovative investor recognizes that the overall risk of his or her portfolio can be reduced by including assets that are uncorrelated to the traditional capital markets, such as bitcoin and its digital siblings.

TRADITIONAL ASSET ALLOCATION

For many years, traditional asset allocation models strictly focused on defining percentages of a portfolio in either stocks or bonds. For instance, the American Association of Individual Investors provides simplified models for three types of investors:[4]

- **Aggressive investors:** 90 percent diversified stock and 10 percent fixed income
- **Moderate investors:** 70 percent diversified stock and 30 percent fixed income
- **Conservative investors:** 50 percent diversified stock and 50 percent fixed income

These three simple models can be used by people of different ages who have different investment time horizons. A whole host of equities can be included within "diversified stock," and even more so for the variety of bonds that can be used for "fixed income." For example, equities can be considered based on the size of the company, the growth characteristics, the valuation, the sector type, geographic exposure, and so on. Similarly, bonds can include government or corporate issues, with varying durations, credit ratings, and tax advantages.

This traditional approach to asset allocation ran aground in 2008, when the financial markets collapsed and investors found that even if they had both stocks and bonds in their portfolio, they all fell together.[5] The average investor felt betrayed by the tried and trusted model of stocks and bonds moving in a noncorrelated fashion. The crash of 2008 shook these investors from their "economic lullaby."[6] In an increasingly globalized world where capital market assets are more closely intertwined, it was becoming clear that twentieth-century diversification models wouldn't cut it for twenty-first-century investing.

While the crash of 2008 was felt by most everyone, it soon surfaced that some people had not only weathered the storm but made significant money by leveraging the strong winds of fortune.[7] Hedge fund managers who had been operating in relative secrecy were now being named as the new "masters of the universe" for their ability to avoid much of the damage of the crash and, for some, to profit greatly from it.

THE RISE OF ALTERNATIVE INVESTMENTS

The financial crisis of 2008 caused many financial advisors and wealth managers to evaluate different approaches to portfolio construction other than solely stocks and bonds. The returns seen by hedge funds during the crisis were identified as examples where nontraditional and alternative investment vehicles had provided positive (in some cases, drastically so) performance returns.

John Paulson became the face of hedge fund billionaires who benefited from the crisis when it was revealed that he had personally earned over $1 billion from his fund management, including the Paulson Advantage Plus Fund (an event-driven fund). This fund alone ranked number one over the period of 2006 to 2008 with an annualized return of nearly 63 percent. Equally successful was James Simons's Renaissance Technologies Medallion Fund with a return of 80 percent in 2008. Becoming a hedge fund manager became all the rage for business-minded students when it was revealed that the top 25 hedge fund managers had earned a total of $22.3 billion in 2007 and $11.6 billion in 2008.[8]

With numbers like these, the world of hedge funds caught the attention of the media. Investors questioned if these managers had something to do with the crash.[9] They also wanted to know what they were doing differently and whether it was something they could do as well.

First, let's understand what we mean by a hedge fund and how they differ among themselves. It's difficult to lump hedge funds together in one group, as they often have different investment objectives and approaches. Historically, one of the easiest ways to spot hedge funds has been their high fee structure. For example, many hedge funds operate under a 2 and 20 model, or sometimes 3 and 30, where they charge a 2 percent annual management fee and take 20 percent of the profits from a year. Other common characteristics include their exclusivity and general secrecy.

Prior to the 2008 financial crisis, investors who took advantage of hedge fund performance and the alternative investments they utilized were typically of ultra-high net worth with sizeable investable assets, given that often the minimum investment was $1 million or more to gain entry. Additionally, investors had to tie up their funds for lengthy periods as part of the agreement with the hedge fund manager.

While mutual funds provide a prospectus that outlines exactly the approach and asset classes to be used, hedge funds are often veiled in secrecy. They might publicly advertise a broad investment strategy, but specifics are often withheld to preserve the secret sauce of the hedge fund. Hedge fund managers demand a high amount of flexibility and tolerance from their clients.

For example, hedge fund managers could buy real estate or take ownership in what they believe to be an undervalued company (either publicly or privately held). If they believe upcoming political changes may favor oil, they could lease oil tankers or make a sizeable investment in a foreign oil partnership. They can also utilize assets such as timber, short positions in stocks (meaning they're betting on the price falling), commodity derivatives, and yes, germane to this book, bitcoin and other cryptoassets.

Even with this lack of transparency and liquidity, affluent investors rushed to hedge funds to chase the performance of managers like Paulson, Simons, and others. An underlying assumption for hedge fund investors was that they needed to be affluent enough to handle the high risk and volatile nature associated with a hedge fund manager's approach and fund assets. For the typical investor, the high asset commitments, illiquidity, and lack of transparency kept hedge funds beyond their reach. Fortunately, the underlying ability to utilize alternative investments in any portfolio is not as elusive as many are made to think.

Alternative Investments Defined

So how does one define an "alternative investment"?

A search online and in dictionaries will present a reader with the perception that accurately defining the term is quite complicated due to the wide range of investments included, ranging from hedge funds to private equity to direct investments in natural resources like gold and timber.[10]

The reality is that classifying alternative investments can be a moving target as investment options and trends change over time. Many investors may already have alternative investment vehicles in their portfolio without specifically referring to them as such. An investment such as an exchange traded fund (ETF) that specializes in arbitrage strategies or futures contracts may look like any other ETF in a portfolio, but it could be considered an alternative investment.[11] Physical holdings in gold, silver, real estate, art collections, or personally-owned businesses are all part of someone's net worth and could also be considered as alternative investments.

A more current and concise way to describe an alternative investment is that it's an asset with its own unique economic and value-based characteristics that are separate from those of the primary investments of stocks and bonds. For an investor, the main concern is to have assets that perform in a noncorrelated fashion to stocks and bonds—which have historically made up most investors' portfolio models—and many alternative assets fit that bill.

If done properly, when the overall market has a severe meltdown as happened in 2008, specific alternative investments within portfolios may not decrease. Equally, in market upturns those same assets may or may not also increase in value; they may lose value, but such is the cost of overall risk reduction. As a small portion of the innovative investor's overall portfolio, alternatives are an effective way to balance risk and provide a cushion in the case of a stock or bond meltdown.

ALTERNATIVE INVESTMENTS AND THE INNOVATIVE INVESTOR

Today's innovative investor can build an investment portfolio and asset allocation strategy with a clear understanding of risk and reward, and the inclusion of alternative investments can help. This has not been lost on wealth management firms that are now looking more aggressively into how alternative invest-ments can be used to improve client returns.

For example, Morgan Stanley has outlined asset allocation models for its high net worth investors with under $25 million in investable assets; those models recommend 56 percent stocks, 19 percent bonds, 3 percent cash, and 22 percent alternatives. For those clients with over $25 million in investable assets, the recommendation is for 50 percent stocks, 19 percent bonds, 3 per-cent cash, and 28 percent in alternatives.[12] Merrill Lynch has recommended allocation models for its typical client that include alternatives near or above 20 percent of a portfolio.[13]

Clearly, the inclusion of alternative investments should not be limited to only high net worth investors. Historically, one of the biggest reasons alterna-tive investments have not been incorporated into retail portfolios is because of their illiquid characteristics. Many retail investors can't guarantee that they won't need to access their funds for 10 years, making many alternatives out of reach. That, however, is changing.

Over the last decade, to address the need for alternative investment options as a way to provide diversification and noncorrelation from the traditional cap-ital markets, wealth management firms have been creating more investment options for the typical investor. The proliferation of ETFs has led to the creation of liquid investments in alternative assets, such as gold, energy resources, and real estate, as well as ways to play the volatility of the market. Because of the easy accessibility of these products through the capital markets, these vehicles and others have found their way into investors' portfolios and onto the recom-mended lists of many financial advisors. The impact of this is seen in a 2015 survey among financial advisors that found they had placed 73 percent of their clients in alternative investments, and that nearly three-quarters of advisors planned to maintain their current alternative investment allocations.[14]

The survey also showed that in terms of asset allocation, most advisors were recommending a range of 6 percent to 15 percent of a client's portfolio in alter-natives. A smaller but not insignificant percentage of advisors recommended 16 percent to 25 percent of their clients' portfolios in alternatives.

Bitcoin and other cryptoassets are alternative assets that can be safely and successfully incorporated into well-diversified portfolios to meet these asset allocation recommendations.[15] However, every alternative investment has its unique set of characteristics, and the innovative investor must understand these.

The potential of bitcoin and other cryptoassets is so great that we believe they should be considered an asset class of their own. We can easily see them more and more commonly used in many innovative portfolios. We explain why we think cryptoassets will increasingly be incorporated into mainstream retail portfolios, first starting with an exploration of how bitcoin's risk, reward, and risk-reward profiles have evolved over the course of its life.

Chapter 7

The Most Compelling Alternative Asset of the Twenty-First Century

B itcoin is the most exciting alternative asset in the twenty-first century, and it has paved the way for its digital siblings to enjoy similar success. In this chapter, we dive into how bitcoin evolved as an asset in the context of absolute returns, volatility, and correlations, concluding with how a small allocation of bitcoin would have affected a portfolio over different holding periods. Because bitcoin can claim the title of being the oldest cryptoasset—giving us the most data to investigate its maturation—understanding its longitudinal market behavior will give us a window into how other cryptoassets may evolve over time.

BITCOIN'S EARLIEST PRICING

Let's go back to the first time a price was established for bitcoin, October 5, 2009, when it was priced at 1,309 bitcoin to the dollar, or 7/100 of a cent per bitcoin. A small website called the New Liberty Standard established the rate based on the amount of money it needed for electricity and rent to maintain the computer that mined bitcoin versus the amount of bitcoin that had been reaped from so doing.

If at that time an investor had tracked down one of the few bitcoin miners in the world and offered $100 for the 130,900 bitcoin implied by that exchange rate, by now that investor would have amassed over $100 million. A single hundred-dollar bill converted into one million hundred-dollar bills: it would have been one of the best investments of all time.

However, having such impeccable timing is an elusive dream for investors. When I (Jack) began investigating bitcoin in August 2013,[1] bitcoin was trading at $135; it had already appreciated significantly from the initial exchange rate of 1,309 bitcoin to the dollar. Yet I decided it was not too late and ultimately made the investment.

Similarly, I (Chris) didn't even consider investing in bitcoin when I first heard about it in 2012. By the time I began considering bitcoin for my portfolio in late 2014, the price was in the mid $300s, having increased 460,000-fold from the initial exchange rate. Like Jack, I also didn't think it was too late and made the jump. While the innovative investor may interpret the current price tag on bitcoin as being too high, consider instead what can be done. We believe it's still early days for cryptoassets.

ABSOLUTE RETURNS

To provide context for bitcoin's behavior in the first eight years of its life, we will compare it to other popular investments from both traditional and alternative asset classes. In terms of absolute returns, long-term comparisons between bitcoin and many other assets make most jaws drop, but it's important to keep *endpoint sensitivity* in mind. Endpoint sensitivity refers to the starting and ending dates chosen for comparison, because over time almost all assets fluctuate considerably in value. Choosing a low starting point and a high ending point will yield drastically different comparisons than a high starting point and low ending point.

We have chosen January 3, 2017, as the ending point of analysis for this chapter, as that was bitcoin's eight-year birthday. While designating a fixed endpoint, we have the flexibility to choose different starting points (including one of bitcoin's most notable peaks in late 2013). By illustrating both high and low starting points, we are able to show the variety of experiences investors could have had depending on when they first bought bitcoin. For those concerned with the cherry-picking of numbers, it should be noted that on January 3, 2017, the price of bitcoin was around $1,000, whereas when this book was entering its final stages of editing, bitcoin had risen past $3,000. We nonetheless have stuck with the $1,000 price of bitcoin for the following comparison in pursuit of intellectual honesty.

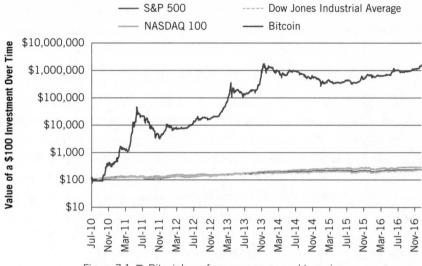

Figure 7.1 ■ Bitcoin's performance compared to major
U.S. stock indices since the start of Mt. Gox
Data sourced from Bloomberg and CoinDesk

To begin with, we examine the longest-term bitcoin prices we have that come from reliable exchange data. Figure 7.1 provides a comparison of bitcoin versus three of the most important stock market indices: the S&P 500, the Dow Jones Industrial Average (DJIA), and the NASDAQ 100, respectively. It assumes a $100 investment was made on July 19, 2010, a few days after Mt. Gox was officially open for business and providing the first widely used exchange services for bitcoin.

These broad market indices represent how the stock markets performed on average, with the S&P 500 representing approximately 80 percent coverage of available U.S. equity market capitalization,[2] the DJIA for 30 of the largest U.S. stocks by market capitalization,[3] and the NASDAQ 100 for big domestic and international companies in sectors that include computer hardware and software, telecommunications, and biotechnology.[4] Note that the graph uses a log scale for the y-axis so that the broad market indices can be seen—in other words, they'd be invisible on a linear scale.

Since July 2010, the three broad indices have done well, with U.S. stocks in a recovery bull market after the financial crisis of 2008. An initial investment of $100 would have grown to $242, $231, and $291, for the S&P 500, DJIA, and NASDAQ 100, respectively. Although equity market returns have been respectable, they have been dwarfed by bitcoin, which has done phenomenally in the same period—an initial investment of $100 grew to nearly $1.3 million by the beginning of January 2017.

LINEAR VS. LOGARITHMIC

Two types of scales are commonly used for representing the change in the price of assets: linear and logarithmic. Linear price scales show unadjusted unit changes in the y-axis. For example, if priced in dollars, $10 in value increase will look the same, whether the asset goes from $10 to $20 or $100 to $110. Logarithmic scales adjust the y-axis—in finance most commonly by factors of 10—which allows *percent* price increases to be compared. For example, on a logarithmic y-axis the price move from $10 to $20 will show up more clearly than the move from $100 to $110, because the former represents a 100 percent price increase while the latter is only a 10 percent price increase. What would look the same on a logarithmic scale, however, is a move from $10 to $20 and a move from $100 to $200. Logarithmic price scales are useful in comparing percent price changes over time, as well as compressing data of widely different values into one chart.

We can also compare these indices to bitcoin by calculating the compound annual growth rates, or the annual appreciation year-over-year. In this comparison, the post-crisis bull market performance is clear, as the S&P 500 provided nearly 15 percent compound annual returns, 50 percent better than the average 9.5 percent it provided investors in the 88 years between 1928 and 2016.[5] Figure 7.2 shows that in spite of the excellent performance of U.S. stock markets, bitcoin was a clear standout in this eight-year period with compound annual returns of 332 percent.

Rather than comparing bitcoin to broad market indices, it may be more fair to compare it to high growth companies riding similar waves of technological innovation. The FANG stocks of Facebook, Amazon, Netflix, and Google have been the darling of many tech analysts over the last few years, outperforming the broad market indices and helping to reshape our increasingly digital world. However, as Figure 7.3 shows, even the FANG stocks were wildly outperformed by bitcoin since Facebook's May 2012 initial public offering (IPO).[6] Once again, note that this chart uses a log scale for the y-axis.

An initial investment of $100 on the day Facebook completed its IPO would have turned into $306, $352, $1,276, and $262 for Facebook, Amazon, Netflix,

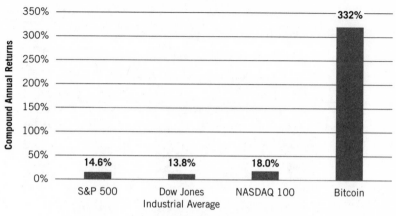

Figure 7.2 ■ Bitcoin's compound annual returns versus
major U.S. stock indices since the start of Mt. Gox
Data sourced from Bloomberg and CoinDesk

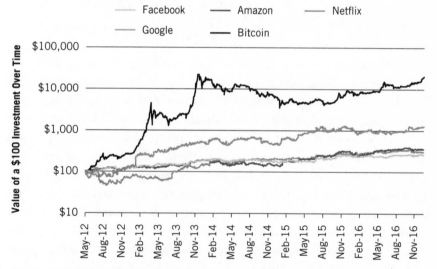

Figure 7.3 ■ Bitcoin's performance compared to the FANG stocks since Facebook's IPO
Data sourced from Bloomberg and CoinDesk

and Google, respectively, by our end date of January 3, 2017. When matched up against these stellar tech names, bitcoin has performed more than an order of magnitude better, with an initial investment of $100 growing to $20,133. On a relative basis, bitcoin has provided capital appreciation 66-fold, 57-fold, 16-fold, and 77-fold that of the FANG stocks, respectively, over this period.

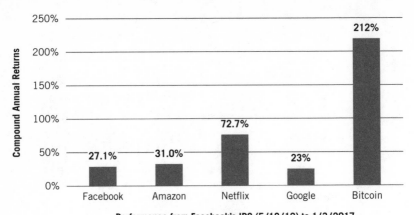

Figure 7.4 ■ Bitcoin's compound annual returns versus
the FANG stocks since Facebook's IPO
Data sourced from Bloomberg and CoinDesk

To provide better context and make the performance of the FANG stocks comparable to the performance of the broad market indices, we can once again convert the above returns into a compound annual rate, as seen in Figure 7.4. Doing so reveals that the FANG names have provided annual returns about double that of the broad market indices over the last few years, with Netflix as the standout for the group. Yet when compared with bitcoin, every other investment pales.

Remember that, as of January 2017, bitcoin's network value was 1/20, 1/22, 1/3, and 1/33 that of the FANG stocks respectively. Therefore, if bitcoin is to grow to a similar size, much opportunity remains. Clearly, it's still early days for bitcoin, and even earlier days for its digital siblings.

If the preceding log graphs all looked relatively similar, that's because they were. Bitcoin's ascent dwarfed that of other assets, and that's on a log scale y-axis. If the y-axis is linear instead, then all the previous graphs condense into Figure 7.5, with Netflix as the only name that moderately differentiates from the rest. We also added assets outside of U.S. equities, including U.S. bonds, U.S. real estate, gold, and oil.[7] Gold and oil investors received a doubly short end of the stick, as by January 3, 2017, they had lost 30 percent and 40 percent of their value, respectively. All other assets provided positive returns since Facebook's IPO.

At this point, innovative investors might ask what if they didn't buy at bitcoin's inception or at Facebook's IPO? Let's address this concern directly by going back to our prior discussion of endpoint sensitivity and seeing what

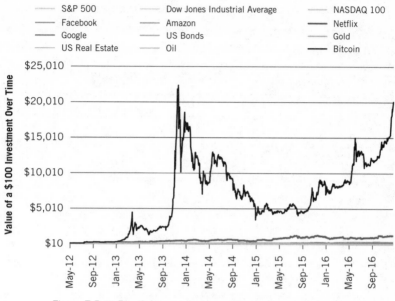

Figure 7.5 ■ Bitcoin's ascent versus other major asset classes
Data sourced from Bloomberg and CoinDesk

would have happened if an investor had picked the worst time to buy bitcoin: at the peak of its astronomical ascent in late 2013.

Worst-Case Scenario for Absolute Returns: Buying at the Top

In late 2013, bitcoin's network value was over $10 billion, making it a significantly investable asset for retail investors even by capital market standards. On November 29, 2013, bitcoin reached $1,242, making one bitcoin worth more than one ounce of gold.[8]

Clearly, bitcoin had risen a long way from its humble roots. If innovative investors had bought at this peak price, their returns would not have been nearly as rosy as if they had bought when Mt. Gox launched or when Facebook IPO'd. In fact, they would have endured an 80 percent loss in value over the following year before bitcoin bottomed in January 2015 and began a long, slow climb back to previous highs. By January 3, 2017, $100 invested in bitcoin at its peak price would only retain $83, while an investment instrument based on the S&P 500, DJIA, or NASDAQ 100 indices would have grown to $133, $133, and $146, respectively (Figure 7.6).

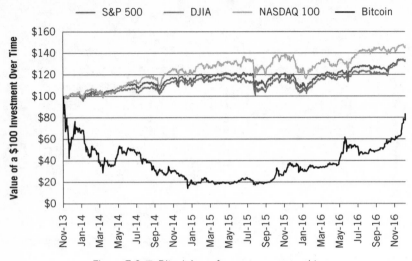

Figure 7.6 ■ Bitcoin's performance compared to
major U.S. stock indices since its November 2013 peak

Data sourced from Bloomberg and CoinDesk

An investor who purchased bitcoin at its peak on November 29, 2013, rather than one of the FANG stocks would have suffered an even more drastic differential in returns. As shown in Figure 7.7, the capital appreciation provided

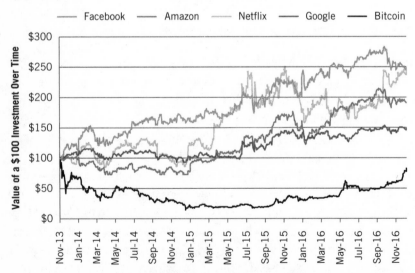

Figure 7.7 ■ Bitcoin's performance compared to
the FANG stocks since its November 2013 peak

Data sourced from Bloomberg and CoinDesk

by Facebook, Amazon, Netflix, and Google would have been 3-fold, 2.3-fold, 2.9-fold, and 1.8-fold that of bitcoin during this time period. While innovative investors who had gotten into bitcoin soon after Facebook IPO'd would have been rewarded for their decision, if they had waited a year and a half they would have been dealing with a vastly different story.

At that same peak in price, innovative investors who chose bitcoin over a nonequity holding—such as bonds, real estate, gold, or oil—would have been the most at peace with their decision (Figure 7.8). The performance of commodities like gold and oil have been far from stellar since November 2013, and in the period up to January 2017, bitcoin actually outperformed oil. The low interest rate environment meant bonds conserved investors' capital but didn't grow it much. In this group, U.S. real estate was the only investment that appreciated on par with the equity markets.

At this point, we have provided insight into some of bitcoin's best and worst returns in its relatively short life. However, throughout this book we will be making the case that we believe there is much more price appreciation potential yet to come from both bitcoin and select cryptocurrencies, cryptocommodities, and cryptotokens.

Dollar cost averaging is a means by which the innovative investor can avoid extreme sensitivity to the starting point of investing. As opposed to taking a

Figure 7.8 ■ Bitcoin's performance compared
to non-equity assets since its November 2013 peak
Data sourced from Bloomberg and CoinDesk

big chunk of money and dumping it all into an investment at once, it often behooves the investor to average in, deploying capital at a measured cadence. In so doing, the investor may buy at the peak but will also be buying all the way to the bottom, ultimately averaging a good price if the underlying investment has long-term potential for capital appreciation.

VOLATILITY

While absolute returns are often the topic of trending conversation, if unaccompanied by an investigation of volatility, investors may be overpaying in risk for their returns. Put another way, they may be undercompensated for the risk they're taking. In this sense, innovative investors must make sure they're being rewarded for the risk in their portfolio.

WHY CRYPTOASSETS ARE TYPICALLY VOLATILE WHEN FIRST LAUNCHED

Upon launch, cryptoassets tend to be extremely volatile because they are thinly traded markets. A thin market refers to the size of the order book, and an order book refers to the list of buys and sells on an exchange. In other words, it's a measure of the number of people wanting to buy and sell at any given moment. Figure 7.9 is an image of an order book for Ethereum (ether) on Poloniex, a widely used cryptoasset exchange.

Each order is one row in an order book, and so the more orders there are, the thicker the book. If there aren't many buys and sells, then the order book is thin. That said, some orders also need to be of sizeable amounts. If all the orders consist of bids to buy or sell $1 of the asset, then it doesn't matter how many orders there are, it will still be a thin order book.

The thinness of the order book is also referred to as the liquidity of the market. If the market is highly liquid, then there are lots of orders and many of them are likely large. In this case, value can be traded easily. If the market is illiquid, or thin, then sizeable price swings with low volume will occur because someone trying to buy (or sell) a lot of the asset will fill all the available sell (or buy) orders, which drives the price up (or down). As a result, in thin or illiquid markets, when investors are bullish they can drive massive swings to the upside, just as when investors turn bearish, strong selling volume can quickly drive the price down.

SELL ORDERS ⇌

Total: 150206.56067270 ETH

Price	ETH	BTC	Sum(BTC)
0.03925597	2.44831756	0.09611108	0.09611108
0.03931000	2.57143699	0.10108319	0.19719427
0.03934598	2.71571324	0.10685240	0.30404667
0.03934600	46.69610000	1.83730475	2.14135142
0.03935194	1.11721950	0.04396475	2.18531617
0.03935884	0.03658613	0.00143999	2.18675616
0.03935888	0.05124561	0.00201697	2.18877313
0.03936000	0.00759279	0.00029885	2.18907198
0.03936354	0.02166923	0.00085298	2.18992496
0.03936789	3.99400000	0.15723535	2.34716031
0.03937493	2.53968705	0.10000000	2.44716031
0.03937499	1.31578947	0.05180920	2.49896951
0.03937600	4.00000000	0.15750400	2.65647351
0.03937772	0.00787320	0.00031003	2.65678354
0.03938999	0.10000000	0.00393900	2.66072254
0.03939423	31.34523000	1.23482120	3.89554374

BUY ORDERS

Total: 4890.35481746 BTC

Price	ETH	BTC	Sum(BTC)
0.03921506	200.84120743	7.87600000	7.87600000
0.03921505	31.31858882	1.22816003	9.10416003
0.03921501	110.34850967	4.32731791	13.43147794
0.03921008	0.07651093	0.00300000	13.43447794
0.03920001	0.57891949	0.02269365	13.45717159
0.03920000	61.30574810	2.40318533	15.86035692
0.03919000	25.51020357	0.99974488	16.86010180
0.03918634	41.73830000	1.63557121	18.49567301
0.03918633	139.22513959	5.45572226	23.95139527
0.03918625	53.58570500	2.09982283	26.05121810
0.03915123	0.12770990	0.00500000	26.05621810
0.03911833	1.27817305	0.05000000	26.10621810
0.03910602	52.17290000	2.04027447	28.14649257
0.03910601	165.79400000	6.48354182	34.63003439
0.03910600	34.95830000	1.36707928	35.99711367
0.03910106	22.94100000	0.89701742	36.89413109

☐ Throttle Updates [1s ⬍]   ☐ Order Grouping [6 decimals ⬍]

Figure 7.9 ■ Order book of buys and sells for ether on Poloniex
Used with permission from Poloniex.com

When cryptoassets are first launched, they have relatively thin order books because the investor base is typically smaller, trading is more infrequent, and orders may be small. This can create volatility in the price of the new asset. However, as news of the asset's merit spreads, interest will increase along with trading volume. The order book will typically fatten and volatility will often decrease.

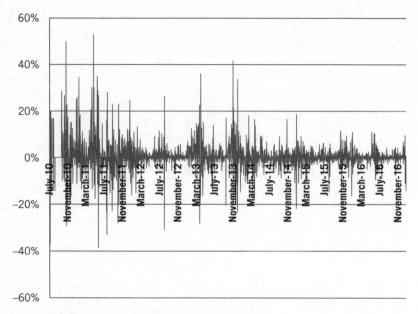

Figure 7.10 ■ Bitcoin's daily percent price changes since the start of Mt. Gox

Data sourced from CoinDesk

One of the easiest ways to visualize the volatility of an asset is to see how much its price changes day to day, or in other words, the daily percent price changes. The bigger the daily percent price changes are, the more volatile the asset is. Figure 7.10 illustrates the daily percent price changes of bitcoin from the time Mt. Gox opened to January 3, 2017.

The graph looks like what a seismometer would produce when measuring ground movements during earthquakes. Early in bitcoin's history there were frequent earthquakes, with the price moving more than 50 percent in a day. Over time, however, the bitcoin seismometer has registered smaller and smaller earthquakes in bitcoin's price. Bitcoin has become more popular and therefore more widely traded, so its market has become more liquid. Therefore, when lots of people choose to buy or sell, the market is able to absorb these changes much more smoothly.

Even though bitcoin's daily percent price changes have decreased dramatically over the years—bringing it into the range of many small capitalization growth stocks—it is still a volatile asset. In Figure 7.11, compare the fluctuation of bitcoin's daily percent price changes in 2016 with that of Twitter and a market stalwart like AT&T.

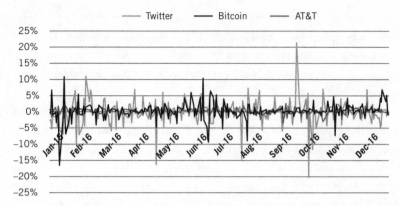

Figure 7.11 ■ Bitcoin's daily percent price changes versus Twitter and AT&T in 2016
Data sourced from Bloomberg and CoinDesk

Twitter experienced three days in 2016 when its price dropped more than 15 percent and one day where it jumped more than 20 percent. Bitcoin had only two days where its price increased more than 10 percent and only one day where it dropped more than 15 percent. AT&T, the slow and steady line in the middle, is a $250 billion company that lumbers along with hardly any price movement.

Volatility is most commonly derived by taking the standard deviation of the daily percent price changes. The bigger this number is, the more the investor can expect significant swings in the price of the asset they're holding and therefore, the riskier the asset is. Figure 7.12 shows the standard deviation of the daily percent price changes of bitcoin, Twitter, and AT&T in 2016.

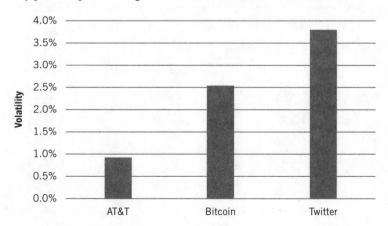

Figure 7.12 ■ Volatility of bitcoin, Twitter, and AT&T in 2016
Data sourced from Bloomberg and CoinDesk

Twitter was 50 percent more volatile than bitcoin in 2016, and bitcoin was nearly three times more volatile than AT&T. The latter is to be expected given bitcoin's network value is less than 5 percent that of AT&T's market cap, and it has been around for less than a decade, while AT&T has been around for more than a century.

In examining FANG stocks, we see an interesting pattern with volatility. Remembering our discussion of modern portfolio theory, historically the most volatile assets have generally been the ones with the greatest returns. This relationship between risk (i.e., volatility) and reward is to be expected: no reward without the accompanying risk. In Figure 7.13 we see that bitcoin's volatility has been the highest, with Netflix coming in second; and these two assets were the best performing. Interestingly, in this period bitcoin's annual returns of 212 percent were threefold that of Netflix's 73 percent, yet bitcoin's volatility was only 35 percent greater than Netflix. Intuitively, it appears bitcoin has had better risk-reward characteristics than Netflix. Similarly, Google, which performed the least well of the FANG stocks with 23 percent returns, also had the lowest volatility at 1.5 percent.

As we learned in the preceding chapter, it's easy enough to directly calculate the risk-reward ratio of different assets. It would appear that in this time period (Facebook's IPO to January 3, 2017) bitcoin has had the best risk-reward ratio of all these assets.

But to make sure, we'll crunch the numbers.

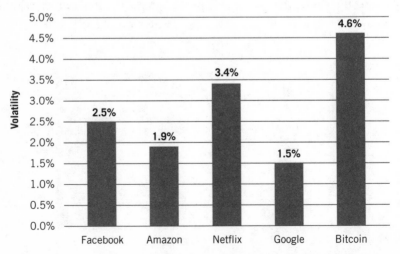

Figure 7.13 ■ Volatility of bitcoin and the FANG stocks since Facebook's IPO
Data sourced from Bloomberg and CoinDesk

SHARPE RATIO

Absolute returns and volatility are important in their own right, but when they're put together they yield the Sharpe ratio, which is an equally important metric for investors to consider. Remember that by dividing the absolute returns[9] by the volatility, we can calibrate the returns for the risk taken. The higher the Sharpe ratio, the more the asset is compensating investors for the risk. This is an extremely important metric in the context of modern portfolio theory, because while an aggressive investor may salivate over sexy returns, the innovative investor is equally aware of the risk necessary to achieve those returns.

As discussed in the previous chapter, by combining returns and volatility into one metric, we can do an apples-to-apples comparison between cryptoassets and other traditional and alternative assets. Currently, cryptoassets often have much higher volatility than other assets, and the Sharpe ratio enables us to understand this volatility in terms of the returns reaped.

It's still important to consider volatility outside of the Sharpe ratio in the context of the investor's time horizon. While some volatile assets will have excellent Sharpe ratios over long time periods, those investments may not be appropriate for someone needing to place a down payment on a house three months from now.

In comparing bitcoin to the FANG stocks, we observed that bitcoin had the highest volatility but also the highest returns by far. Interestingly, its Sharpe ratio was not just the highest but significantly so. Bitcoin compensated investors twice as well for the risk they took than Facebook did and 40 percent better than Netflix, its closest contender (see Figure 7.14).

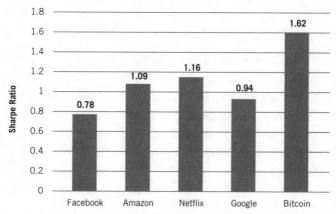

Figure 7.14 ■ Sharpe ratio of bitcoin and the FANG stocks since Facebook's IPO

Data sourced from Bloomberg and CoinDesk

Bitcoin and the FANG four's Sharpe ratio comparison clearly illustrates the importance of combining solid returns and low volatility. While Facebook's annual returns were just shy of Amazon's and better than Google's, its volatility was significantly greater than both. Therefore, since its IPO Facebook has compensated investors least well for the risk they've taken.

As we saw in Figure 7.11, "Bitcoin's daily percent price changes," bitcoin's daily swings have dampened significantly over time, meaning its volatility is less. However, simultaneous with decreasing volatility, bitcoin's annual appreciation has calmed as well. In Figure 7.15, we once again see the relationship between risk and reward playing out as we view bitcoin's Sharpe ratio every full year from 2011 through 2016.

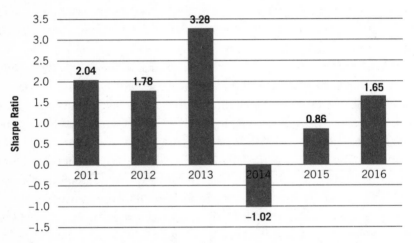

Figure 7.15 ■ Bitcoin's annual Sharpe ratios since the start of Mt. Gox
Data sourced from CoinDesk

The year 2014 was the only time bitcoin had a negative Sharpe ratio, when it lost 60 percent of its value from the start to the end of the year. Recall that 2014 was the year of bitcoin's painful decent from its late 2013 high to its early 2015 low, with Chinese regulations, Mt. Gox implosions, and Silk Road associations plaguing the price of the asset.[10] Meanwhile, 2016 was bitcoin's best risk-adjusted return year since 2013. Digging into the comparison between 2013 and 2016, it's remarkable that 2013's Sharpe ratio was only double that of 2016, even though bitcoin's returns in 2013 were so much greater, as shown in Figure 7.16.

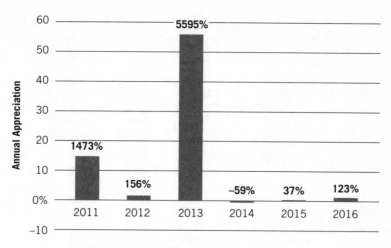

Figure 7.16 ■ Bitcoin's annual appreciation
Data sourced from CoinDesk

With capital appreciation in 2013 at 45 times greater than that of 2016, it would be reasonable to expect bitcoin in 2013 to have had a Sharpe ratio many times greater than in 2016. However, this is where both daily volatility and the way the Sharpe ratio is calculated come into play.[11] First, volatility in 2013 was triple that of 2016, which implies investors were taking three times as much risk in 2013 as in 2016. This allowed 2016 to have much lower returns but still have a risk-reward ratio within the same ballpark as 2013. Second, the Sharpe ratio is calculated using average weekly returns, not total capital appreciation over the year.

The Sharpe ratio is also revealing when comparing bitcoin to the broader market indices of the S&P 500, the DJIA, and the NASDAQ 100. We already know these indices had lower annual returns than bitcoin and the FANG stocks, but they also had lower volatility given they were made up of diversified baskets of stocks, and diversification helps reduce volatility. Furthermore, these indices are made up of large market cap[12] names, especially the DJIA. As we saw with AT&T, many of these large cap stocks have been around for a long time and are relatively steady when compared with fast-moving tech names. Figure 7.17 shows a comparison of bitcoin's Sharpe ratio to the aforementioned three broad market indices, using the same period that we used for comparing the absolute returns of these assets: July 19, 2010 through January 3, 2017.

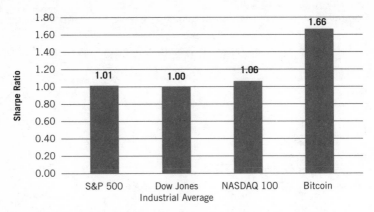

Figure 7.17 ■ Bitcoin's Sharpe ratio compared
to major U.S. stock indices since the start of Mt. Gox
Data sourced from Bloomberg and CoinDesk

Once again, this chart reveals how absolute returns are tempered by volatility when calculating the Sharpe ratio. Although bitcoin's Sharpe ratio is roughly 60 percent higher than the three broad market indices, this is a far cry from its absolute returns, which were roughly 20 times greater than the broad market indices on an annual basis during the same period.

In Figure 7.18 we compare bitcoin's Sharpe ratio in 2016 to that of the broad market indices. Because 2016 was bitcoin's lowest year of volatility (in the range of a small- to mid-cap stock), it is the most appropriate period to compare it to equities. What's most surprising is bitcoin's Sharpe ratio in 2016 was almost as high as its overall Sharpe ratio since the launch of Mt. Gox, the

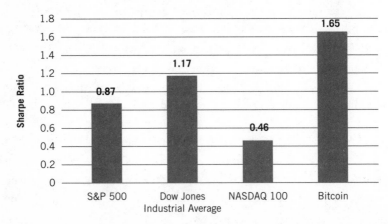

Figure 7.18 ■ Bitcoin's Sharpe ratio compared to major U.S. stock indices in 2016
Data sourced from Bloomberg and CoinDesk

first exchange that gave mainstream investors access to bitcoin (1.65 for 2016 vs. 1.66 since Mt. Gox).

Some people are apt to think that the best years to be a bitcoin investor are past. However, looking at the Sharpe Ratio, 2016 had risk-adjusted returns that were as good as those of an investor who bought bitcoin when the mainstream first had the opportunity to do so.

CORRELATION

Diversification is accomplished by selecting a variety of assets that have low to negative correlation with one another. A group of stocks is inherently more diversified than a single stock, and therefore the volatility should be lower.

Cryptoassets have near-zero correlation to other capital market assets. The best explanation for this is that cryptoassets are so new that many capital market investors don't play in the same asset pools. Therefore, cryptoassets aren't dancing to the same rhythm of information as traditional capital market assets, at least not yet.

Correlation Coefficient	Effects of Diversification on Risk
+1.0	No risk reduction is possible
+0.5	Moderate risk reduction is possible
0	Considerable risk reduction is possible
−0.5	Most risk can be eliminated
−1.0	All risk can be eliminated

Figure 7.19 ■ The correlation coefficient and effects of diversification on risk
Source: *A Random Walk Down Wall Street*, Burton G. Malkiel, 2015

Figure 7.19 clearly shows that if an asset is zero correlated to other assets in a portfolio, then "considerable risk reduction is possible." In quantitative terms, reducing risk can be seen by a decrease in the volatility of the portfolio.

If an asset merely reduces the risk of the overall portfolio by being lowly to negatively correlated with other assets, then it doesn't have to provide superior absolute returns to improve the risk-reward ratio of the overall portfolio. Since the Sharpe ratio is returns divided by risk, if the risk gets smaller, then the denominator gets smaller, making the Sharpe ratio bigger. The returns don't have to change at all.

However, it is possible for an asset to be added to a portfolio that both decreases the risk of the portfolio and increases the returns. Finding assets that can do this is rare and almost feels like cheating the laws of risk-reward. After all, we've already learned that the more rewarding an asset is, the riskier it likely is. But with a portfolio we are not talking about a single asset but rather a group of them. It is the way in which a new asset behaves with the preexisting group of assets in a portfolio that is the key to both reducing risk and increasing returns.

CRYPTOASSETS AS THE SILVER BULLET OF DIVERSIFICATION

Most people would reasonably expect that if they added bitcoin to their portfolio it would increase the absolute returns but it would also make the portfolio significantly riskier (more volatile). However, it's important to remember that bitcoin's propensity toward volatility proved true early in its life when volume was low (thin). In contrast, the past few years have been more nuanced: bitcoin's volatility has calmed, yet it retains a low correlation with other assets. In some years, bitcoin even provided the magical and elusive combination mentioned above of increasing the returns while also decreasing risk within a portfolio.

The question is how bitcoin's low to negative correlation with other capital market assets would have affected the volatility of a portfolio in which it was included. To perform our analysis, let's use the definition of a *moderate investor* laid forth by the American Association of Individual Investors (AAII).[13] Per the AAII, a moderate investor allocates 70 percent to stocks and 30 percent to bonds, a common asset allocation model. The innovative investor can also be moderate and diversify beyond stocks and bonds into alternative assets, such as bitcoin. Innovative yet moderate investors interested in bitcoin could do so by taking a small piece of their equity portfolio, say 1 percent, and purchasing bitcoin. In this way, they maintain their overall risk profile because equities are riskier than bonds, and so swapping one risky asset with another risky asset is a reasonable adjustment.

We built a model to simulate how a 70 percent equities–30 percent bonds portfolio would have behaved in comparison to a 1 percent bitcoin–69 percent equities–30 percent bonds portfolio. For equities, we used the S&P 500 index, and for bonds we used a broad-based U.S. bonds index known as the Bloomberg Barclays U.S. Aggregate Bond Index.

We calculated using quarterly rebalancing to maintain the original percentage target. As assets rise and fall, over time their percentages in a portfolio change. It's common practice to reassess each quarter and make small buy and sell transactions to reset the target percentages. For example, an investor that purchased a 1 percent position in bitcoin four years ago would have had a whopping 32 percent allocation by the start of 2017, as shown in Figure 7.20. The difference between a 1 percent and 32 percent portfolio allocation creates a drastically different risk profile and would likely not be appropriate for all. Hence the importance of rebalancing.

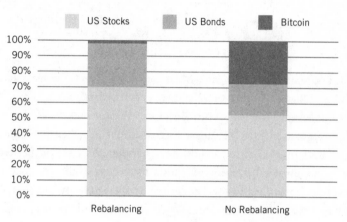

Figure 7.20 ■ The effects of rebalancing versus not rebalancing a portfolio
Data sourced from Bloomberg and CoinDesk

What if the innovative investor had deployed 1 percent of his or her equity capital into bitcoin at the start of 2013, peak of 2013, and start of 2015, done quarterly rebalancing, and held until our designated end date of January 3, 2017? Interestingly, while a 1 percent investment in any asset might seem insignificant, when done in bitcoin the results were definitive.

At the start of 2013, bitcoin was around $10 a coin and still had a tumultuous 2013 and 2014 in front of it. As a result, it's not surprising that there was an increase in both the absolute returns of the portfolio and the volatility. As can be seen in Figure 7.21, compound annual returns proved superior with a 1 percent allocation to bitcoin and volatility was 4 percent higher. In this case the volatility was worth it, because the bitcoin portfolio had a 22 percent greater Sharpe Ratio, offering more return for the risk taken (note that comparison calculations in the text were made using unrounded numbers, while the tables show rounded numbers).

To underscore the significance of compound annual returns 3.2 percent greater over a four-year period, we look at the end results. If both portfolios started at $100,000, the outperforming bitcoin portfolio would have accu-

Four-Year Holding Period (January 2013 to January 2017)

Metric	Base Case	1% Equity —> Bitcoin
Weekly Volatility	1.13%	1.18%
Sharpe Ratio	1.28	1.57
Compound Annual Returns	10.8%	14.0%

Figure 7.21 ■ Comparative performance of a four-year portfolio
with and without a 1 percent allocation of bitcoin
Data sourced from Bloomberg and CoinDesk

mulated approximately $170,000, while the one without bitcoin reached only about $150,000, a difference of $20,000 over four years.

Now comes the true test of bitcoin: if an investor had decided to deploy a 1 percent allocation into bitcoin at its November 29, 2013 peak and held it until the start of 2017, what would have happened? It would be reasonable to expect that even a 1 percent allocation to bitcoin would put a drag on the returns of the portfolio and also lower the Sharpe ratio. However, here is where the power of rebalancing and dollar cost averaging would have come into play. An investor would have endured one year of sliding prices (2014) before then enjoying two years of rising prices (2015 and 2016). By rebalancing quarterly, the investor would have been gradually adding to the bitcoin portion of the portfolio to make up for the continually lower percentage due to its falling price. In effect, the investor would have been dollar cost averaging down. As a result, the compound annual returns of this period are about equal for the two portfolios. More surprisingly, the portfolio with bitcoin would have had lower volatility! The power of diversification is becoming evident, and it leads to a marginally superior Sharpe ratio for the investor who held bitcoin as a 1 percent position in his or her portfolio during this period (see Figure 7.22).

Three-Year Holding Period (November 29, 2013 to January 2017)

Metric	Base Case	1% Equity —> Bitcoin
Weekly Volatility	1.17%	1.16%
Sharpe Ratio	0.89	0.90
Compound Annual Returns	7.5%	7.6%

Figure 7.22 ■ Comparative performance of a portfolio since November 2013
with and without a 1 percent allocation of bitcoin
Data sourced from Bloomberg and CoinDesk

However, it is the two-year period between 2015 and 2017 that really shines. Shown in Figure 7.23, the portfolio with a 1 percent allocation of bitcoin would have been less volatile, while improving compound annual returns by 0.6 percent, ultimately yielding a Sharpe ratio 14 percent better. Operating in the wild, innovative investors would have experienced the joy of a golden asset that both decreased volatility *and* increased returns when added to their portfolio, providing a double boost to the Sharpe ratio.

Two-Year Holding Period (January 2015 to January 2017)

Metric	Base Case	1% Equity —> Bitcoin
Weekly Volatility	1.24%	1.22%
Sharpe Ratio	0.54	0.61
Compound Annual Returns	4.7%	5.3%

Figure 7.23 ■ Comparative performance of a two-year portfolio
with and without a 1 percent allocation of Bitcoin
Data sourced from Bloomberg and CoinDesk

In the previous chapter, we explored the necessary use of tools such as modern portfolio theory and asset allocation to build an effective investment portfolio and to identify appropriate and compelling investment options for the innovative investor. In this chapter, we've looked through the lens of modern portfolio theory at bitcoin as an investment over time. The next chapters will address the broad characteristics of bitcoin and its digital siblings as an entirely new asset class with which the capital markets must reckon.

Chapter 8

Defining Cryptoassets as a New Asset Class

Thus far, we've covered the birth of Bitcoin, the rise of blockchain as a general purpose technology, a brief history of cryptoassets at large, the keys to portfolio management, and how bitcoin would have performed in the context of modern portfolio theory over its first eight years of life. What the innovative investor now needs is a framework to understand the general patterns to be expected of all cryptoassets going forward. To set the foundation for that framework, we need to first define what type of asset a cryptoasset is.

Are bitcoin and its digital siblings to be defined as commodities, as the Commodities Futures Trading Commission seems to believe?[1] Or are they better thought of as property, as the Internal Revenue Service has set forth?[2] The Securities and Exchange Commission has thus far steered clear of applying a specific label to all cryptoassets, though in late July 2017 it did release a report detailing how some cryptoassets can be classified as securities, with the most notable example being The DAO.[3]

While it's a great validation of cryptoassets that regulators are working to provide clarity on how to classify at least some of them, most of the existing laws set forth suffer from the same flaw: agencies are interpreting cryptoassets through the lens of the past.

What further complicates the situation is that not all cryptoassets are made equal. Just as there is diversity in equities, with analysts segmenting companies depending on their market capitalization, sector, or geography, so too is there diversity in cryptoassets. Bitcoin, litecoin, monero, dash, and zcash fulfill the three definitions of a currency: serving as a means of exchange, store of value, and unit of account. However, as we've seen, many other cryptoassets function as digital commodities, or cryptocommodities. These cryptocommodities include ether, storj, sia, and golem. Meanwhile, there are myriad cryptotokens for end-user-specific applications, such as augur, steem, singularDTV, or gamecredits. Moreover, all cryptoassets are alive with code that morphs based on the evolution of use cases and the value-add that the core open-source developers feel their cryptoasset can best fulfill.

How can a regulator possibly hope to put a cryptoasset in a category that is centuries old, when these assets are redefining themselves and breaking their own boundaries every couple of years, if not every couple of months?

They can't.

The point is not to bash regulators but to show how hard it is to classify a brand-new asset class, especially when it is the first digital native asset class the world has seen.

WHAT IS AN ASSET CLASS, ANYWAY?

While people accept that equities and bonds are the two major investment asset classes, and others will accept that money market funds, real estate, precious metals, and currencies are other commonly used asset classes,[4] few bother to understand what is meant by an asset class in the first place.

Robert Greer, vice president of Daiwa Securities, wrote "What Is an Asset Class, Anyway?"[5] a seminal paper on the definition of an asset class in a 1997 issue of *The Journal of Portfolio Management*. According to Greer:

> An asset class is a set of assets that bear some fundamental economic similarities to each other, and that have characteristics that make them distinct from other assets that are not part of that class.

Still fuzzy. Greer then goes on to define three superclasses of assets:

- Capital assets
- Consumable/transformable assets
- Store of value assets

Greer has the following to say about how to identify each superclass from the others (boldface ours):

Capital Assets

One thing all these capital assets have in common. **A capital asset might reasonably be valued on the basis of the net present value of its expected returns.** Therefore, everything else being equal (which it never really is), a financial capital asset (such as a stock or a bond) will decline in value as the investor's discount rate increases, or rise as that rate decreases. This economic characteristic unifies the superclass of capital assets.

Consumable/Transformable (C/T) Assets

You can consume it. You can transform it into another asset. It has economic value. But it does not yield an ongoing stream of value. . . . The profound implication of this distinction is that C/T assets, not being capital in nature, cannot be valued using net present value analysis. This makes them truly economically distinct from the superclass of capital assets. **C/T assets must be valued more often on the basis of the particular supply and demand characteristics of their specific market.**

Store of Value Assets

The third superclass of asset cannot be consumed; nor can it generate income. Nevertheless, it has value; it is a store of value asset. One example is fine art. . . . A broader and more relevant example is the category of currency, either foreign or domestic . . . store of value assets, can serve as a refuge during uncertainty (U.S. Cash), or offer currency diversification to the portfolio. [*Author note:* He does not define how to price it.]

Greer's superclasses are not clear-cut, as some assets can fall into two camps. For example, precious metals are both C/T assets and store of value assets. They are used in the circuitry of electronics or transformed into ornate forms of decoration (C/T asset), and they are also held solely as bars of value, not meant for consumption or transformation of any kind (store of value asset).

Cryptoassets most obviously fall into the C/T realm because they have utility and are consumed digitally. For example, developers use ether to gain access to Ethereum's world computer, which then can perform operations on smart contracts stored in Ethereum's blockchain. Hence, ether is consumed in the operation of a world computer. Then there is "attention," the fuel of advertising, which is leading to the creation of blockchain-based attention markets. Steemit is a social media platform with the native cryptoasset steem that rewards content creators and curators. Steem creates an economic system that rewards creators for new, quality content because that content enhances the platform, thereby increasing the value of steem.

While many cryptoassets are priced by the dynamics of supply and demand in markets, similar to more traditional C/T assets, for some holders of bitcoin—like holders of gold bars—it is solely a store of value. Other investors use cryptoassets beyond bitcoin in a similar way, holding the asset in the hope that it appreciates over time. Therefore, one could make the case that cryptoassets are like precious metals in that they belong to two superclasses of assets.

According to Greer, beneath these superclasses, there are classes. And within the classes, there are *subclasses*. These classifications can help innovative investors understand the different ways in which their investments relate to one another, and enable them to best diversify their portfolios.

For example, within the superclass of capital assets there is the class of *equities*, and within the class of equities there are subclasses like *large-cap value* or *small-cap growth*. Cryptoassets are a class that falls between the C/T and store of value superclasses. Within the cryptoassets class there are the subclasses of cryptocurrencies, cryptocommodities, and cryptotokens.

ETFS AND MUTUAL FUNDS ARE WRAPPERS, NOT ASSET CLASSES

It should be noted that when we talk about asset classes we are not doing so in the context of the investment vehicle that may "house" the underlying asset, whether that vehicle is a mutual fund, ETF, or separately managed account. With the growth of financial engineering and securitization of nearly every asset—and especially with the growing popularity of ETFs—one may find every type of asset at some point housed within an ETF. For example, ETFs for bitcoin and ether are already in the filing process with the SEC. For the purpose of our definition of asset classes, we are distinguishing the asset class from the form within which they are traded.

Delineating the separation between asset classes is no easy task. Greer gives us one solid point to distinguish assets, the economic similarities, but then leaves the rest to "characteristics that make them distinct." We've reviewed the academic literature further in order to crystallize the difference between asset classes. Much of the thinking in this chapter grew out of a collaboration between ARK Invest and Coinbase through late 2015 and into 2016 when the two firms first made the claim that bitcoin was ringing the bell for a new asset class.[6]

KEY DIFFERENTIATORS BETWEEN ASSET CLASSES

In our investigation of economic characteristics, we find the main differences come down to governance, supply schedule, use cases, and basis of value. Beyond economic similarities, asset classes also tend to have similar liquidity and trading volume profiles. Remember that a liquidity profile refers to how deep the order book of the markets is, while trading volume refers to how much is traded daily. Lastly, asset classes differ in their marketplace behavior, the most important of which include risk, reward, and correlation with other assets.

A general pattern exists of assets belonging in the same class behaving in a similar fashion. While each unique asset in a class will behave slightly differently from others, they resemble one another more closely than they resemble assets from other classes.

Brand-new assets within a class will differ in their behavior from more mature assets in the same class. Differences in maturity are particularly relevant for cryptoassets, with its oldest asset being only eight years old and newborns arriving on a weekly cadence.

At the moment, cryptoassets are best described as an emerging class. Their economic characteristics of governance, supply schedule, use cases, and basis of value are relatively fixed from the genesis of any particular cryptoasset. What will change more over time are the liquidity profile and marketplace characteristics as these assets mature. The remainder of this chapter will focus on the economic characteristics of cryptoassets, while the next chapter will dive into the progression of liquidity profiles and marketplace characteristics of different cryptoassets over time, and how those trends compare with other assets.

ECONOMIC CHARACTERISTICS OF AN ASSET CLASS

For the innovative investor, evaluating cryptoassets requires similar analysis as other assets. The starting point is to recognize and identify those economic characteristics that qualify them as their own asset class. We believe that this can be done by evaluating them on the basis of four criteria.

How Are They Governed?

Just as countries are governed, so too are assets. Typically, there are three layers of governance for assets of all kinds: the procurers of the asset, the people holding the asset, and a regulatory body or multiple regulatory bodies to oversee the behavior of the procurers and the holders.

For example, a typical equity has the management of the underlying company, the shareholders of the company, and the SEC as a regulatory overseer.

Energy commodities and their associated derivatives, such as oil and natural gas, are arguably more complex. The governance of the procurers is often much more dispersed and global in nature, as are the holders of the physical commodities. For the financial derivatives of these commodities, in the U.S. the Commodities Futures Trading Commission (CFTC) provides a layer of regulatory cohesiveness, while the SEC plays the same role for ETFs, mutual funds, and other fund structures that are composed of these assets.

Currency, a somewhat more controversial asset class, also has a unique governance profile. First, a central bank controls its distribution, while the people of the country, global businesses, and international creditors often dictate the exchange rate and use of the currency (though a controlling nation can manipulate these arenas). Regulatory bodies vary by nation, and there are international regulatory bodies like the International Monetary Fund if the currency of a nation hits choppy water.

Cryptoassets adhere to a twenty-first century model of governance unique from all other asset classes and largely inspired by the open source software movement. The procurers of the asset and associated use cases are three pronged. First, a group of talented software developers decide to create the blockchain protocol or distributed application that utilizes a native asset. These developers adhere to an open contributor model, which means that over time any new developer can earn his or her way onto the development team through merit.

However, the developers are not the only ones in charge of procuring a cryptoasset; they only provide the code. The people who own and maintain the computers that run the code—the miners—also have a say in the development of the code because they have to download new software updates. The developers can't force miners to update software. Instead, they must convince them that it makes sense for the health of the overall blockchain, and the economic health of the miner, to do so.[7]

The Seattle Public Library
Northeast Branch
Visit us on the Web: www.spl.org

Check out date: 02/04/22

xxxxxxxxx9923

Cryptoassets : the innovative invest
0010091889286   Due date: 02/25/22
book

TOTAL ITEMS: 1

Renewals: 206-386-4190
TeleCirc: 206-386-9015 / 24 hours a day
Online: myaccount.spl.org

* * * * * * * * * * * * * * * * * * * *

*Keep up to date on Library reopening
plans: www.spl.org/RoadToReopening*

VALD

DAV

xxxxxxxx9923

2/2/2022

Item: ï¿½0010091889286 ((book)

In addition to the developers and miners, there is a third level of governance among the procurers: the companies that offer services that interface between the cryptoasset and the broader public. These companies often employ some of the core developers, but even if they don't, they can assert significant influence over the system if they are a large force behind user adoption.

After the three groups of procurers, there are the holders or the end users who buy the cryptoasset for investment purposes or to gain access to the utility of the underlying blockchain architecture. These users are constantly providing feedback to the developers, miners, and companies, in whose interest it is to listen, because if users stop using the cryptoasset, then demand will go down and so too will the price. Therefore, the procurers are constantly held accountable by the users.

Last, there is an emerging regulatory landscape for cryptoassets. However, regulators are still considering exactly how they want to handle this emerging asset class.

What Is the Supply Schedule?

The supply schedule of an asset can be influenced by its three layers of governance, but the procurers typically have the strongest hand. For example, with equities there is an initial share issuance via an initial public offering (IPO). The IPO helps the management of the underlying company raise cash from the capital markets and get broader exposure for their company's brand. The company can continue to issue shares, via stock-based compensation or secondary offerings, but if they do so at too high a quantity, their investors may rebel because their ownership of the company is becoming diluted.

Bonds, on the other hand, are markedly different from equities. Once a company, government, or other entity issues a bond, that is a claim upon a fixed amount of debt. There is no negotiating on that debt except in the case of default. That same entity may issue more bonds going forward, but unless that issuance is an indicator of economic distress, typically a follow-on issuance of bonds will have little effect on a prior set of issued bonds.

Depending on the energy commodity, there can be varied supply schedules, though nearly all of them are calibrated to balance market supply and demand and to avoid supply gluts that hurt all procurers. For example, with oil, there's the famous Organization of the Petroleum Exporting Countries (OPEC), which has had considerable control over the supply levels of oil.

The central banks that control currency supply have even more control than OPEC. As the world has witnessed since the financial crisis of 2008 and 2009, a central bank can choose to issue as much currency in the form of quantitative easing as it wants. It does this most often through open market operations, such as buying back government issued bonds and other assets to inject cash into the economy. Central bank activity can lead to drastic increases in the supply of a fiat currency, as we have seen in the U.S. dollar. Figure 8.1 shows a comparison of the supply schedules of bitcoin, the U.S. dollar, and gold.[8]

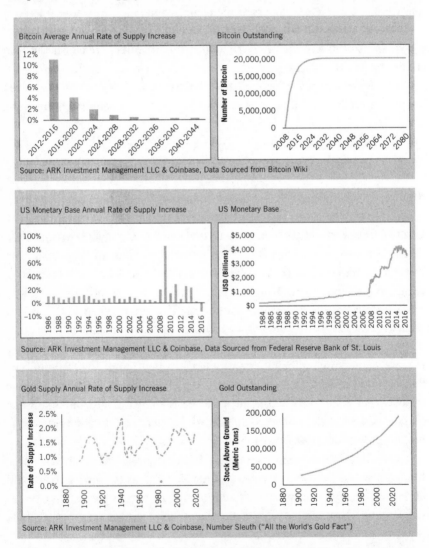

Figure 8.1 ■ Comparison of supply schedules of bitcoin, the U.S. dollar, and gold

Precious metals have long been valued for their scarcity and aesthetic appeal, even though, as metals, most are largely inferior to other more common metals. Their malleability makes them impossible to use for structural support as they can easily be deformed. However, due to their scarcity and now near universal acceptance as a form of beauty, they have come to be considered a relatively safe store of value. Notice also, Figure 8.1 reveals that gold's supply is on an inflationary schedule. In other words, each year more gold is pulled out of the ground than the year before, much to the surprise of many gold bugs.

Cryptoassets, like gold, are often constructed to be scarce in their supply. Many will be even more scarce than gold and other precious metals. The supply schedule of cryptoassets typically is metered mathematically and set in code at the genesis of the underlying protocol or distributed application.

Bitcoin provides for a maximum of 21 million units by 2140, and it gets there by cutting the rate of supply inflation every four years. Currently, the supply schedule is at 4 percent annually, in 2020 that will be cut to 2 percent annually, and in 2024 it will drop to 1 percent annually. As discussed earlier, Satoshi crafted the system this way because he needed initially to bootstrap support for Bitcoin, which he did by issuing large amounts of the coin for the earliest contributors. As Bitcoin matured, the value of its native asset appreciated, which means less bitcoin had to be issued to continue to motivate people to contribute. Now that Bitcoin is over eight years old, it provides strong utility to the world beyond as an investment, which drives demand. Over time, next to zero bitcoin will be issued, but the aim is for the network to be so big by then that all contributors get paid a sufficient amount via transaction fees, just like Visa or MasterCard.

Many other cryptoassets follow a similar model of mathematical issuance, though they differ widely in the exact rates. For example, Ethereum initially planned to issue 18 million ether each year in perpetuity. The thinking was that as the underlying base of ether grew, these 18 million units would become an increasingly small percentage of the monetary base. As a result, the rate of supply inflation would ultimately converge on 0 percent. The Ethereum team is currently rethinking that issuance strategy due to an intended change in its consensus mechanism. Choosing to change the issuance schedule of a cryptoasset from the plan at time of launch is more the exception than the norm, though since the asset class is still young we are not surprised by such experimentation.

Steemit's team pursued a far more complicated monetary policy with its platform, composed of steem (STEEM), steem power (SP), and steem dollars (SMD). The founding team initially chose STEEM to increase in supply by 100 percent per year. While they incorporated a wrinkle that would decrease the total units outstanding by periodically dividing it to combat outrageously large numbers, they quickly discovered that even this modification would not be enough to avoid an unsustainably high rate of inflation and devaluation of the platform. They have also chosen to modify their monetary policy post-inception.

Steemit is an example of why innovative investors should investigate the monetary policy of a platform to make sure it makes economic sense and avoid being caught in a situation similar to the STEEM bubble that we will detail in Chapter 10. As each individual cryptoasset matures, we expect the monetary policy to ossify into its mathematically metered intent.

How Are They Used?

Governance and supply schedules play an important role in the use cases of an asset. For equities and bonds, the use cases are straightforward. Equities allow a company to raise capital from the capital markets via issuance of shares, while bonds allow a company to raise capital via the issuance of debt. Currencies are clear-cut in their use cases as well, serving as a means of exchange, store of value, and unit of account.

Commodities are where use cases can become more diverse. The use cases for metals or semiconducting agents changes as technology progresses. For example, silicon was once a forgotten element, but with the age of semiconductors it has become vital, causing arguably the most innovative valley in the world to be named after it (though there is no physical silicon to be taken from the ground there).

Cryptoassets can be likened to silicon. They have come upon the scene due to the rise of technology, and their use cases will grow and change as technology evolves. Currently, bitcoin is the most straightforward, with its use case being that of a decentralized global currency. Ether is more flexible, as developers use it for computational gas within a decentralized world computer. Augur facilitates prediction markets on a decentralized system, economically compensating (or punishing) individuals for telling the truth (or lies).

Then there are the trading markets, which trade 24/7, 365 days a year. These global and eternally open markets also differentiate cryptoassets from the other assets discussed herein.

In short, the use cases for cryptoassets are more dynamic than any preexisting asset class. Furthermore, since they're brought into the world and then controlled by open-source software, the ability for cryptoassets to evolve is unbounded.

What Is the Basis of Value?

As Greer mentioned in his definition of superclasses, capital assets like equities and bonds are valued based on the net present value (NPV) of all future cash flows. With net present value, Greer refers to the idea that a dollar tomorrow is worth less than a dollar today. For example, if an investor puts $100 in a savings account and earns a 5 percent annual return (in the good old days), then one year from now that $100 will be worth $105. Therefore, investors either want the $100 today, or the $105 a year from now, but they don't want the $100 a year from now or they've effectively lost money.

C/T assets are priced by market dynamics of supply and demand, as are the more liquid store of value assets like currencies. However, it should be noted with currencies that the governance of the issuing nation can meddle with the exchange rate, and therefore basis of value, of the currency. Value assets like fine art are the hardest and most subjective to value, as often beauty is in the eye of the beholder.

Cryptoassets have two drivers of their basis of value: utility and speculative.

Digital units of bitcoin don't exist beyond unspent transaction outputs—or credits—in bitcoin's blockchain. Therefore, a significant portion of the basis of value is what the underlying blockchain enables the users of the assets to do; in other words, bitcoin's utility value.

Utility value refers to what the underlying blockchain is used for, and therefore what the demand is for its asset. For example, Bitcoin's blockchain is used to transact bitcoin and therefore much of the value is driven by demand to use bitcoin as a means of exchange. Similarly, bitcoin can be used as a store of value, so a percentage of the bitcoin outstanding is demanded for that use case. All these use cases temporarily bind bitcoin, drawing it out of the supply of bitcoin outstanding. The more that people want to use bitcoin, the more they'll have to pay to get access to it.

On top of utility value, there's a speculative value to a cryptoasset. Since cryptoassets are all under a decade old, much is still left to be seen regarding how each will develop, which is where speculative value comes into play.

Speculative value is driven by people trying to predict how widely used a particular cryptoasset will be in the future. It's similar to newly publicly traded companies, where much of the market capitalization of the company is based on what investors expect from it in the future. As a result, the multiple of sales at which the company is valued is much greater than the multiple of sales that a more mature company will trade at. For example, a young, fast-growing company with $100 million in revenue may be worth $1 billion, whereas a much older company that is hardly growing may have $500 million in sales and also be worth $1 billion. With these two companies, the younger one has greater investor speculation about the future cash flow of the company baked into what it's worth, while with the older company, investors are valuing it much more closely to its current revenue situation because they know more or less what they'll be getting going forward.

With cryptoassets, much of the speculative value can be derived from the development team. People will have more faith that a cryptoasset will be widely adopted if it is crafted by a talented and focused development team. Furthermore, if the development team has a grand vision for the widespread use of the cryptoasset, then that can increase the speculative value of the asset.

As each cryptoasset matures, it will converge on its utility value. Right now, bitcoin is the furthest along the transition from speculative price support to utility price support because it has been around the longest and people are using it regularly for its intended utility use cases. For example, in 2016, $100,000 of bitcoin was transacted every minute, which creates real demand for the utility of the asset beyond its trading demand. A great illustration of bitcoin's price support increasingly being tied to utility came from Pantera Capital, a well-respected investment firm solely focused on cryptoassets and technology. In Figure 8.2 we can see that in November 2013 bitcoin's spec-

Figure 8.2 ■ Comparison of bitcoin's price with its utility value
Source: https://medium.com/@PanteraCapital/bitcoin-continues-exponential-growth-in-2016
-blockchain-letter-february-2017-9445c7d9e5a2

ulative value skyrocketed beyond its utility value, which is represented here by transactions per day using Bitcoin's blockchain (CAGR is the compound annual growth rate).

Speculative value diminishes as a cryptoasset matures because there is less speculation regarding the future markets the cryptoasset will penetrate. This means people will understand more clearly what demand for the asset will look like going forward. The younger the cryptoasset is, the more its value will be driven by speculative value, as shown in Figure 8.3. While we expect cryptoassets to ossify into their primary use cases over time, especially as they become large systems that support significant amounts of value, their open-source nature leaves open the possibility that they will be tweaked to pursue new tangential use cases, which could once again add speculative value to the asset.

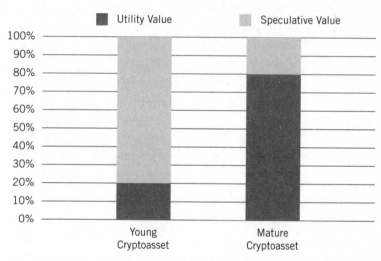

Figure 8.3 ■ The maturation of a cryptoasset from speculative to utility value

Speculative value in young markets is hard to estimate and can be dangerous to play with, as often only a few investors have a good basis for the future value of the asset, while the rest follow the movement of the market.

Benjamin Graham uses a famous example in his classic investing book *The Intelligent Investor*, where he personifies the market as Mr. Market, who is prone to oscillation between dark and ebullient moods. When Mr. Market is dark, he'll throw assets around, damaging their value to beneath their utility value. When Mr. Market is ebullient, he'll pay most any price for assets, driving them far above their utility value with hefty speculative premiums. Mr. Market is a fictional representation of the movement of crowds, and Graham suggests that investors do their fundamental work on the asset and from there ignore the moods of Mr. Market. Speaking of Mr. Market, let's discuss how cryptoasset marketplace behavior evolves over time.

Chapter 9

The Evolution of Cryptoasset Market Behavior

I n the previous chapter, we discussed what differentiated asset classes from one another. We identified economic characteristics, liquidity and trading volume profiles, and marketplace behavior, as key differentiators. The economic characteristics covered in Chapter 8 are largely well defined at the launch of an asset, though any given cryptoasset's economic characteristics may evolve more than a stock, and certainly more than a bond, given the nature of its open-source software.

Inarguably, the liquidity and trading volume profiles along with the marketplace behavior of an asset class—and individual examples within an asset class—mature considerably over time. For example, in 1602 when the United Dutch Chartered East India Company (Dutch East India Company, for short) became the first company to issue stock,[1] the shares were extremely illiquid. When first issued, no stock market even existed, and purchasers were expected to hold on to the shares for 21 years, the length of time granted to the company by the Netherlands' charter over trade in Asia. However, some investors wanted to sell their shares, perhaps to pay down debts, and so an informal market for the stock (the very first stock market) developed in the Amsterdam East India House. As more joint-stock equity companies were founded, this informal location grew, and was later formalized as the Amsterdam Stock Exchange, the oldest "modern" securities exchange in the world.[2] Despite the structure of the shares of the Dutch East India Company not changing much, their market liquidity and trading volumes changed considerably.

Similarly, when bitcoin, the first cryptoasset and therefore the crypto-analogue to the Dutch East India Company, was "issued" through the mining process, there was no market to transact or trade bitcoin. For much of 2009, there were hardly any bitcoin transactions, even though a new batch of 50 bitcoin was minted every 10 minutes. It wasn't until October 2009 that the first recorded transaction of bitcoin for the U.S. dollar took place: 5,050 bitcoin for $5.02, paid via PayPal.[3] This transaction was sent from one of Bitcoin's earliest proselytizers, Martti Malmi, to an individual using the name NewLibertyStandard, who was trying to set up the world's first consistent place of exchange between bitcoin and the U.S. dollar.[4]

To say it was an exchange in the sense of the word that we think of today would be an overstatement. NewLibertyStandard's attempt to create a trading location for bitcoin was sparsely populated and illiquid, yet the idea was there. It wouldn't be until the summer of 2010 that a formidable place of exchange would come into existence. In short, the bitcoin markets took time to develop, just as those for stocks or any other asset class.

The asset can stay the same, but the functioning markets around it and the way the asset changes hands can morph considerably. For example, currently the bond markets are undergoing significant changes, as a surprising amount of bond trading is still a "voice and paper market," where trades are made by institutions calling one another and tangible paper is processed. This makes the bond market much more illiquid and opaque than the stock market, where most transactions are done almost entirely electronically. With the growing wave of digitalization, the bond markets are becoming increasingly liquid and transparent. The same can be said of markets for commodities, art, fine wine, and so on.

Cryptoassets have an inherent advantage in their liquidity and trading volume profile, because they are digital natives. As digital natives, cryptoassets have no physical form, and can be moved as quickly as the Internet can move the 1s and 0s that convey ownership. The rapidity with which cryptoassets can be moved sets them apart from other asset classes—especially alternative assets like art, real estate, and fine wines—and should enable more liquid markets much earlier in their developmental history.

Correlations between assets are also relevant in the evolution of an asset class. Recall from Chapter 6 that correlation refers to the prices of assets moving together. With the globalization of markets, correlations have largely increased as national economies are attached at the hip. Many still turn to gold in risk-off periods, when they want something safe from the groupthink trading in the bond and equity markets.

As of April 2017, the aggregate network value for cryptoassets was so small on a relative basis, storing less than $30 billion in value, that they had yet to penetrate most traditional investor capital pools. Even though they are growing at an incredible clip, separation between cryptoasset markets and traditional investor capital pools still largely remains the case. As a result, cryptoassets currently have little correlation with traditional assets. However, we increasingly see signs of correlation between bitcoin and the broader capital markets (either negative or positive correlation), which makes sense as bitcoin is the most well-established cryptoasset and will likely be the first for traditional investors to venture into.

Over time, we expect increasing correlations (once again, either negative or positive) between cryptoassets and other asset classes, as overlap between the entities using these investments increases. The transition from an emerging asset class to a mature asset class involves being accepted by the broader capital markets.

It's critical for the innovative investor to understand the liquidity and trading volume profiles of cryptoassets and how they change as they mature. Given bitcoin's status and tenure, we'll begin there. Then for comparison, we'll pull in relevant examples from other top cryptoassets by market cap, such as ether, dash, ripple, monero, and litecoin.

BITCOIN'S LIQUIDITY AND TRADING VOLUME PROFILE

Bitcoin's liquidity has improved dramatically over time, and exchanges have grown from just Mt. Gox in July 2010 to over 40 as of the start of 2017.[5] Equally, the order books of individual exchanges have matured. For example, consider that on the first day Mt. Gox traded bitcoin, only 20 were traded, totaling 99 cents of value. On opening day Mt. Gox had an extremely thin order book. Now sites such as Bitcoinity.org provide metrics like, "Spread 100 BTC [%]," showing how much the price of bitcoin would move on different exchanges if 100 bitcoin were bought.[6]

In Figure 9.1, we see that there are five exchanges where placing a trade for 100 bitcoin (at the time, worth about $100,000) would not move the price more than 1 percent—and this was only for U.S. dollar-denominated order

Bitcoin exchanges

	Name	Rank	Volume [BTC]	Spread [%]	Spread 10 BTC[%]	Spread 100 BTC [%] ▲	Volatility (stddev)	Trades per minute
1	lakeBTC	189	83,761	0.13	⑧ 0.17	❶ 0.25	⑷ 1.44	⑧ 6.66
2	Bitfinex	❶ 6,025	❶ 425,505	❷ 0.03	❶ 0.11	❷ 0.54	⑺ 1.56	⑺ 6.53
3	Gemini	777	72,553	⑧ 0.05	❷ 0.12	❸ 0.66	❶ 1.24	1.22
4	itBit	❸ 3,060	73,374	0.10	0.25	⑹ 0.77	❷ 1.30	0.94
5	Bitstamp	❷ 3,627	❷ 195,757	⑺ 0.08	⑸ 0.20	⑸ 0.93	1.57	⑼ 4.09
6	GDAX	⑸ 1,766	⑹ 159,044	❶ 0.03	⑹ 0.19	1.02	❸ 1.42	❶ 9.09
7	BTC-e	⑷ 2,195	❸ 160,654	0.13	0.45	1.26	1.81	❷ 8.40
8	Bit-x	698	⑨ 97,547	0.43	0.68	1.45	2.33	2.22
9	Kraken	796	59,676	0.19	0.41	1.77	1.81	1.56

Figure 9.1 ■ Comparing the effect that the purchase of 100 bitcoin
has on prices among different exchanges
Source: Annotation of Bitcoinity.org screenshot

books. As can be seen in the upper-right tab, one can compare order books for
different currency pairs, like the yuan, yen, euro, and so on.

Greater liquidity is created from more trading activity, as there are more
people buying and selling bitcoin. Global trading volumes since the opening
of Mt. Gox have increased exponentially.[7] On January 5, 2017, bitcoin trading
activity clocked in at over $11 billion and bitcoin broke through $1,000 a coin
for the second time in its history (see Figure 9.2).

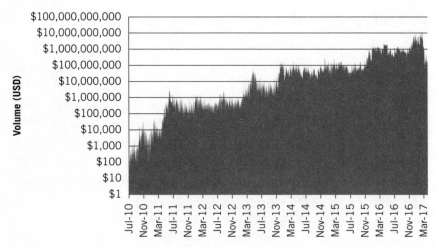

Figure 9.2 ■ Bitcoin's trading volume history
Data sourced from CryptoCompare

Just as trading equities evolved from an informal venue in Amsterdam to trading hundreds of billions of dollars daily in exchanges all over the world, so too has bitcoin evolved. We now have tens of exchanges globally trading hundreds of millions to billions of dollars daily. This increase in trading volume is a function of increased interest, which has driven maturation in bitcoin markets.

THE EVOLUTION OF CRYPTOASSET TRADING VOLUMES

Other cryptoassets show similar trends as they mature, but because they're younger than bitcoin, their variability in volume and liquidity is greater. For example, in 2016, Monero experienced a sizeable increase in notoriety—largely because its privacy features began to be utilized by a well-known dark market[8]—which sent its average trading volume skyrocketing. In December 2015, daily volume for the asset was $27,300, but by December 2016 it was $3.25M, well over a hundredfold increase. The price of the asset had appreciated more than 20-fold in the same period, so some of the increase in trading volume was due to price appreciation, but clearly a large amount was due to increased interest and trading activity in the asset. Figure 9.3 shows monero's historic trading volume.

To varying degrees, ether, dash, litecoin, ripple, and other cryptoassets have shown similar increases in trading volume as they have matured. Many

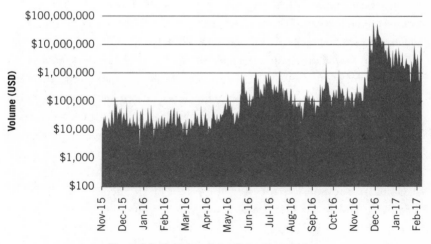

Figure 9.3 ■ Monero's trading volume history
Data sourced from CryptoCompare

cryptoassets will enjoy significant boosts in trading volumes upon sizeable price appreciation because a rising asset catches the attention of more investors and traders. Such a pattern is easily visible in monero in Figure 9.3. However, once the cryptoasset settles down into a price range, its trading volume will often settle into a new range as well. Some cryptoasset traders will then look for increases in volume as an early indicator that interest is picking up and that a move in the asset's price could be on the horizon.

Regardless of whether or not traders are right, burgeoning interest, trading volumes, and market liquidity all point to a maturing cryptoasset. If sustained, all of these are good indicators of health for the innovative investor to be aware of. If, however, the rise in trading volumes looks too steep and there is little news as to why, then that is reason to be wary. As we will cover in the next two chapters on speculation, sometimes volumes that rise too far and too fast can be a sign of manipulation or overheating markets.

REGULATORY IMPACT ON MARKET LIQUIDITY

While the innovative investor can generally expect assets with real value to mature and increase in liquidity and trading over time, external factors that impact markets can significantly dampen trading volume. Investors become skittish and at times regulation can forcibly clamp down on overenthusiasm. What helps an asset through these difficult periods is the diversity and depth of the exchanges and trading pairs offered globally.

On January 6, 2017, the day after bitcoin hit an all-time high trading volume of $11 billion in one day and crossed the $1000-a-coin mark for the second time in its life, the People's Bank of China (PBoC) announced it was investigating bitcoin trading on Chinese exchanges.[9] Shortly after, the PBoC issued new regulations for the trading of bitcoin on exchanges within the country, including curtailing margin trading, requiring trading fees, and demanding stronger anti–money laundering and know-your-customer protocols. All of these requirements were understandable and have helped to legitimize bitcoin, but they did lead to a noticeable decline in Chinese trading volume, which for much of 2016 was still greater than 90 percent of trading volumes worldwide in bitcoin.[10]

China was responsible for over 90 percent of all bitcoin trading volume worldwide, and now the PBoC was placing restrictions on this activity. The situation was eerily similar to a late 2013 incident, when the PBoC rolled out new regulations after bitcoin crossed the $1,000 mark for the first time.[11] Bitcoin's price crashed then, and continued to decline for over a year, and many feared the same would happen after the PBoC's commentary in 2017. While the price did initially fall precipitously, within a month it had recovered, and would shortly move to all-time highs. This was a very different reaction than 2013.

Bitcoin's price resilience in 2017, compared to the devastating price impact in 2013, reveals a valuable lesson for the innovative investor on the importance of trading volumes, exchange diversity, and trading pair diversity. In December 2013, trading volumes averaged $60 million, whereas in December 2016 they averaged $4.1 billion. Hence, there was significantly more market depth leading into the PBoC announcement in 2017 than there was in 2013. Furthermore, in 2013 bitcoin trading occurred on a much more limited number of exchanges (most activity was at Mt. Gox). Currency pair diversity was not nearly as robust either, both through different fiat currencies or other cryptoassets.

In 2017, bitcoin was able to recover quickly because market liquidity, exchange diversity, and trading pair optionality came through in spades. As a result, when the PBoC issued its regulations, there were plenty of other investors and traders outside of China to pick up the slack, leading to an inversion in market share of fiat currencies used to trade bitcoin, as shown in Figure 9.4. The Chinese yuan's percent of market share fell from 90+ percent to less than 10 percent.

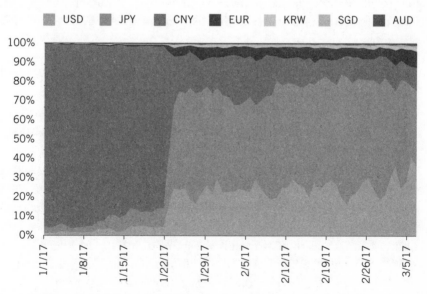

Figure 9.4 ■ Share of bitcoin trading volume in various currency pairs, highlighting the drop in the Chinese yuan's share in January 2017

Data sourced from CryptoCompare

The increase of dollar and yen trading in bitcoin is dramatic after January 22, 2017. Traders of bitcoin weren't rattled by the Chinese regulations for long, and increased investments from the United States and Japan filled the void and buoyed bitcoin's price.

TRADING PAIR DIVERSITY AS A SIGN OF MATURITY FOR CRYPTOASSETS

Balancing the diversity of exchanges and trading pairs is important for the robustness of any asset, including cryptoassets. Learning from bitcoin's reliance on too few currencies and exchanges early in its young life, we can now follow the trading pair diversity of other cryptoassets, especially with regard to fiat currency pairs.

Fiat currency pairs are particularly important for cryptoassets because they require significant integration with preexisting financial infrastructures. Due to high levels of required compliance, only a small number of cryptoasset exchanges offer the capability to accept fiat currency or connect to investors' bank accounts. These exchanges, such as Bitstamp, GDAX, itBit, Gemini, Kraken, and a few others, are hesitant to provide access to all cryptoassets, as they do not want to encourage trading in those that are not reputable. Given their caution, it is a stamp of approval for a cryptoasset to be added to their platforms.

Ethereum's ether provides a study on how exchanges adding a cryptoasset can increase the diversity of the trading pairs used to buy the asset. If our hypothesis on the importance of fiat currencies in cryptoasset trading holds, then as an asset grows in maturity and legitimacy, it should have more diversity in its trading pairs, with particularly strong growth in fiat currencies being used to buy the asset.

That has certainly been the case with ether. In Figure 9.5 we can see that over the course of 2016 the diversity in trading pairs used to buy it has grown significantly. The dollar has shown particular strength, and overall fiat currencies have increased from less than 10 percent of ether's trading volume in the spring of 2016 to nearly 50 percent in the spring of 2017.

We encourage the innovative investor to monitor the increase of trading pair diversity as a way to check the growing robustness and maturity of a single cryptoasset within the broader asset class. CryptoCompare.com is a good tool to identify these trends.

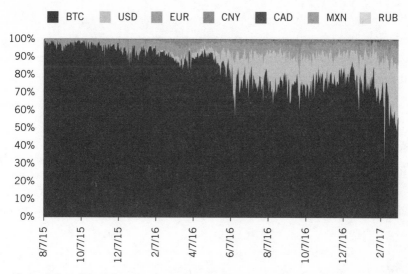

Figure 9.5 ■ Ether's increase in trading pair diversity and the use of fiat onramps
Data sourced from CryptoCompare

DECREASING VOLATILITY AS A CRYPTOASSET MATURES

Greater trading volumes, liquidity, exchange diversity, and trading pair diversity all lead to more resilience in the market. The cryptoasset is better able to absorb shocks without wild price swings—or at least with price swings that are diminishing in severity over time—which translates into a decrease in volatility.

We should expect to see decreasing volatility in cryptoassets when we plot this volatility over time. Since we already covered bitcoin's decreasing volatility in Chapter 7, we will showcase the other cryptoassets here. Figures 9.6, 9.7, and 9.8 show the volatility of ether, ripple, and monero over time. The following figures were made using CryptoCompare data, which provides similar graphs for other cryptoassets.[12]

From these trends, we can infer that this declining volatility is a result of increased market maturity. Certainly, the trend is not a straight line, and there are significant bumps in the road, depending on particular events. For example, monero had a spike in volatility in late 2016 because it experienced a significant price rise. This shows that volatility is not only associated with a tanking price but also a skyrocketing price. The general trend, nonetheless, is of dampening volatility (while not pictured in the following figures, Q2 and Q3 of 2017 were quite volatile for cryptoassets, underscoring that decreasing volatility will not unfold in a straight line).

Figure 9.6 ■ Ether's decreasing daily volatility

Data sourced from CryptoCompare

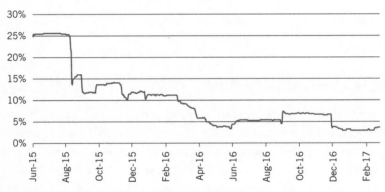

Figure 9.7 ■ Ripple's decreasing daily volatility

Data sourced from CryptoCompare

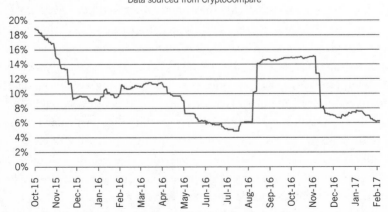

Figure 9.8 ■ Monero's decreasing daily volatility

Data sourced from CryptoCompare

In Figure 9.9, we compare bitcoin, ether, and dash's volatility since the end of 2015. Bitcoin has the lowest volatility because its markets are the most liquid and it has the greatest diversity of support from different exchanges and asset trading pairs. While bitcoin has sustained its low volatility, ether has come down significantly, and dash has varied widely. We included dash because we posit that it will continue to have problems with volatility over time. While it is gaining in acceptance, which should decrease its volatility, its software architecture creates a liquidity problem by requiring masternodes (entities similar to miners, but unique to Dash's architecture) to lock up a large amount of the dash outstanding. Such a requirement impedes the liquidity of dash's markets, thereby making the markets more prone to volatility.

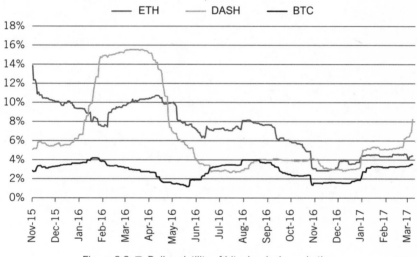

Figure 9.9 ■ Daily volatility of bitcoin, dash, and ether

Data sourced from CryptoCompare

Interestingly, just because an asset has a rapid price increase doesn't mean it must do so in a volatile manner. For example, through 2016, bitcoin more than doubled in price but decreased in volatility. Its daily gains and occasional losses were close enough to the mean not to register as overly volatile. Such behavior can indicate big traders are taking positions in an asset; often they gauge how much they are moving the price of an asset and make sure not to do so above a certain percentage point. In this way, they minimize volatility and slowly ease into a big position over a series of days, weeks, or months.

As these assets mature and their volatility decreases, recall that this can help boost the Sharpe ratio. Recall that since the Sharpe ratio is absolute returns[13] divided by volatility, if volatility comes down, then the returns don't have to be as stupendously good for the Sharpe ratio to still be a standout.

MARKETPLACE BEHAVIOR: CORRELATIONS

As an asset class is first emerging, it will be uncorrelated with the broader capital markets because there is not much overlap between the early adopters of that asset and the broader capital market investors. This is exactly what we saw with bitcoin when it was first invented and was only known to a small core group of developers and adopters (see Figure 9.10).

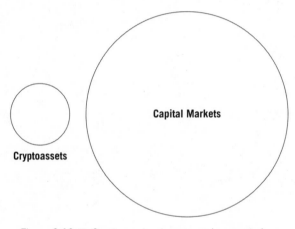

Figure 9.10 ■ Cryptoassets as an emerging asset class

At that time, with minimal overlap between bitcoin and capital market investors, bitcoin's correlation with other common asset classes was close to zero; events that made the broader capital markets move had no effect on bitcoin, and vice versa (see Figure 9.11).

As bitcoin's use grew, so too did its fame. It is now routinely discussed in publications such as the *Wall Street Journal*, the *New York Times*, and *Forbes* on a near-weekly basis. As a result, not only has it become part of the conversation, it's also becoming an investment vehicle for a larger audience within the broader capital markets.[14] A graphical depiction of the increased reach of cryptoassets can be seen in Figure 9.12.

Bitcoin's increased acceptance among capital market investors explains why it has surged on news that could be detrimental to other markets, such as Brexit, the surprise Trump election win, and the devaluation of the Chinese

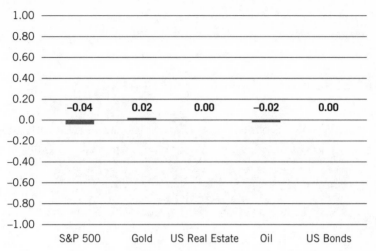

Figure 9.11 ■ Bitcoin's average 30-day rolling correlation with other major assets from January 2011 to January 2017

Data sourced from Bloomberg and CoinDesk

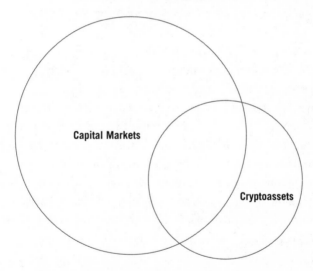

Figure 9.12 ■ Cryptoassets as a mature asset class

yuan.[15] Despite the many PBoC interventions, Chinese citizens used bitcoin to protect themselves against the erosion in value of their national currency. Figure 9.13 holds the key to inferring such behavior. On the left side of the figure, the y-axis shows the number of Chinese yuan needed to buy one dollar. As this number increases, the value of the Chinese yuan decreases, because more yuan are needed to buy one dollar. On the right side of the figure, the

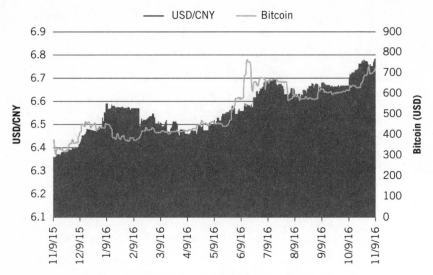

Figure 9.13 ■ Bitcoin's price history in relation to the devaluation of the Chinese yuan

Source: https://www.washingtonpost.com/news/wonk/wp/2017/01/03/
why-bitcoin-just-had-an-amazing-year/?utm_term=.64a6cfdf7398

price of bitcoin is shown. As the yuan decreases in value, the price of bitcoin increases. Such a correlation implies that people are likely buying bitcoin to protect themselves from further devaluation of the yuan.

While we expect to see bitcoin become increasingly correlated—either positively or negatively—with other broadly used asset classes, as new cryptoassets are born, they will likely have a low to zero correlation with the broader capital markets. At best, what they will show is some form of correlation with bitcoin, as it is of the same asset class. It should be expected that examples within an asset class will move together in some fashion. For example, leading up to the decision on the Winklevoss bitcoin ETF on March 10, 2017, bitcoin became increasingly correlated with ether and monero, and increasingly negatively correlated with litecoin (see Figure 9.14).

Since litecoin is such a close derivative of bitcoin, investors likely became concerned that people would rotate out of litecoin and move into bitcoin if the bitcoin ETF was approved. Ether and monero, on the other hand, are significantly different cryptoassets and therefore are held as complementary to bitcoin in a crypto portfolio. As bitcoin rose and fell, so too did these assets. This reinforces the need for the innovative investor to become knowledgeable about these assets' specific characteristics and recognize where correlations may or may not occur.

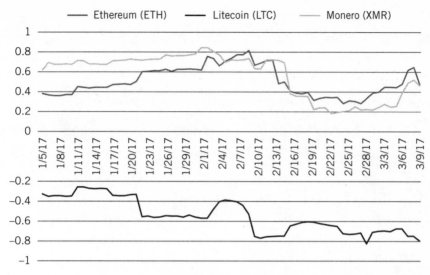

Figure 9.14 ■ Bitcoin's correlation with ether, litecoin, and monero, leading up to the SEC's rejection of the Winklevoss ETF

Data sourced from CryptoCompare

We expect to see more of this correlation trend play out. At best, newer cryptoassets will show some behavior tied to bitcoin and its siblings, either positively or negatively. Then as the cryptoasset grows, so too will its capital pool, and soon enough this will overlap with more traditional assets, strengthening its price relationship with the broader capital markets.

Although we're seeing maturation of these assets and greater overlaps with others, it's fair to consider bitcoin and cryptoassets to be in their early stages. There is still a lack of understanding by most investors. Innovative investors may be more educated on this topic than most, but they will encounter those who see cryptoassets as speculative pump-and-dump vehicles or worse. The next two chapters will address these arguments by putting cryptoassets in the context of the history of past investment bubbles, scams, and speculation.

Chapter 10

The Speculation of Crowds and "This Time Is Different" Thinking

O n its path to maturity, bitcoin's price has experienced euphoric rises and harrowing drops, as have many cryptoassets. One of the most common complaints among bitcoin and cryptoasset naysayers is that these fluctuations are driven by the Wild West nature of the markets, implying that cryptoassets are a strange new breed that can't be trusted. While each cryptoasset and its associated markets are at varying levels of maturity, associating Wild West behavior as unique to cryptoasset markets is misleading at best.

Equities, which many consider to be transacted on the most transparent, efficient, and fair markets in the world, had a rocky first couple of centuries. Yes, centuries. Not only were these markets prone to mass speculation, as people raced to buy and sell based on mostly fabricated rags-to-riches stories, but many times the markets were rigged against participants. Misleading prospectuses, manipulation of share prices, false accounting, and issuance of forged paper shares all led to losses.[1] The reality is that some of the most trusted markets in the world today also had Wild West beginnings.

By examining the most famous examples of markets gone wrong, specifically the sequence of events, the innovative investor is better informed by history to protect present and future wealth. When patterns reappear, it's a good time to exit right, or at least reassess one's investment strategy. This thinking is prudent with regard to any investment, including a venture into cryptoassets.

These examples also show that cryptoassets are not going through bizarre growing pains unique to them. Instead, they are experiencing the same evolutionary process that new asset classes over hundreds of years have had to go through as they matured. For those interested in a thorough history of such events, we highly recommend Edward Chancellor's *Devil Take the Hindmost: A History of Financial Speculation*.

While the way in which markets become dangerous to investors changes over time, and often becomes less insidious the more the asset and its associated markets mature, the potential for markets to destabilize never disappears. Much of the world learned that lesson during the financial crisis of 2008.

Broadly, we categorize five main patterns that lead to markets destabilizing:

- The speculation of crowds
- "This time is different"
- Ponzi schemes
- Misleading information from asset issuers
- Cornering

The first two will be detailed in this chapter, while the latter three we reserve for the next chapter. In addition to historical examples from decades past, we also give examples of how these patterns have manifested in cryptoasset markets.

THE SPECULATION OF CROWDS

While often given a bad name, speculation in and of itself is not a bad thing. For millennia, speculation has been integral to markets and trading, with some of the earliest evidence coming from second-century BC Rome.[2] The root of the word speculate comes from the Latin specular, which means "to spy out, watch, observe, examine, explore."[3] Speculators are keenly focused on the movement of the market, observing its swings and taking action accordingly.

Speculators, generally, differ from investors in the duration they intend to hold assets. They do not buy an asset with the intent to hold it for years. Rather, they buy the asset for an abbreviated period before selling it likely to the next speculator. Sometimes they do this to capitalize on short-term information they believe will move the market, other times they do it because they expect to ride the momentum of the market, regardless of its fundamentals. In short, they try to profit within the roller-coaster ride.

In comparison, the innovative investor diligently investigates the fundamentals of value for investing, and exits that investment when the markets no longer appear rational.

In our view, no matter the investment, it's important to discern when one is investing and when one is speculating. Benjamin Graham and David Dodd attempted to define the difference between investing and speculation in their book *Security Analysis*[4]: "An investment operation is one which, upon thorough analysis, promises safety of principal and a satisfactory return. Operations not meeting these requirements are speculative."

In his book *The Intelligent Investor*,[5] Graham recognized that speculation would always be present in the investing world, but he saw a need to distinguish between "good" and "bad" speculation.[6] He wrote, "There is intelligent speculation as there is intelligent investing. But there are many ways in which speculation may be unintelligent."

While speculators have often been scorned, they were perhaps most famously denigrated by Franklin D. Roosevelt in his inaugural address on March 4, 1933. As America was struggling through the Great Depression, which many pinned on the stock market crash of 1929, there was strong resentment against speculators. Every crisis loves a scapegoat. In his speech, Roosevelt called them "money changers" to invoke religious judgment:

> Primarily this is because rulers of the exchange of mankind's goods have failed through their own stubbornness and their own incompetence, have admitted their failure, and have abdicated. Practices of the unscrupulous money changers stand indicted in the court of public opinion, rejected by the hearts and minds of men.
>
> True they have tried, but their efforts have been cast in the pattern of an outworn tradition. Faced by failure of credit they have proposed only the lending of more money. Stripped of the lure of profit by which to induce our people to follow their false leadership, they have resorted to exhortations, pleading tearfully for restored confidence. They know only the rules of a generation of self-seekers. They have no vision, and when there is no vision the people perish.
>
> The money changers have fled from their high seats in the temple of our civilization. We may now restore that temple to the

> ancient truths. The measure of the restoration lies in the extent
> to which we apply social values more noble than mere monetary
> profit.[7]

While Roosevelt's judgment is understandable, market realities show that speculation has its place in the investment world. Speculators often jump on opportunities more quickly than does a typical investor, which begins the process of pricing new information into the value of an asset. In seeking to profit from opportunity, speculators help drive the search between buyers and sellers for a mutually agreed upon price. When a shortage of an asset is on the horizon, whether it be energy commodities or electronic hardware, speculators will quickly bid up the price of that good. As a result, more suppliers are drawn to the market, accelerating the alleviation of the shortage in classic supply and demand economics.

When it comes to innovation, such as the introduction of railroads, automobiles, or the Internet, speculation served to allocate money to the rapid buildout of the infrastructures necessary to support these sweeping innovations. Speculators are the ones who first allocate money because they have the highest tolerance for risk and are always on the lookout for new information. While speculation typically ends with a supply glut because too much money eventually pours into the innovation, the glut is often temporary. The arrival and implementation of copious amounts of capital may lead to an excess of capacity, but as the innovation gains mass adoption over the following decades, the abundance of infrastructure proves useful. Such was the case with the rapid buildout of railways in Europe in the mid-1800s and the deployment of fiber optic cables to support the Internet in the 1990s.

Single speculators, or small groups of them, typically do not destabilize markets. It is when the groups turn into crowds that the negative ramifications build. In this sense, the vitriol should not be directed so much at speculation, but instead at crowd behavior that overtakes the capital markets.

Crowd theory was pioneered by Gustave Le Bon, whose most famous work was *The Crowd: A Study of the Popular Mind*. In his later book *The Psychology of Revolution*, Le Bon wrote:

> Man, as part of a multitude, is a very different being from the
> same man as an isolated individual. His conscious individual-
> ity vanishes in the unconscious personality of the crowd. . . .

> Among the other characteristics of crowds, we must note their infinite credulity and exaggerated sensibility, their short-sightedness, and their incapacity to respond to the influences of reason. Affirmation, contagion, repetition, and prestige constitute almost the only means of persuading them. Reality and experience have no effect upon them.[8]

These characteristics are dangerous in the context of a market. Credulity, or to be more direct, gullibility, leads the masses to readily believe what they are told, whether by fellow speculators or the management behind different assets coming to market.

Credulity is often what draws individual speculators to the crowd, and once there, the speculator is trapped within groupthink. The four characteristics of persuasion Le Bon mentions only exacerbate the situation: *Affirmation* leads the credulous to more strongly believe in their strategies when the market continues to go up, and that thinking spreads like a *contagion*. This pattern is *repeated*, again and again, as the speculators chase the returns of the most *prestigious* of assets. Unfortunately, when the market turns and the prestige is gone, the contagion of terror spreads just as quickly through the speculative crowd.

Tulipmania

The most famous instance of mass speculation in a commodity happened in the Dutch Republic in the 1630s. As with most periods of mass speculation, the time was right. With their merchants fueling trade, the Dutch enjoyed the highest salaries of any in Europe, financial innovation was in the air, and money was free-flowing. Shares of the Dutch East India Company had been rewarding shareholders handsomely for their investments.[9] Fueled by enthusiasm, wealthy citizens poured money into properties, leading to a robust housing market. The ongoing appreciation of asset values created an excess of wealth to fund further asset purchases, setting up a positively reinforcing feedback loop into asset bubble territory.[10]

While the wealthy sowed the grounds for an asset bubble, initially not everyone could take part. Dutch East India shares were expensive and illiquid, making them inaccessible to all but the rich, and the same went for prized properties.

A tulip, on the other hand, was much more affordable. Yet due to a quirk of nature, an affordable tulip had the potential to morph into one that would make its owner rich. A virus transmitted by aphids turned solid-colored tulips into a prized variegated variety, with streaks of lighter hues through darker colors, resembling flames.[11] The cause of such variegation was not known at the time and so lent itself to speculation, as people tried to predict which tulips would develop the unique coloration.

On the other side of the transformation, however, was death, as the virus eventually killed the tulip. Speculators, therefore, passed the tulips around like hot potatoes, hoping they could sell them to the next speculator for a higher price, until the last person was left with a claim on a dead tulip.

Tulips had promised value since their introduction to Europe in the mid-1500s, but it was not until 1634 and the spread of the virus that prices increased exponentially, causing what is commonly referred to as Tulipmania. What began with small groups of speculators turned into crowds of speculators, as outsiders from other countries were drawn to Dutch tulip markets upon hearing stories of the immense riches to be gained. Meanwhile, the experienced withdrew from participation or shunned the tulip trade, as explained by Chancellor:

> The wealthy amateur bulb collectors, who had long shown a readiness to pay vast sums for the rarer varieties, withdrew their custom as prices began to soar, while the great Amsterdam merchants continued investing their trading profits in town houses, East India stock, or bills of exchange—for them, tulips remained merely an expression of wealth, not a means to that end.[12]

Since much of a tulip's life is spent as a bulb and not a blossom, it lends itself to a futures market, which the Dutch called a windhandel, or the wind trade.[13] A futures market is where a buyer and a seller agree to the future price of a good. When that specific time arrives, the buyer must pay the seller the agreed upon amount.

However, in those days, waiting for that agreed-upon time was not fast enough for the crowds of speculators. The tulip futures contracts themselves were traded, sometimes as many as 10 times in a day.[14] Considering these trades were made person to person, 10 trades in a day was representative of a liquid and frenzied market.

With the futures market, the value of tulips could be abstracted even more. People didn't have to worry about the actual delivery of the tulip—they just had to make sure they could sell the contract for a higher price than they themselves had bought it for. While the frenzy over tulips had been building for a few years, the mania peaked during the winter of late 1636 and early 1637, when the tulip bulbs were still dormant in the ground. Therefore, the period of greatest speculation during Tulipmania was not accompanied by a single blossoming tulip changing hands.[15]

Two factors made the crowd speculation even worse. According to a study in *The Economist*, government officials were in on the action themselves and moved to change the futures contracts to options. The result was that:

> Investors who had bought the right to buy tulips in the future were no longer obliged to buy them. If the market price was not high enough for investors' liking, they could pay a small fine and cancel the contract. The balance between risk and reward in the tulip market was skewed massively in investors' favour. The inevitable result was a huge increase in tulip options prices.[16]

The second factor was that much of the trade began to be financed by notes of personal credit. Therefore, not only were the bulbs not changing hands, neither was physical money. Transactions were made on simple promises to deliver money in the future.

It should be clear to the innovative investor that the delusion of value here was created by the frenzy of a crowd. As Chancellor points out, "By the later stages of the mania, the fusion of the windhandel with paper credit created the perfect symmetry of insubstantiality: most transactions were for tulip bulbs that could never be delivered because they didn't exist and were paid for with credit notes that could never be honored because the money wasn't there."

Cheap credit often fuels asset bubbles, as seen with the housing bubble that led to the financial crisis of 2008. Similarly, cryptoasset bubbles can be created using extreme margin on some exchanges, where investors are effectively gambling with money they don't have.

Back to tulips. At that time, the guilder served as currency in the Dutch Republic. Paper money didn't exist; instead, metal that held real value was used. Each guilder contained 0.027 ounces of gold. Therefore, 37 guilders held an ounce of gold, and 592 guilders contained a pound of gold. The highest recorded amount paid for a tulip was 5,200 guilders, or the equivalent of nearly nine pounds of gold.[17] At that time, an average year's work yielded 200 to 400 guilders, and modest town houses could be bought for 300 guilders. The tulip that fetched nine pounds of gold was worth the equivalent of 18 modest town houses: speculators were paying for single tulips with what would take them over a decade to pay off, and with money they didn't have.

It all came crashing down in February 1637. Spring was approaching, and tulips would be blossoming soon. Contractual dates would soon require the conversion of the notes of credit into real money. The merchants that drove the economic machine were largely unaffected, because they had "continued investing their trading profits in town houses, East India stock, or bills of exchange."[18] While it was the wealth of these merchants that caused the masses to yearn for similar riches, the merchants were unscathed by the crash they precipitated. The crash did not set off a recession throughout the economy, which was one saving grace of Tulipmania.

It was the common people, less experienced in investing, that had been swept up in the madness of the crowd who were the hardest hit. Fights over the amount due per contract ensued. A little over a year after the bubble burst, the Dutch government stepped in to declare that the contracts could be settled for 3.5 percent of their initial value. While a marked improvement over paying the full contract, 3.5 percent of the most expensive tulip would still require a year's work for some unlucky citizens.

The Speculation of Crowds Comes to Cryptoassets

As with Tulipmania, cryptoassets are vulnerable to the speculation of crowds. This is especially true as people fixate on the incredible returns some early bitcoin investors enjoyed and hope that the latest cryptocurrency, cryptocommodity, or cryptotoken will make them rich too.

However, remember that just because the unfettered enthusiasm of a crowd takes an asset to unreasonable highs doesn't mean the asset itself is flawed. Tulips are still enjoyed and sold worldwide. And as we saw with the tech and telecom boom, there were gems such as Amazon and Salesforce that would reward their patient investors spectacularly for years to come. The investors who got burned were the ones who bought because everyone else was buying, and then sold because everyone else was selling. The best way to avoid getting burned in this manner is to do proper due diligence and have an investment plan that is adhered to. If the urge is to buy the asset because everyone else is buying it and it keeps going up, then it's likely best to walk away from any consideration of that investment. Speculative bubbles are particularly dangerous when there is no underlying long-term value proposition to the asset. In these cases, it's as bad as gambling (or worse, as there's an illusion of value).

We sometimes hear skeptical investors warn of the dangers of bitcoin. Nout Wellink, the former president of the Dutch Central Bank, is famous for saying, "This is worse than the tulip mania. At least then you got a tulip, now you get nothing."[19] While we understand that some may have a hard time grasping that something with no physical form could have value, at this point in its life, bitcoin is a far cry from tulips.

The key to understanding bitcoin's value is recognizing it has utility as "Money-over-Internet-Protocol" (MoIP)—allowing it to move large amounts of value to anyone anywhere in the world in a matter of minutes—which drives demand for it beyond mere speculation. While tulips have aesthetic appeal, it is a stretch to argue that their utility is on par with MoIP in the digital age. It's important to investigate the underlying utility of any other cryptoasset that the innovative investor may be considering.

That said, bitcoin has had periods when crowds momentarily overtook the markets. These times are worthwhile to examine and learn from, and it's important to note that bitcoin has always recovered from these periods of mass speculation, a major differentiator from tulips. There are six periods over the last eight years when the crowd temporarily controlled the bitcoin market. The innovative investor will take note that the power of crowds to move bitcoin's markets has been moderating over time. We include this dive into bitcoin's speculative past to help inform future investigation of cryptoassets as they come to market and inevitably get swept up in periods of mass speculation.

Bitcoin Bubbles

When Mt. Gox was established, bitcoin finally became accessible to the mainstream. Prior to this point, bitcoin holders had mostly been computer and cryptography wizzes, acquiring bitcoin as a function of running the computers that supported the network. Figure 10.1 shows the price action of bitcoin on a log scale since the start of Mt. Gox. Recall that charts with log scales are good at showing the percent price appreciation of an asset over time. On a linear scale, the early years of bitcoin's price appreciation would be less evident.

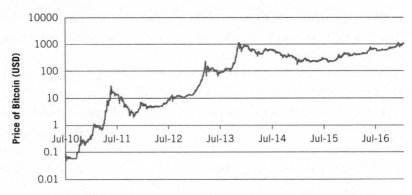

Figure 10.1 ■ Bitcoin's price action from Mt. Gox until early 2017

Data sourced from CoinDesk

What is immediately apparent is bitcoin's price appreciation in the year following the opening of Mt. Gox. When Mt. Gox opened, bitcoin was worth less than $0.10, and just a year later it was worth over $10. While $10 may not sound like much, consider that in the period of a year bitcoin increased 100-fold, meaning that a $100 investment had turned into $10,000.

Another significant leg up was in November 2013, when bitcoin made its infamous run past the price of $1,000 per coin for the first time. While many people new to the space think that was bitcoin's first bubble, in fact, it had many bubbles before that. Figure 10.2 shows the percentage change in bitcoin's

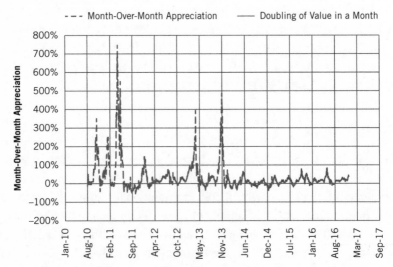

Figure 10.2 ■ Bitcoin's history of doubling price in a one-month period

Data sourced from CoinDesk

price over 30-day periods, or what is known as month-over-month appreciation. It becomes clear that bitcoin has experienced six one-month periods when it doubled in price.

Three of these doublings happened in the year after the opening of Mt. Gox. The last ascent during this period was the most phenomenal, when on May 13, 2011, the price increased more than 700 percent over the previous month. While there were respective drivers to these price runs, by and large they were fueled by the ability of more mainstream users to gain access to bitcoin through Mt. Gox. Small pieces of information created snowball effects that took the market by storm.

To understand how these bubbles unfolded, it is helpful to quantify certain aspects. First, we will define a *bitcoin bubble cycle* as being recognizable on the first day that bitcoin's price has doubled from its price 30 days prior. The bubble ends when the price stops falling from the month prior, firming up with month-over-month gains for three straight days. These bubbles are visible on bitcoin's price chart in Figure 10.3.

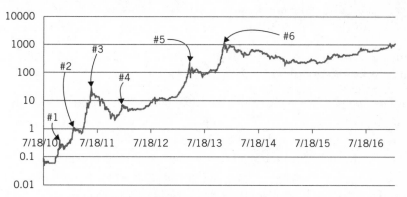

Figure 10.3 ■ Bitcoin's price bubbles
Data sourced from CoinDesk

Price bubbles after the launch of Mt. Gox peaked at the following prices on the following dates:

- November 6, 2010: $0.39
- February 9, 2011: $1.09
- June 8, 2011: $29.60
- January 8, 2012: $7.11
- April 9, 2013: $230
- December 4, 2013: $1,147

Clearly, the time periods soon after the launch of Mt. Gox were particularly exciting, but also at times harrowing. On the other side of every peak there is a dangerous trough, and bitcoin investors in these bubbles were not spared. Within the period defined as a bitcoin bubble, the average decline from peak price to trough price was 63 percent. The bubbles that peaked in June 2011 and December 2013 were particularly devastating, with losses of 93 percent and 85 percent respectively.

More insidious than the precipitous nature of the losses is how they unfolded compared to the rises. Sharp rises are often characterized by investor exuberance, quickly escalating as more and more jubilantly pile in. The falls, on the other hand, are sustained excruciation. The pattern is qualitatively visible in Figure 10.3, as the ascent to the peak of a bubble is like a rocket taking off, while the decent is more like a parachute drifting to the ground.

The longer duration of descents as opposed to ascents is important for the innovative investor to keep in mind, as sometimes it may feel like the drop from the peak of a bubble will never end. Immature investors will typically cry out in defeat when they can't tolerate further losses. Sadly, these last cries of capitulation are often when a bear market is getting ready to turn around.

The Steemit Bubble

A large number of cryptoassets other than bitcoin have gone through similar stratospheric ascents, fueled by the speculation of crowds, and corresponding descents. A good example was in the middle of 2016, when the new blockchain architecture Steemit caught everyone's attention. Its premise was to provide an open publishing or blogging platform on which authors who wrote good articles and posts were rewarded by readers with the cryptoasset steem. Steemit served as a decentralized Reddit of sorts, with flavors of the blogging site Medium mixed in. The architecture was supported by a convoluted, albeit innovative, flow of monetary policy between miners, content creators, content curators, and more.

On July 1, 2016, the total network value of Steemit was around $16 million. Two weeks later it was around $350 million, a more than 20-fold increase.[20] Such rapid changes in price are almost always fueled by mass speculation and not fundamental growth. Behavior changes slowly, and many of the use cases put forth by cryptoassets will require the mainstream to adapt to these new platforms. Speculators, on the other hand, move quickly.

As shown in Figure 10.4, steem's price in bitcoin terms would fall from its mid-July peak by 94 percent three months later, and by 97 percent at the end of the year. This doesn't mean the platform is bad. Rather, it shows how the speculation and excitement about its prospects fueled a sharp rise and fall in price.

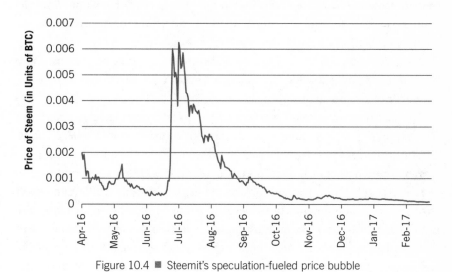

Figure 10.4 ■ Steemit's speculation-fueled price bubble

Data sourced from CryptoCompare

The Zcash Bubble

One of the most meteoric rises and crashes was the October 2016 rollout of the new privacy-focused cyptocurrency zcash (ZEC). Few cryptocurrencies have been more anticipated than this one, and rightfully so, given its strong engineering team. Ethereum's Vitalik Buterin was an advisor and described Zcash as providing the "advantages of using a public blockchain, while still being sure that their private information is protected."[21] Two well-regarded cryptoasset investment firms, Pantera Capital and Digital Currency Group, were involved with Zcash as well. Zcash technology targeted the privacy-centric vertical that dash and monero occupied, both of which were in the top 10 of cryptocurrencies in terms of network value when zcash was released. The excitement was palpable.

Integral to the ensuing price bubble was how the Zcash team structured the issuance of zcash, which they did with good intention. As we discussed in Chapter 5, they chose to follow an issuance model similar to bitcoin's, which meant that upon launch of its blockchain there would be zero units of zcash outstanding. From zero units outstanding, all units would be issued organically through miners competing to add blocks to Zcash's blockchain and getting paid with newly minted zcash via coinbase transactions. The Zcash team had implemented a further tweak, known as a *slow-start*, that would limit the initial size of coinbase transactions[22] to miners. The slow-start was intended as a safety feature in case there were any bugs in Zcash's code. This prudent model was markedly different from the crowdsale model that many cryptoassets have been pursuing (which will be discussed further in Chapter 16), but it also drastically limited the initial supply.

Zcash frenzy was stoked further by the recent increase in popularity of futures trading of cryptoassets. One exchange known as BitMEX began offering futures prior to the launch of zcash, which spiked to 10 bitcoin per zcash.[23]

The combination of limited initial supply with widespread demand led to a classic supply shortage that boosted the price of zcash. On the first day of trading, the coin momentarily achieved a price of 3,300 bitcoin, or more than $2 million dollars per zcash, on Poloniex.[24] Within two days it had crashed below 1 bitcoin per zcash and continued to fall, closing out 2016 at a price of .05 bitcoin per zcash, or roughly $48.[25] While zcash has since stabilized and continues to hold great promise as a cryptoasset, its rocky start was caused by mass speculation.

Words of Warning for the Innovative Investor Tempted by Bubbles

Robert Shiller, author, professor, and Nobel Prize winner, defined a bubble as "a social epidemic that involves extravagant expectations for the future."[26] We've talked much about the expectations for the future of cryptoassets.

However, we also believe innovative investors must be grounded in common sense in order to identify proper investments from improper ones, and they need to recognize when buying opportunities exist and when the madness of the crowd has taken over. When a cryptoasset is skyrocketing, it can be hard to resist the urge to jump in and ride the rocket. However, the timing can be precarious, and spotting the end of a bubble is not easy. By the time the bubble is popping and the speculation of crowds has turned on itself, it's often too late. Alan Greenspan encapsulated the idea nicely: "You can spot a bubble. They're obvious in every respect. But it is impossible for the majority of participants in the market to call the date when it blows. Every bubble by definition deflates."[27]

"THIS TIME IS DIFFERENT"

When asset markets are taken over by mass speculation and prices reach nose-bleed territory, a common refrain can often be heard: "This time is different." Typically, the logic goes that the markets have evolved from more primitive years, and financial engineering innovations have led to robust markets that can't possibly crash. Time and again this thesis has been refuted by subsequent market crashes. In their well-regarded book *This Time Is Different: Eight Centuries of Financial Folly*, Carmen Reinhart and Kenneth Rogoff deliver a 300-page tour de force to prove that this time is never different.

They describe how "this time is different" thinking was used to justify the sustainability of jubilant markets prior to the 1929 crash that led to the Great Depression. Proponents of "this time is different" thinking claimed that business cycles had been cured by the creation of the Federal Reserve in 1913. The thinking was that the Federal Reserve could use monetary policy to boost economies when production and consumption were flagging, and they could reel in markets when they showed signs of overheating. Others pointed to increasing free trade, declining inflation, and scientific methods being applied to corporate management that were leading to much more accurate production and inventory levels.[28]

In the October 16, 1929, issue of the *New York Times*, Yale economist Irving Fisher declared, "Stock prices have reached what looks like a permanently high plateau."[29] His proclamation would go down as the worst stock tip in history, as eight days later the market dropped by 11 percent. On October 28, it would fall another 13 percent, and on October 29 another 12 percent. A month after this declaration was printed in the *New York Times*, Fisher went broke and the Dow had lost almost half its value prior to the crash.[30]

Similar thinking characterized the tech-and-telecom boom in the late 1990s and early 2000s. As eloquently described by Chancellor:

> The 1990s bull market was accompanied by the reappearance of a new era ideology similar to that of the 1920s. Known as the "new paradigm," or the "Goldilocks economy" (like the porridge in the fairy tale it was neither too hot nor too cold), the theory suggested that the control of inflation by the Federal Reserve, the decline in the federal deficit, the opening of global markets, the restructuring of corporate America, and the widespread use of information technology to control inventory stock levels had

> combined to do away with the business cycle. Point for point, this
> was a reiteration of the new era philosophy of Irving Fisher's day.[31]

Similar to the 1920s, in the 1990s stock analysts and investment managers rationalized the expensive markets with the claim that the old methods of valuing companies no longer applied. There were new methods that justified the nosebleed prices.[32]

The Same Patterns Persist

The idea of valuation, which we will tackle in the next chapters, is a particularly challenging one for cryptoassets. Since they are a new asset class, they cannot be valued as companies are, and while valuing them based on supply and demand characteristics like that of commodities has some validity, it doesn't quite suffice. As a result, we predict that as the space grows, and likely to dizzying levels, we'll once again hear the refrain that old methods of valuation no longer apply. When the innovative investor hears that refrain, it will be important to stay on high alert and investigate if the new method of valuation really makes sense.

Throughout this book, we've tried to stay on message that the innovative investor may be a new class of investor, just as cryptoassets are a new asset class. However, we've also been reminding readers of lessons to be learned from the past and time-tested tools of portfolio and asset analysis. Ignoring these important lessons will lead people into the trap of thinking that not only are things different this time, but that they are different from other investors as well.

Generally, these traps follow a pattern: initially, there may be support for the underlying price appreciation, as with most fundamental innovations. But that price appreciation and the story behind it can become a self-fulfilling prophecy. People become entranced by stories of their friends and family making easy money, even when they knew little about what they bought. In times like these (as in Tulipmania), many subscribe to the "greater idiot" ideal: people can make money so long as they are able to sell the asset at a higher price to an idiot greater than them. A key indicator of the unsustainability of mass speculation is when new and inexperienced entrants stream into the markets.

Bubbles are typically worsened by cheap credit, as financial institutions provide speculators the means to take out loans so they can buy more of the asset than they could with cash on hand. In this sense, the financial institutions buy into the speculative bubble as they see the opportunity to make money, just as the institutions around them are making money off loans to frenzied speculators. Both individual speculators and financial institutions providing cheap credit fall into the rut of crowd theory and convince themselves that "this time is different."

To make matters worse, when markets are overheating is usually when misleading asset issuers, Ponzi operators, and market manipulators come out to play. For that reason, we'll turn to these three themes in the next chapter.

Chapter 11

"It's Just a Ponzi Scheme, Isn't It?"

The example of Tulipmania and similar events should remind the innovative investor that bubbles can appear quickly and violently, especially in cryptoassets. These patterns have been repeated in bitcoin's bubbles, steem's stratospheric summer rise, and zcash's postrelease run. Given the emerging nature of the cryptoasset markets, it's important to recognize that there is less regulation (some would say none) in this arena, and therefore bad behavior can persist for longer than it may in more mature markets.

As activity grows in the bitcoin and cryptoasset markets, investors must look beyond the madness of the crowd and recognize that there are bad actors who seek easy prey in these young markets. The growth of new cryptoassets and new investment products around them create a rapidly evolving marketplace in which financial criminals can exploit profit-seeking motives, especially if the innovative investor doesn't perform proper due diligence. This chapter will focus on Ponzi schemes, misleading asset issuers, and the cornering of markets (also known as "pump and dump" schemes).

As we've mentioned, those who lack an understanding of bitcoin and cryptoassets often express their disdain and ignorance with the proclamation, "It's just a Ponzi scheme." So let's start there.

PONZI SCHEMES

Ponzi schemes, also referred to as pyramid schemes, are the most dangerous type of misleading asset. While it got its name from Charles Ponzi, an Italian who lived from 1882 to 1949, it existed before he was born; he just made it famous.

The idea is simple: new investors pay old investors. As long as there are enough new investors, old investors will continue to be rewarded handsomely. For example, if an operator of a Ponzi scheme offered 20 percent returns into perpetuity, some investors would be duped into initially believing the operator. Call this "Batch A" of investors. The operator would encourage Batch A investors to tell their friends, who would become Batch B of even newer investors. The money Batch B investors invested would pay the 20 percent returns promised to the Batch A investors who brought them into the scheme. From there, Batch A and Batch B go and solicit Batch C, telling Batch C about this amazingly easy and rewarding investment product. The capital from Batch C goes to pay Batch A and Batch B, and so the Ponzi cycle continues indefinitely until there are not enough new investors to keep it going. The scheme falls apart when people realize no real value has been created, and everything is founded upon a scheme to dupe new investors into paying old investors. Tragically, investors often don't realize they are duping one another, and it is the operator of the Ponzi scheme who makes out handsomely.

Before we turn to cryptoassets, let's look at how Ponzi schemes have played out in traditional assets.

Many think of bonds as a safe investment with steady cash flows. If they are issued by a government, then they also have the full backing of that government. As we will soon see, bonds have not always been safe, and in what has been labeled the first emerging market boom, many bonds turned out to be Ponzi schemes.[1]

For about a century after the equity bubbles brought on by the Mississippi Company[2] and South Sea Schemes[3] (we'll cover the shady dealings of these companies in the next section), British investors stuck close to government-issued bonds.[4] During the Napoleonic Wars from 1803 to 1815, the British government issued over 400 million pounds of bonds, providing plenty of opportunity to bond investors. However, once peace reigned again, the British government had less need to borrow, and therefore the supply of government bonds shrank.[5]

At about the same time, South America was in the throes of rebellion against Spain, leading to the creation of new countries with a need for capital to build their infrastructure and join the developed world. An English newspaper claimed, "We may indulge the brightest hopes of these Southern Republics. They have entered upon a career of endless improvement. And . . . will soon attain the knowledge and freedom and civilization of the happiest states of Europe."[6]

The opportunity to make money was the focus of hungry British investors, and it was fueled by stories of how British innovation would make these regions economic powerhouses, and that fabled gold and silver mines were up for grabs.

Investors ended up dumping millions into these exotic and high-yielding loans, with little to no information on where the money ended up. For the most part, bonds were issued repeatedly to budding countries such as Chile, Colombia, and Peru, with the newer issues going to pay off the older issues in classic Ponzi finance. As put forth by Chancellor in his book, *Devil Take the Hindmost: A History of Financial Speculation*:

> The payment of interest from capital, otherwise known as "Ponzi finance," created the illusion of viability although no money was ever actually sent from South America to service the loans (to which it must be added that the borrowing countries received only a tiny fraction of the total sums for which they contracted).[7]

In other words, not only did very little of the money raised in Europe ever make it to South America for its intended purpose, but little to no money was ever sent from South America back to Europe to pay for the dividends the bonds promised. In one famous instance, there wasn't even the possibility of repayment, as the bonds were floated for an imaginary country called Poyais. These Poyaisian bonds remain the only bond for a fake country to be issued on the London Stock Exchange.

As with all Ponzi finance, the South American loan bubble had to burst, which it did in 1826. Every newly founded South American country defaulted on its debt, except for Brazil, in what has become known as "The First Latin American Debt Crisis."[8] Not only would this bubble hurt European investors, it would hurt South America for decades to come, arguably even to the present as the region has been marred by continued defaults. For example, Chile, Colombia, and Peru have spent 27.5 percent, 36.2 percent, and 40.2 percent of their sovereign lives in default or rescheduling, never quite able to escape the early precedent that was set.[9]

The Bitcoin Ponzi Myth

Criticisms of bitcoin and cryptoassets being Ponzi schemes have been circulating since bitcoin first hit investors' radar screens.[10] However, this criticism is deeply misinformed, and the World Bank has joined us in this opinion. In a 2014 report it states:

> Contrary to a widely-held opinion, Bitcoin is not a deliberate Ponzi. And there is little to learn by treating it as such. The main value of Bitcoin may, in retrospect, turn out to be the lessons it offers to central banks on the prospects of electronic currency, and on how to enhance efficiency and cut transactions cost.[11]

Historical Ponzi schemes require a central authority to hide the facts and promise a certain annual percent return. Bitcoin has neither. The system is decentralized, and the facts are out in the open. People can sell any time, and they do, and no one is guaranteed any return. In fact, many longtime advocates of the space warn people not to invest more money than they're willing to lose. Any good Ponzi operator would never say as much.

How to Spot a Ponzi Scheme Disguised as a Cryptoasset

The Ponzi scheme is a specific and easily identifiably structure that isn't applicable to Bitcoin but could be to some phony cryptoassets. While a truly innovative cryptoasset and its associated architecture requires a heroic coding effort from talented developers, because the software is open source, it can be downloaded and duplicated. From there, a new cryptoasset can be issued wrapped in slick marketing. If the innovative investor doesn't do proper due diligence on the underlying code or read other trusted sources who have, then it's possible to fall victim to a Ponzi scheme.

A new cryptoasset called OneCoin was met with much interest due to its promise of providing a guaranteed return to investors. When the words "guaranteed return" appear, the innovative investor should always see an instant red flag. All investors should always be deterred by an investment that purports a guarantee (although annuities or other insurance-backed investments may qualify).

Millions of dollars poured into OneCoin, whose technology ran counter to the values of the cryptoasset community: its software was not open source (perhaps out of fear that developers would see the holes in its design), and it was not based on a public ledger, so no transactions could be tracked.[12]

The community responded with reports of OneCoin as a Ponzi scheme. One of the best articles on the topic, which received nearly 300,000 views and over 1,000 comments, was loud and clear: "Buyer Beware! The Definitive OneCoin Ponzi Exposé."[13] The Swedish Bitcoin Foundation stepped up to the plate as well, with warnings about OneCoin as a "pyramid" and a "fraud." The Financial Conduct Authority in the United Kingdom also warned investors against OneCoin.[14] The swift action revealed the strength of a self-policing, open-source community in pursuit of the truth.

To warn investors against Ponzi schemes like OneCoin, the SEC released a memo titled "Investor Alert: Ponzi Schemes Using Virtual Currencies." The memo warned that cryptoassets can be an easy way for scammers to disguise pyramid schemes.[15] Investors should still consider this alert, not in thinking of bitcoin as a scam but in recognizing that scams may masquerade as cryptoassets. Here are a few of the most important ways to recognize a Ponzi scheme:

- Overly consistent returns
- Secretive and/or complex strategies and fee structures
- Difficulty receiving payments
- Comes through someone with a shared affinity

Just as investors duped by the allure of Latin American bonds should have been more cautious, the innovative investor needs to keep an eye out for new cryptoasset issues that don't quite smell right.

We will go more deeply into specific vetting strategies regarding cryptoassets in later chapters, but two "smell tests" are easy to begin with. First, do a quick Google search for "Is _____ a scam?" If nothing pops up, then check to see if the project's code is open source. This can best be accomplished by searching for, "_____ GitHub," as most of these projects use GitHub as their platform for collaboration. If nothing pops up with signs of the code on GitHub, then the cryptoasset is likely not open source, which is an immediate red flag that a cryptoasset and investment should be avoided.

MISLEADING INFORMATION FROM ASSET ISSUERS

Ponzi schemes are a particularly perverse form of misleading information from asset issuers. However, sometimes the way in which issuers mislead investors is subtler. As markets mature over time, there is more regulation on what information asset issuers must provide and by whom that information must be verified and audited. With cryptoassets, however, these standards are not yet in place. To get an idea of what havoc misleading asset issuers can create, we'll examine an example from early equities markets.

About 80 years after Tulipmania, in the early 1700s, the first international bull market came to rise.[16] Kick-started by infamous entities such as John Law's Mississippi Company in France and John Blunt's South Sea Company in Britain, the equity markets were whipped into a buying frenzy fueled largely by duplicity. Both the Mississippi Company and South Sea Company had convoluted structures and were heavily marketed as pursuits to establish a presence and exploit trade in the burgeoning Americas, even though they had only marginal success in doing so. Both Blunt and Law used elaborate and unproven financial engineering to advance the price of their companies' stocks at all costs.

Law's scheme was particularly intricate and dangerous, as it involved controlling France's first central bank, in addition to the Mississippi Company, which was the country's largest enterprise. Law won his way into a place of financial power in France with promises to resolve the country's financial woes, which were dire: the government was on the verge of its third bankruptcy in less than a century. Part of Law's scheme involved issuing shares in the Mississippi Company, the proceeds of which were then used to pay down the national debt. It depended on artificially inflating the share price of the Mississippi Company, of which he was also the largest shareholder. Such pressure and vast control allowed Law to manipulate shareholders into believing the company's prospects were great. The company was in charge of setting up colonies for trade in the Louisiana territory, which spanned the equivalent of nearly a quarter of the present-day United States, with New Orleans intended to be its centerpiece. To recruit colonists to develop the area and lay the foundation of trade that would lead to future profits for the company, he shared "rosy visions of the colony as a veritable Garden of Eden, inhabited by friendly savages, eager to furnish a cornucopia of exotic goods for shipment to France."

Law's promises entranced investors and colonists alike, but the dreams he spoke of were illusions, with no prospect of near-term profits, and therefore little basis for the rising share prices of the Mississippi Company. When the colonists arrived in the Louisiana territory what they found "was a sweltering, insect-infested swamp. Within a year 80 percent of them had died of starvation or tropical diseases like yellow fever."

Meanwhile, Law tinkered with other monetary policy experiments to prop up the shares of his company and pay down the national debt, such as doubling the supply of paper money in France in a little over a year. Law grew his power to the point where, "It was as if one man was simultaneously running all five hundred of the top U.S. corporations, the U.S. Treasury and the Federal Reserve System."[17]

JOHN LAW: CONVICTED MURDERER AND COMPULSIVE GAMBLER

The French would have done well to better investigate the priors of John Law before handing him control of the country's finances. If they had done proper due diligence, they would have discovered he was a compulsive gambler and convicted murderer. In the 1690s he had escaped from prison in London— where he was awaiting a death sentence—and fled to Amsterdam. At the time, Amsterdam was a pioneer in new market structures, with the trading of stock in the Dutch East India Company and establishment of the world's first central bank as gleaming examples. Law studied these systems closely, which gave him the knowledge necessary to pull off his elaborate scheme in France.[18] The innovative investor would be wise to learn from France's mistake and always take the time to investigate the priors of cryptoasset developers and advisors before putting money into the assets they create. Fortunately, today it's quite easy to find information on just about anyone through Google searches.

While Law duped French investors and government officials for a few years, by the middle of 1720 it was clear his financial engineering was unsustainable. Shareholder losses were brutal, as the Mississippi Company would fall 90 percent in value by the end of 1720, leading to public outrage and a worsening of France's financial woes. Law's machinations stunted France's financial development for generations, as its population remained gun-shy of paper money and stock markets, thereby losing out on the positives that came with responsible innovation in markets.

Law's grand Mississippi Company was best described in a cartoon that read:

> This is the wondrous Mississippi land,
> Made famous by its share dealings,

Which through deceit and devious conduct,
Has squandered countless treasures.
However men regard the shares,
It is wind and smoke and nothing more.[19]

Misleading Cryptoassets

One of the most important actions innovative investors can take to protect themselves from misleading characters is to do their homework on the backgrounds of the main parties involved in a cryptoasset, especially if it's been newly issued. If not much can be found about the specific characters involved, that's immediately a bad sign, as it means the creators don't want to be identified or held accountable for what happens with that asset.

Next, investigate the materials the cryptoasset team members have created. If their website, white paper, or other materials are filled with typos, formatting mistakes, or anything else that shows a lack of care, then take this also as a warning. A team who doesn't care enough to present themselves well, likely doesn't care if they mislead investors.

Many conversations and much information flow takes place on Reddit, Twitter, in Slack Channels, and so on, not on the well-manicured pages of tech and investing websites. The lack of easily accessible information and standardization of necessary information are weaknesses of the cryptoassets space. It is the reason, after all, that you are reading this book.

THE FINE LINE BETWEEN MISLEADING AND A MISTAKE

Dash, a coin that rose to fame in late 2016 and early 2017 due to its stratospheric price increase, had what many would call a misleading issuance. In the first 24 hours that the coin went live, over 1.9 million dash were mined, which was not part of the original plan. While Dash's founder supplied explanations—mainly that this was caused by an inadvertent software bug—a concern many still hold is that the Dash team misled new investors.[20] As of March 2017, those first 24 hours still account for nearly 30 percent of the coins outstanding.

This is a situation in which the innovative investor must discern the difference between a misleading issuer and an honest mistake. We believe that Dash's initial distribution could have been corrected, just as its competing anonymity cryptoasset, Monero, did, when it was forked off from Bytecoin to solve for an unfair distribution of coins. The Dash team could have relaunched to ensure a fair initial distribution. That said, Dash has worked to overcome its rocky beginning and at the start of April 2017 was one of the top four cryptoassets in network value.[21] The asset is backed by a few interesting innovations, and its team has successfully navigated to a position of increasing mainstream acceptance.

Misleading statements don't even have to come from the progenitors of cryptoassets; they can come from people who claim to manage the assets for investors. We have seen many deceptive investment offerings that purport to take investors' money and place it into cryptoasset funds that will provide "guaranteed" returns. For example, there's a "Bitcoin Mutual Fund" website that promises to provide 700 percent returns over a range of periods, from 2 hours to 48 hours, depending on the amount of money invested.[22] The website is full of mistakes in spelling and grammar in the text, which provide another red flag beyond the guaranteed returns. This is the equivalent of Law's Louisiana swampland.

CORNERING

Cornering a market refers to when one or more investors work to drive the price of an asset up or down significantly. In the cryptoasset space, they are frequently referred to as "pump and dump" schemes, where loosely coordinated groups work to pump up the price of a cryptoasset, exploiting crowd behavior, before quickly selling to realize their profits. As with the other examples in this chapter, cornering is nothing new in the history of markets.

In 1869, Jay Gould, who was a prototype of the "Robber Baron" and one of the most vilified men in nineteenth-century America,[23] decided he wanted to corner the gold market.[24] Cornering the gold market was a particularly dangerous proposition at the time, as gold remained the official currency of international trade, and the value of gold in the United States was largely dictated by the federal government.

When Ulysses S. Grant became president of the United States in March 1869, the country was still dealing with the ramifications of the Civil War that had ended four years prior.[25] One of the biggest problems was the national debt the country had accrued in fighting the war, which led many to doubt the government's credit worthiness. To re-instill faith, one of the first actions Grant took was to sign a law that stated the federal government would buy back U.S. bonds in "gold or its equivalent."[26] If the government were to buy bonds with gold, the supply of gold in the market would increase, meaning that the price of gold would decrease. Gold quickly fell to $130 an ounce, its lowest point since 1862.[27]

Gold has been valued by civilizations over hundreds of centuries, and for a savvy investor, a drop in price typically signifies a time to buy. Gould was not satisfied, however, with buying gold and holding it patiently until he could sell at a higher price and make an earnest profit. He had an ulterior motive for driving gold up. He believed it would cause currency devaluation, which would create an export boom that would benefit the Erie Railroad,[28] a company in which he was intimately involved. Furthermore, there was the clear opportunity to benefit from buying low and selling high.

Knowing that the federal government could control the price of gold with its open market operations, Gould devised a plan to convince Grant, and thereby the federal government, not to sell the gold it intended to. Since the federal gold reserves were north of $100 million, which was greater than the amount of gold in circulation, Gould rightly realized that controlling the federal government meant controlling the price of gold in U.S. markets.[29] If he could convince the government not to sell its gold, then there would be less supply in the market, thereby driving the price up. The price would go up even more if Gould could freely buy it without having to worry about a government dump.

Gould found the pawn he needed in Abel Corbin, who was involved in politics and was married to Grant's sister, Jennie. Gould befriended Corbin, and with the extra persuasion of a bribe, captured the ally he needed to sway the government's open market operations. Corbin first used his political influence to appoint General Daniel Butterfield to the post of U.S. sub-Treasurer in New York. Butterfield was instructed to alert Corbin to any government gold sales in advance, which would protect Gould from being surprised by any government actions.[30] Both Corbin and Butterfield were promised $1.5 million stakes in the scheme, aligning their interests with Gould's.[31]

More important than Butterfield, through the summer of 1869 Corbin worked his way into the president's confidence with the singular goal of convincing him to cease selling gold. Corbin also succeeded in getting Gould and Grant to converse at social gatherings, allowing Gould to provide his convoluted rationale that a rising gold price would be for the nation's benefit.[32] Corbin eventually succeeded, getting word from Grant on September 2 that he planned to stop gold sales for the month.[33]

Gould had been stockpiling gold throughout August in anticipation of this favorable verdict, and upon receiving the news, he kicked it into overdrive. He enlisted a wealthy ally, Jay Fisk, with whom he had pulled off other illegal market feats. With the added funds of Fisk, Gould pumped even more money into the gold market, driving up the price.[34]

In mid-September, however, the cabal overplayed its hand. They first tried to bribe the president's private secretary, and when that failed Corbin wrote a letter to Grant, checking to see if the president planned to continue with his strategy of not selling gold through the month. Upon getting the letter on September 19, Grant became suspicious of foul play and instructed his wife to write to Mrs. Corbin to convince her husband to steer clear of the ruse.[35]

Unsurprisingly, Mr. Corbin was dismayed that Grant was catching on to the plot. Upon learning of the situation, Gould knew he could no longer depend on Grant to hold the nation's gold. Under the cover of Fisk's continued buying, Gould started unloading the gold he had acquired.

While the Gold Exchange had been rising continuously throughout September, on September 24, 1869, it peaked and would go down as "Jay Gould's Black Friday." Gould had employed a dozen brokers to continue quietly selling his gold, while his partner Fisk pushed the gold market to $160, a 20 percent rise from its bottom earlier in the year. Shortly thereafter, Butterfield's broker started selling gold, which alerted those at the exchange that the federal government was likely on its way to a sale. Sure enough, an hour after gold hit $160, an order came in from the federal government to sell $4 million of gold. While Gould and Fisk quietly slipped out of the exchange, panic ensued, as detailed by Chancellor: "The rapid fluctuations bankrupted thousands of margin holders, mobs formed in Broad Street and outside Gould's brokerage office, and troops were put on alert to enter the financial district."[36]

As with most panics, the contagion spread from the Gold Exchange. Because of Gould's cornering of the market, stock prices dropped 20 percent, a variety of agricultural exports fell 50 percent in value, and the national economy was disrupted for several months.[37] Gould exited with a cool $11 million profit from the debacle, and scot-free from legal charges.[38] It is all too common that characters like Gould escape unscathed by the havoc they create, which then allows them to carry on with their machinations in other markets.

In the cryptoasset markets, characters toying with asset prices can often obfuscate their identity through the veil of the Internet, which unfortunately makes it even easier for them to escape. Often, they will target small and relatively unknown assets, which makes it important for the innovative investor who ventures into these smaller markets to pay particular attention to the details of those assets and the characters associated with them.

Beyond the Gold Exchange in 1869, examples of the cornering of commodities markets have continued to surface. In 1980, the Hunt brothers, who had been left billions by their wealthy oil-mogul father, attempted to corner the silver market. With inflation levels starting the year off at 14 percent, one of the highest levels on record,[39] the brothers believed silver would become a haven against inflation the way gold was, and they intended to own as much of it as they possibly could. Using the commodities markets and leverage, the brothers rapidly amassed $4.5 billion worth of silver (much of it being flown to Switzerland in specially designed planes under armed guard),[40] pushing the price to nearly $50 per ounce. Ultimately, the U.S. government had to step in to prevent further manipulation, which ultimately ruined the brothers' ploy and fortunes, as silver dropped back to $11 per ounce on March 27, 1980.[41]

Other notable instances of cornering markets reveal that this vulnerability spans asset classes:

- In 1929 over a hundred companies listed on the NYSE were cornered.[42]
- From April 1987 to March 1989, the Tokyo Stock Exchange estimated that one out of every 10 companies listed on its exchange was cornered.[43]
- In the middle of 1991, Salomon Brothers was caught trying to manipulate U.S. Treasuries, widely regarded as one of the safest investment instruments in the world.[44]
- In the mid-1990s, Yasuo Hamanaka pushed the cost of copper on the London Metals Exchange up by over 75 percent to $3,200 and was rewarded with a seven-year prison sentence.

Pumping, Dumping, and Cornering Cryptoassets

Cryptoassets that have small network values are particularly susceptible to the cornering of their markets. For example, at the start of April 2017, the 200 smallest cryptoassets had markets of less than $20,000. Therefore, a bad actor could come in with $10,000 and buy up half the assets outstanding. This increased buying pressure will drive up the price of the asset, which tends to draw curiosity from others. If several speculators are in collusion, then they will work together to drive up the price of these small cryptoassets, while spreading hype on different social media platforms (a tweet or two from an "influencer" is enough).

The intent is to lure unknowing speculators to take the bait and buy the asset based on what they think is genuine market interest. The innovative investor who does due diligence would never buy solely based on market interest, and for good reason. The colluders will slowly work to exit their positions, while the inertia of enthusiasm leads more unknowing speculators to continue buying, as we saw with Gould. These pump-and-dumps, or P&Ds, are unfortunately becoming common in the smaller cryptoassets.

Cornering is also important to consider in crowdsales, especially if the founding team has given itself a significant chunk of the assets. While crowdsales will be further detailed in Chapter 16, the key takeaway for now is that if the founding team gives themselves too much of the assets outstanding, then they have immense power over the market price of the cryptoasset and this is potentially concerning.

Control over the asset supply goes beyond crowdsales and founders, as it can spread to the miners or other entities required to support a cryptoasset. This is where it becomes important to consider the monetary policy of a cryptoasset. For example, one of the concerns with Dash is that it created a supply structure prone to cornering. In addition to miners, in Dash there are entities called *masternodes*, which are also controlled by people or groups of people. Masternodes play an integral role in performing near instant and anonymous transactions with Dash. However, as a security mechanism, the entity has to bond at least 1,000 dash to be a masternode.[45] Bond is a fancy word for hold, but it's a term commonly used in the cryptoasset space to imply that those assets can't move. If the masternode moves those bonded dash, and subsequently holds less than 1,000 dash, then that person or group can no longer be a masternode.

Given that there were over 4,000 masternodes in March 2017, that means 4 million dash were bonded, or illiquid. With just over 7 million dash available on the market, that 4 million means that roughly 60 percent of the supply is unavailable. Add to that the nearly 2 million dash that were instamined in the first 24 hours, and it implies that 6 million of the 7 million dash available are likely under the control of power players in the space, leaving only 15 percent of the remaining dash in free-floating markets.

The situation is arguably only worsening, as masternodes receive 45 percent of each block reward, which means that of the new supply of dash, they are receiving almost 50 percent. Since they already own 60 percent of the supply outstanding, this gives the masternodes significant ability, and since they hold lots of dash, incentive, to corner the market.

The innovative investor needs to carefully examine the supply schedules and who newly minted cryptoassets are being issued to. Fortunately, once the blockchain is live, because it's a distributed and transparent ledger, it's easy to see address balances. Often there are sites that will show the amount held by the top addresses, such as the Bitcoin Rich List.[46] For Bitcoin, two addresses hold between them 227,618 bitcoin, or roughly 1.4 percent of the total outstanding. Another 116 addresses hold a total of 2.87 million bitcoin, or 19 percent of the total outstanding, which is sizeable. Unlike dash, however, these holders aren't necessarily receiving nearly half of the newly minted bitcoin, and so their ability to push the price upward is less. Lastly, it should be noted that a single person can have multiple bitcoin addresses, so each address is not necessarily a distinct entity.

•   •   •

In closing, there are many tricks of the trade, whether it be mass speculation, misleading asset issuers, Ponzi finance, or cornering, with much of it justified by "this time is different" thinking. However, these are not new tricks—they have existed for centuries and in all asset classes. The best way for innovative investors to avoid these traps when considering cryptoassets for their portfolio is to perform proper due diligence on the fundamentals and ignore the whims of the crowd. Understanding which fundamentals are most important for long-term growth takes us to the next chapter on a framework for investigating cryptoassets.

Part III

HOW

Chapter 12

Fundamental Analysis and a Valuation Framework for Cryptoassets

With an awareness of the many tricks that can be played on investors in emerging markets, it's time to develop a framework for innovative investors to evaluate a cryptoasset for their portfolio. Each cryptoasset is different, as are the goals, objectives, and risk profiles of each investor. Therefore, while this chapter will provide a starting point, it is by no means comprehensive. It's also not investment advice. Since this space is moving at light speed, our intent is not to say, "Buy this, sell that." Remember, in the process of writing this book, we watched the aggregate network value of cryptoassets jump from approximately $10 billion to north of $100 billion and hundreds of new cryptoassets come to market.[1]

Investors need to judge for themselves what to do. Our goal is to provide a basis for what to look for when first investigating cryptoassets. Then, using knowledge from chapters past, how to begin contemplating whether a specific cryptoasset fits their risk-profile and overall investment strategy and if it will help them achieve their financial goals and objectives.

In Chapter 15, we discuss investment products that take the bulk of operational weight off the investor. If someone wants exposure to this new asset class but doesn't want his or her fingers in the wires all the time, a growing number of investment options are becoming available, like cryptoasset managers and publicly traded vehicles like the Bitcoin Investment Trust. Even with those products, innovative investors will need to know enough to ask the right questions and be assured that the vehicle they've put their hard-earned money into is an appropriate investment.

Fortunately, many of the same tools for assessing any investment can be used for individual cryptoassets as well. Fundamental analysis will reveal if an investment is worthy of long-term capital allocation, while technical analysis will assist with the timing of buys and sells. Much has been written about these two schools of investing thought, and they're often pitched as being diametrically opposed.[2] We believe they can be used together, especially if innovative investors want to be actively involved in their portfolios.

Fundamental analysis involves looking at the intrinsic value drivers of an asset. For example, with stocks, fundamental analysis involves the evaluation of a company's operating health through close examination of its income statement, balance sheet, and cash flow statement, while placing these factors in the context of its long-term vision and macroeconomic exposure. Metrics like price to earnings, price to sales, book value, and return on equity are derived through fundamental analysis to determine the value of a company and compare it with its peers.

Fundamental analysis can be a time-consuming process that requires access to the latest data not only for a company but also as it relates to an industry and the economy overall. Many times, an investor and even a financial advisor will depend on analysts to crunch these numbers to provide insights into relevant assets. In the traditional capital markets, an entire industry is based on this process, known as sell-side research. Currently, there is no such thing as sell-side research for cryptoassets, and this will require innovative investors to scour through the details on their own or rely on recognized thought leaders in the space. We'll do our best to arm investors with the resources to do this analysis so they aren't scared away from the effort.

As it pertains to evaluating cryptoassets, the process of conducting fundamental analysis is different from stocks because cryptoassets are not companies. The assets may have been created by a company or group of individuals, and an understanding of that company or those individuals is vital, but the cryptoassets themselves should be valued more as commodities, with markets priced by the balance of supply and demand.

In this chapter we discuss applying fundamental analysis to the founding characteristics of a cryptoasset. This includes examining:

- White paper

- Decentralization edge
- Valuation
- Community and developers
- Relation to digital siblings
- Issuance model

In the next chapter, we focus on applying fundamental analysis to the ongoing network health of these assets, including metrics on miners, developers, companies, and users. Together, these foundational and network fundamentals generate a unique fundamental analysis approach to cryptoassets that will help the innovative investor make well-informed investment decisions. We'll round out these framework chapters by including an examination of how technical analysis can be used for further benefit, specifically to identify appropriate times to invest or liquidate.

WHERE TO START: THE WHITE PAPER

Since cryptoassets are supported by open-source code, with transparent and accessible communities, there is typically an abundance of information available on an asset. Any cryptoasset worth its mustard has an origination white paper. A white paper is a document that's often used in business to outline a proposal, typically written by a thought leader or someone knowledgeable on a topic. As it relates to cryptoassets, a white paper is the stake in the ground, outlining the problem the asset addresses, where the asset stands in the competitive landscape, and what the technical details are.

Satoshi outlined Bitcoin in his white paper, and since then most creators of cryptoassets have followed the same process. Some of these white papers can be highly technical, though at the very least, perusing the introduction and conclusion is valuable. White papers can often be found on the website created for the cryptoasset.

VAGUENESS IS NOT YOUR FRIEND

A cryptoasset white paper may include a lot of technical information and be difficult to read all the way through. Many times, the team developing the cryptoasset will have a website that has a brief description of what the asset intends to do and how it intends to do it. Even if not everything described is understood, if the description lacks specificity and seems intentionally vague, that may be a sign to avoid the asset. Investors should feel comfortable briefly explaining the asset in some manner to a friend who may or may not be knowledgeable on the subject. If the investor can't do that, it may be appropriate to consider a different cryptoasset.

DECENTRALIZATION EDGE

When reading the white paper, the first question to ask is: What problem does it solve? In other words, is there a reason for this cryptoasset and its associated architecture to exist in a decentralized manner? There are lots of digital services in our world, so does this one have an inherent benefit to being provisioned in a distributed, secure, and egalitarian manner? We call this the *decentralization edge*. Put bluntly by Vitalik Buterin, "Projects really should make sure they have good answers for 'why use a blockchain.'"[3]

A number of cryptoasset-based projects focus on social networks, such as Steemit[4] and Yours,[5] the latter of which uses litecoin. While we admire these projects, we also ask: Will these networks and their associated assets gain traction with competitors like Reddit and Facebook? Similarly, a cryptoasset service called Swarm City[6] (formerly Arcade City) aims to decentralize Uber, which is already a highly efficient service. What edge will the decentralized Swarm City have over the centralized Uber?

In the case of Steemit and Yours, we understand content creators will get directly compensated. This may draw more quality content to the platform, which will thereby drive more use. In the case of Swarm City, the drivers won't be losing 20 to 30 percent of every fare to a centralized service, so over time, more drivers may come to the platform. As more drivers come to the platform, there may be increased availability of Swarm City cars, and therefore the service may be more beneficial to the end user. Just as with Steemit and Yours, a greater volume of providers and consumers increases the value of the platform over time.

However, are these factors enough to gain traction over Reddit, Facebook, and Uber over the long term? The innovative investor should perform similar thought experiments with any cryptoasset under consideration and be convinced that its associated architecture will provide long-term value and isn't simply riding a hype-wave[7] with the intent of gaining funding while providing little value over time.

THE POWER OF AGE: THE LINDY EFFECT

The *Lindy effect* is often used to gauge the potential life expectancy of technologies. Unlike humans, where the longer someone lives, the more likely that death is approaching, the longer technologies live, the less likely they are to die soon. The reason is that technologies build momentum, and over time many other technologies are built around them, which continues to drive underlying support. The most important technologies become intractable to our daily lives, or at least sticky on a decadal scale. Even culturally, it will take time for the technology to fade deep into obsolescence.

The same applies to cryptoassets. The longest-lived cryptoasset, bitcoin, now has an entire ecosystem of hardware, software developers, companies, and users built around it. Essentially, it has created its own economy, and while a superior cryptocurrency could slowly gain share, it would have an uphill battle given the foothold bitcoin has gained.

On the other hand, a newly launched cryptoasset is little known, making the community supporting it much more fragile. If a major flaw is exposed, or the cryptoasset undergoes some other form of duress, the community may quickly disperse. Many members may move to support other cryptoassets, while others may try again, launching a slightly altered cryptoasset, applying the lessons learned. In other words, with a new cryptoasset there is much less sunk cost, which makes it easier for people to let go and move on to something else. For a great example of how quickly a new cryptoasset can rise and fall, recall what happened with The DAO.

However, if a cryptoasset has strong community engagement and achieves success early on, it can create a solid foothold that can benefit it over time. Ethereum seems to be a good example. The demise of The DAO significantly impacted Ethereum (which The DAO was built on), but through leadership and community involvement, the major issues were addressed, and as of April 2017 Ethereum stands solidly as the second largest cryptoasset in terms of network value.[8]

UNDERSTANDING A CRYPTOASSET'S VALUATION

One of the most common questions is: What gives a cryptoasset value? After all, these assets have no physical manifestation. Since they are born of software, the value is derived from the community and the marketplace that naturally develops around the asset. Broadly, there are two kinds of value that the community places on any kind of cryptoasset: utility value and speculative value.

Utility Value and Speculative Value

Utility value refers to the use of the cryptoasset to gain access to the digital resource its architecture provisions and is dictated by supply and demand characteristics. For bitcoin, its utility is that it can safely, quickly, and efficiently transfer value to anyone, anywhere in the world. All it takes is typing in the person's bitcoin address and clicking send, a functionality that all exchanges and wallets provide (which we cover in Chapter 14). Bitcoin's utility in sending value using the Internet is similar to that of Skype, which can safely, quickly, and efficiently transmit anyone's voice and image to anyone, anywhere in the world.

The innovative investor might say: "OK, I understand that bitcoin can have utility as MoIP, just as Skype has utility as VoIP, but how does that translate to bitcoin being worth $1,000 a coin?" Bitcoin's utility value can be determined by assessing how much bitcoin is necessary for it to serve the Internet economy it supports. To conceptually understand how bitcoin has value, we will use a couple of simplified examples. From there the innovative investor can use this scaffolding to dive deeper into valuations.

Let's start with a hypothetical Brazilian merchant who wants to buy US$100,000 worth of steel from a Chinese manufacturer. While this particular merchant is hypothetical, adoption of bitcoin by Latin American merchants has been well documented.[9] The merchant wants to use bitcoin because it will allow her to transfer that money within an hour as opposed to waiting a week or more. Therefore, the Brazilian merchant buys US$100,000 worth of bitcoin and sends it to the Chinese manufacturer. While the manufacturer is waiting for that transaction to be incorporated into Bitcoin's blockchain, that bitcoin is frozen, temporarily drawn out of the available supply of bitcoin.

Now imagine there are 99,999 other merchants wanting to do the same thing. In total, among all these merchants, there is demand for US$10 billion worth of bitcoin (100,000 people wanting to send US$100,000 each), simply because it is more expedient at moving money between Brazil and China than other available payment methods. US$10 billion worth of demand with bitcoin trading at $1,000 converts to 10 million coins being temporarily frozen or drawn out of the available supply of bitcoin.

But consider that a significant amount of bitcoin is also being held by investors. Those investors do not plan to sell their bitcoin for some time because they are speculating that due to its utility as MoIP, demand will continue to rise and so too will its value. Currently, roughly 5.5 million bitcoin, or US$5.5 billion worth at the price of US$1,000 per coin, is held by the top 1,000 addresses recorded in Bitcoin's blockchain.[10] That means on average each of these addresses is holding US$5.5 million worth of bitcoin, and it's fair to assume that these balances are not those of merchants waiting for their transactions to complete. Instead, these are likely balances of bitcoin that entities are holding for the long term based on what they think bitcoin's future utility value will be. Future utility value can be thought of as speculative value, and for this speculative value investors are keeping 5.5 million bitcoin out of the supply.

At the start of April 2017, there were just over 16 million bitcoin outstanding. Between international merchants needing 10 million bitcoin, and 5.5 million bitcoin held by the top 1,000 investors, there are only roughly 500,000 bitcoin free for people to use. A market naturally develops for these bitcoin because maybe another investor wants to buy-and-hold 5 bitcoin, or a merchant wants to send US$100,000 of bitcoin to Mexico. Since these people must buy that bitcoin from someone else, that someone else needs to be convinced to let that bitcoin go, and so a negotiation begins. On a broader scale, all these negotiations occur on exchanges around the world, and a market to value bitcoin is made.

If demand continues to go up for bitcoin, then with a disinflationary supply schedule, so too will its price (or velocity). However, at a certain point some investors may choose to exit their investments because they feel that bitcoin has reached its maximum value. In other words, those investors no longer feel bitcoin has any speculative value left, and instead its price is only supported by current utility value. With only utility value left, then there is no reason for the investor to continue to hold the asset as it has reached its maximum potential and is unlikely to appreciate any further. To perform the calculation that may lead an investor to believe bitcoin's maximum value has been reached, we need to introduce two more concepts: the velocity of money and discounting.

Velocity in the Context of Valuation

The concept of velocity is a necessary tool in understanding the opportunity that exists for bitcoin's value to increase as it fills more needs around the world. Velocity is used to explain the turnover of fiat currencies, and is described succinctly by the Federal Reserve Bank of St. Louis:

> The velocity of money is the frequency at which one unit of currency is used to purchase domestically-produced goods and services within a given time period. In other words, it is the number of times one dollar is spent to buy goods and services per unit of time. If the velocity of money is increasing, then more transactions are occurring between individuals in an economy.[11]

The velocity of a currency is calculated by dividing the Gross Domestic Product (GDP) for a certain period by the total money supply. For example, if the GDP is $20 trillion, but there are only $5 trillion worth of dollars available, then that money needs to turn over four times, or have a velocity of four, in order to meet demand on any given year. Currently, the velocity of the USD is a little north of 5.[12]

For bitcoin, instead of looking at the "domestically produced goods and services" it will purchase in a period, the innovative investor must look at the internationally produced goods and services it will purchase. The global remittances market—currently dominated by companies that provide the ability for people to send money to one another internationally—is an easily graspable example of a service within which bitcoin could be used.

About US$500 billion is transmitted annually through the remittances market. Assuming that bitcoin serviced that entire market, then to figure out the value of one bitcoin, one would need to assume its velocity. Say bitcoin's velocity is 5, similar to that of the U.S. dollar. Then dividing that $500 billion by a velocity of 5 would yield a total value of bitcoin of $100 billion. If, at this point, we are at the maximum of 21 million bitcoin, and this is the only use for bitcoin, then that $100 billion divided by 21 million units would yield a value per bitcoin of $4,762.

Clearly, this is an overly simplistic example because bitcoin will not service the entire remittances market. Instead, there needs to be an assumption about the percentage of the remittance market that bitcoin will service. Let's assume it will service 20 percent, and so each bitcoin will need to store $952 dollars to meet its demand within the remittance market described ($952 = $4,762 × 20%).

Importantly, the use cases for bitcoin are additive, as are the values demanded. For example, the global financial gold market is worth US$2.4 trillion,[13] so if bitcoin were to take a 10 percent share of that market it would need to store a total value of US$240 billion. Now, holding bitcoin as digital gold has a velocity of 1 because it's not turning over: it's just being held each year. In other words, there's no need to divide the value that must be stored by velocity as we had to do with remittances. Thus, at a steady state with 21 million units of bitcoin outstanding, each unit of bitcoin would need to store $11,430 worth of value to meet the demand of 10 percent of the investable gold market ($11,430 = $240B / 21M).

If each bitcoin needs to be worth $952 to service 20 percent of the remittance market and $11,430 to service the demand for it as digital gold, then in total it needs to be worth $12,382. There is no limit to the number of use cases that can be added in this process, but what is extremely tricky is figuring out the percent share of the market that bitcoin will ultimately fulfill and what the velocity of bitcoin will be in each use case.

Also, note that in this example we used the assumption of a steady state bitcoin supply at 21 million units, which will not be reached until 2140. When trying to piece together the fundamental value of the cryptoasset, it is important to consider the time frame and the units of that cryptoasset that will be available by that time, as some assets can have extremely high rates of inflation initially.

Discounting in the Context of Valuation

The next concept necessary for determining the present value of one bitcoin is discounting future values back to the present. For example, if you deposit $100 in a bank account that yields a 5 percent compounded annual rate, then in one year you will have $105. In two years, you will have $110.25 because you earn 5 percent on your $105. Therefore, you either want $100 now or $110.25 in two years—both are worth the same to you.

Analysts use the discounting method to figure out how much they should pay for something now if it is expected to be worth more in the future. Discounting is simply the reverse of accruing interest. For example, in this example, if $110.25 is divided by 1.05 once, and then divided by it again it will yield $100. In other words, $110.25 is divided by $(1.05)^2$ to get back to $100, as opposed to multiplying $100 by $(1.05)^2$ to get to $110.25. Such a method can be applied to much longer periods as well. For example, if someone offered to give the innovative investor $150 in 10 years or $100 now, then if there was a perfectly safe way to earn 5 percent the innovative investor should take the $100 now because $150 divided by (1.05^{10}) equals $92 today.

Taking the concepts of supply and demand, velocity, and discounting, we can figure out what bitcoin's value should be today, assuming it is to serve certain utility purposes 10 years from now. However, this is much easier said than done, as it involves figuring out the sizes of those markets in the future, the percent share that bitcoin will take, what bitcoin's velocity will be, and what an appropriate discount rate is. The discount rate should be a function of risk, which often for cryptoassets is 30 percent or more. This is more than double what common discount rates are for risky stocks.[14]

If we take the hypothetical value of bitcoin as \$12,382, and assume it will reach that utility value in 10 years, then with a discount rate of 30 percent that means the present value of each bitcoin is worth \$898 per bitcoin [\$898 = \$12,380 / (1.3^{10})]. Hence, at a current price of \$1,000 per bitcoin, the asset would be *overvalued* because investors are paying too much for it at \$1,000 when it really should only be worth \$898 given future expectations.

Now, this model has many assumptions and flaws, and a common refrain for such models is "*Garbage in, garbage out.*" For example, we give only two potential use cases, we had no justification for the percent market share bitcoin would take, and to derive the original price of \$12,382 we made the assumption that 21 million bitcoin would be available. In reality, we will be roughly 95 percent of the way to 21 million bitcoin outstanding in ten years, again highlighting the importance of considering the future supply of a cryptoasset when digging into fundamental values. It is easy to manipulate models to show that an asset is under- or overvalued, but these models are nonetheless useful to give investors some bearing on what they are paying for.

For even the most diligent innovative investor, valuing prospective crypto-assets is not a palatable task. However, just as there exists a big business in selling valuation research on stocks, so too will there be a business for valuing cryptoassets. Already there have been reports, such as those from Spencer Bogart at Needham & Company, as well as Gil Luria at Wedbush, that look at the fundamental value of bitcoin. Figure 12.1 shows a fundamental valuation report that Gil put together on bitcoin in July 2015 to give some idea of how complex these models can become.

The valuations these analysts produce can be useful guides for the innovative investor, but they should not be considered absolute dictations of the truth. Remember, "Garbage in, garbage out." We suspect that as opposed to these reports remaining proprietary, as is currently the case with much of the research on equities and bonds, many of these reports will become open-source and widely accessible to all levels of investors in line with the ethos of cryptoassets.

SUPPLY

$ Billion

	2014A	2015E	2016E	2017E	2018E	2019E	2020E	2021E	2022E	2023E	2024E	2025E
Total Bitcoin in Circulation (End of Year)	13,125,000	15,000,000	16,025,000	16,656,000	7,287,000	17,918,000	18,410,000	18,725,000	19,041,000	19,357,000	19,687,500	20,343,750
% of total		71.43%	76.31%	79.31%	82.32%	85.32%	87.67%	89.17%	90.67%	92.18%	93.75%	96.88%
Held for Investment or Dormant %	50%	50%	48%	46%	44%	42%	41%	39%	38%	36%	35%	33%
Held as Working Capital %	50%	50%	52%	54%	56%	58%	60%	61%	63%	64%	66%	67%
Bitcoin Available for Transactions	6,562,500	7,500,000	8,333,000	8,994,240	9,680,720	10,392,440	10,953,950	11,422,250	11,900,625	12,388,480	12,895,313	13,562,568

DEMAND

$ Billion

	2014A	2015E	2016E	2017E	2018E	2019E	2020E	2021E	2022E	2023E	2024E	2025E
Online Payments	1,500	1,725	1,984	2,281	2,624	3,017	3,379	3,785	4,239	4,747	5,317	5,955
Remittances	435	457	480	504	529	555	583	612	643	675	709	744
Micro Transactions	540	567	595	625	656	689	724	760	798	838	880	924
Unbanked	4,305	4,435	4,568	4,705	4,846	4,991	5,141	5,295	5,454	5,618	5,786	5,960
Other	1,829	1,902	1,978	2,057	2,140	2,225	2,314	2,407	2,503	2,603	2,707	2,816
Growth Rates												
Online Payments		15%	15%	15%	15%	15%	12%	12%	12%	12%	12%	12%
Remittances		5%	5%	5%	5%	5%	5%	5%	5%	5%	5%	5%
Micro Transactions		5%	5%	5%	5%	5%	5%	5%	5%	5%	5%	5%
Unbanked		3%	3%	3%	3%	3%	3%	3%	3%	3%	3%	3%
Other		4%	4%	4%	4%	4%	4%	4%	4%	4%	4%	4%
Bitcoin Share												
Online Payments	0.02%	0.04%	0.08%	0.17%	0.34%	0.67%	1.35%	2.70%	5.39%	7.00%	9.00%	10.00%
Remittances	0.01%	0.03%	0.09%	0.27%	0.54%	1.08%	2.16%	4.32%	8.64%	17.28%	18.50%	20.00%
Micro Transactions	0.01%	0.003%	0.09%	0.27%	0.54%	1.08%	2.16%	4.32%	8.64%	17.28%	18.50%	20.00%
Unbanked	0.001%	0.003%	0.01%	0.03%	0.08%	0.24%	0.73%	1.46%	2.92%	5.83%	7.50%	10.00%
Other	0.01%	0.02%	0.04%	0.08%	0.16%	0.32%	0.64%	1.28%	2.56%	5.12%	7.50%	10.00%
Capacity Supported by Bitcoin												
Online Payments	$ 0.32	$ 0.7	$ 1.7	$ 3.8	$ 8.8	$ 20.3	$ 45.6	$ 102.1	$ 228.6	$ 332.3	$ 478.5	$ 595.5
Remittances	$ 0.04	$ 0.1	$ 0.4	$ 1.4	$ 2.9	$ 6.0	$ 12.6	$ 26.4	$ 55.5	$ 116.6	$ 131.1	$ 148.8
Micro Transactions	$ 0.05	$ 0.2	$ 0.5	$ 1.7	$ 3.5	$ 7.4	$ 15.6	$ 32.8	$ 68.9	$ 144.8	$ 162.7	$ 184.7
Unbanked	$ 0.04	$ 0.1	$ 0.4	$ 1.3	$ 3.9	$ 12.1	$ 37.5	$ 77.2	$ 159.0	$ 327.6	$ 434.0	$ 596.0
Other	$ 0.18	$ 0.4	$ 0.8	$ 1.6	$ 3.4	$ 7.1	$ 14.8	$ 30.8	$ 64.1	$ 133.3	$ 203.1	$ 281.6
Total	$ 0.64	$ 1.5	$ 3.8	$ 9.8	$ 22.6	$ 53.0	$ 126.1	$ 269.3	$ 576.2	$ 1,054.6	$ 1,409.4	$ 1,806.6
Assumed Annual Velocity												
Online Payments	12	12	12	12	12	12	12	12	12	12	12	12
Remittances	12	12	12	12	12	12	12	12	12	12	12	12
Micro Transactions	12	12	12	12	12	12	12	12	12	12	12	12
Unbanked	6	6	6	6	6	6	6	6	6	6	6	6
Other	6	6	6	6	6	6	6	6	6	6	6	6
Bitcoin Monetary Base Required												
Online Payments	$ 0.03	$ 0.06	$ 0.14	$ 0.32	$ 0.74	$ 1.69	$ 3.80	$ 8.50	$ 19.05	$ 27.69	$ 39.88	$ 49.63
Remittances	$ 0.00	$ 0.01	$ 0.04	$ 0.11	$ 0.24	$ 0.50	$ 1.05	$ 2.20	$ 4.63	$ 9.72	$ 10.92	$ 12.40
Micro Transactions	$ 0.00	$ 0.01	$ 0.04	$ 0.14	$ 0.30	$ 0.62	$ 1.30	$ 2.74	$ 5.74	$ 12.06	$ 13.56	$ 15.39
Unbanked	$ 0.01	$ 0.02	$ 0.07	$ 0.23	$ 0.71	$ 2.21	$ 6.81	$ 14.04	$ 28.92	$ 59.57	$ 78.90	$ 108.36
Other	$ 0.03	$ 0.07	$ 0.14	$ 0.30	$ 0.62	$ 1.29	$ 2.69	$ 5.60	$ 11.65	$ 24.23	$ 36.92	$ 51.19
Total BTC Monetary Base Required	$ 0.08	$ 0.18	$ 0.44	$ 1.10	$ 2.61	$ 6.31	$ 15.66	$ 33.08	$ 69.99	$ 133.28	$ 180.18	$ 236.97

VALUATION

	2014A	2015E	2016E	2017E	2018E	2019E	2020E	2021E	2022E	2023E	2024E	2025E
Bitcoin Monetary Base Required / Bitcoins Available for Transactions	$12	$24	$53	$123	$269	$608	$1,429	$2,896	$5,881	$10,758	$13,973	$17,473
		11/4/2015	1	2	3	4	5	6	7	8	9	10

BTC Price $462
PV $USD/BTC $604
Discount Rate 40%

<= present value of the price per BTC required to support the expected level of economic activity in 2025

Figure 12.1 ■ A fundamental valuation of bitcoin over 10 years (Source: Gil Luria, Director of Research at D.A. Davidson & Co.)

GET TO KNOW THE COMMUNITY AND THE DEVELOPERS

After a valuation analysis is done, or at the very least current value is contemplated, the best thing the innovative investor can do is to know and understand the cryptoasset developers and surrounding community. As peer-to-peer technologies, all cryptoassets have social networks. Reddit, Twitter, and Slack groups are valuable information channels, though we hesitate to give more guidance than that as each community is different, and communication channels are always changing. Another extremely valuable and often underappreciated or unknown resource is Meetup.com groups.

In getting to know the community better, consider a few key points. How committed is the developer team, and what is their background? Have they worked on a previous cryptoasset and in that process refined their ideas so that they now want to launch another? For example, this could be similar to what happened with Vitalik Buterin in his decision to move on from Bitcoin and start Ethereum, which was something fundamentally new. Or is there something more sinister going on? If any of the developers have a questionable track record, especially concerning involvement in the fishy launch of past cryptoassets, then exercise extreme caution. Remember John Law. Information about the core members behind a cryptoasset can be found through Google searches, LinkedIn, and Twitter, as well as by spending time on the forums related to these assets (they're good for at least a chuckle or two as well). If information cannot be found on the developers, or the developers are overtly anonymous, then this is a red flag because there is no accountability if things go wrong.

RELATION TO DIGITAL SIBLINGS

Next, the innovative investor should ask: How is the cryptoasset related to its ancestors? Is it a fork of another coin? If so, what aspects are being changed, and why do those changes justify an entirely new asset? A frequent argument that Bitcoin Maximalists—people who believe bitcoin will be the only cryptoasset that survives—purport is that all other cryptoassets display features that Bitcoin will someday absorb. There is some merit to this point, as Bitcoin's open-source roots make it flexible, but it is by no means a view we ascribe to. We do, however, encourage innovative investors to put their Bitcoin Maximalist thinking cap on every time they're investigating a new cryptoasset, as it forces important questions to be asked.

We expect to see an increasing number of cryptoassets that are built on the platform of another asset, which is an important consideration in the arena of digital siblings. As we covered in Chapter 5, Ethereum, which we defined as a cryptocommodity, is a common platform for dApps and their associated cryptotokens. Whether this relation is for better or worse depends on the situation. In the DAOsaster, The DAO had a significantly negative impact on Ethereum. On the other hand, the successful creation and implementation of cryptotokens like Augur or SingularDTV, which are also built on Ethereum, can have a positive impact on all assets involved. As Ethereum grows as a platform for other cryptoassets, it will be important to keep an eye on the quality of the dApps that are built on it, and how the Ethereum team handles its relationship with these dApps. If Ethereum gets big enough, there may eventually be those who call themselves Ethereum Maximalists!

ISSUANCE MODEL

The current and ongoing rate of supply increase is extremely important to consider. If a cryptoasset has a high rate of supply issuance, as bitcoin did in its early days, then that can erode the asset's value if its utility isn't growing in line with expectations. The total planned supply of the asset is also integral to the cryptoasset's individual units preserving value over time. If too many units will ultimately be issued, that will erode the value of the asset in the future.

Next, consider if the distribution is fair. Remember that a premine (where the assets are mined before the network is made widely available, as was the case with bytecoin) or an instamine (where many of the assets are mined at the start, as was the case with dash) are both bad signs because assets and power will accrue to a few, as opposed to being widely distributed in line with the egalitarian ethos.

As much as these comments about premines and instamines can sound black and white, the reality is there may be appropriate reasons for different issuance models. Issuance models are evolving as developers sort through the *cryptoeconomics* of releasing cryptoassets to support decentralized networks. As with central banks and traditional economics, people are feeling their way toward what works. Furthermore, the issuance model of cryptoassets is always subject to change. For example, Ethereum started with one planned issuance model, but is deciding to go with another a couple years into launch.[15] Such changes in the issuance model may occur for other assets, or impact those assets that are significantly tied to the Ethereum network.

While we have covered a few issuance models in detail, like those of Bitcoin and Monero, the most important aspect is that the issuance model fits the use case. With Dogecoin we saw that it needed lots of units outstanding for it to function as a tipping service, which justifies it currently having over 100 billion units outstanding, a significantly larger amount than Bitcoin. With many people turning to bitcoin as gold 2.0, an issuance model like Dogecoin's would be a terrible idea.

• • •

The next avenue to pursue information often depends on the maturity of the cryptoasset. For Bitcoin, more than eight years worth of conversation and writing on the trials and tribulations of the asset exist, plus constant improvements to its underlying code. For Ethereum, there's clearly less information, as it was announced five years after Bitcoin's network had been up and running. Many cryptoassets, especially in the cryptotoken vertical, are even newer than Ethereum.

The creation of new cryptoassets is occurring at an increasing, some would say alarming, pace. New releases are the ones that require the most due diligence. We caution all but the most experienced innovative investors to venture into these riskier assets. We have dedicated an entire chapter, Chapter 16, to the history and investigation of cryptoassets being launched in 2017 and beyond.

In the next chapter, we will investigate the network health of cryptoassets, which can also be thought of as operating fundamentals. Operating fundamentals are the metrics that show a cryptoasset with a functioning architecture is gaining traction and fulfilling its potential. Since these fundamentals can also influence the price, we will conclude the chapter with a discussion of market technicals to identify the best opportunities to buy, sell, or trade a cryptoasset.

Chapter 13

Operating Health of Cryptoasset Networks and Technical Analysis

A cryptoasset that is already operating provides a wealth of information, which can be used to build upon the foundational information we discussed in the last chapter. Such information leads us deep into the operational fundamentals: those aspects of a cryptoasset that reveal how it is working day-to-day and year-to-year in the real world.

Recall how we first described blockchain architecture as a stack of hardware, software, applications, and users. Specific metrics can be investigated from each of these four layers that will reveal the ongoing growth of an operating cryptoasset, or lack thereof. For a healthy and thriving asset, the one universal law is that these metrics should be growing. If a cryptoasset is in its early days and it's not growing, then its future is likely not going to be bright.

We describe in detail the operating fundamentals for each of the four layers. We close off the chapter with a practical discussion of technical analysis and how the innovative investor can use these tools to help the timing of both cryptoasset purchases and sales.

MINERS

One of the most important, but often overlooked, indicators of a cryptoasset's ongoing health is the support of the underlying security system. For proof-of-work based systems, such as Bitcoin, Ethereum,[1] Litecoin, Monero, and many more, security is a function of the number of miners and their combined compute (or hashing) power.

Since miners are the ones validating transactions and building the asset's blockchain, their combined compute power needs to be robust enough to fend off attackers that want to trick the network into processing invalid transactions. The only way attackers can process invalid transactions is if they own over half of the compute power of the network, so it's critical that no single entity ever exceeds 50 percent ownership. If they do, then they can perform what's referred to as a *51 percent attack*, in which they process invalid transactions. This involves spending money they don't have and would ruin confidence in the cryptoasset. The best way to prevent this attack from happening is to have so many computers supporting the blockchain in a globally decentralized topography that no single entity could hope to buy enough computers to take majority share.

Buying and maintaining these computers is costly, and miners are not volunteering their time and money out of altruism. Instead, more computers are only added to the network when more entities see the ability to profit from doing so. In other words, miners are purely economically rational individuals—mercenaries of compute power—and their profit is largely driven by the value of the cryptoasset as well as by transaction fees. Therefore, the more the price goes up, and the more transactions are processed, the more likely new computers will be added to help support and secure the network.[2] In turn, the greater hardware support there is for the network, the more people will trust in its security, thereby driving more people to buy and use the asset.

A clearly positively reinforcing cycle sets in that ensures that the larger the asset grows, the more secure it becomes—as it should be. The security should be different for a pawn shop with $3,000 in the cash register versus a Wells Fargo branch with $2 million in the vault. The same goes for the security of a cryptoasset with a network value of $300,000 versus $3 billion.

Hash Rates as a Sign of Security

One way to determine the relative safety of a cryptoasset is through its hash rate. A cryptoasset's hash rate is representative of the combined power of the mining computers connected to the network. For example, Figures 13.1 and 13.2 show Bitcoin's hash rate and Ethereum's hash rate over time, both of which display hyper growth characteristics.

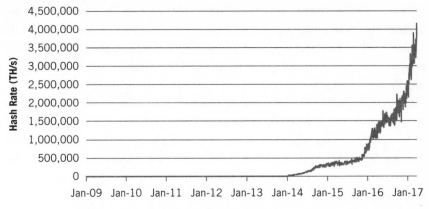

Figure 13.1 ■ Bitcoin's hash rate rise since inception

Data sourced from Blockchain.info

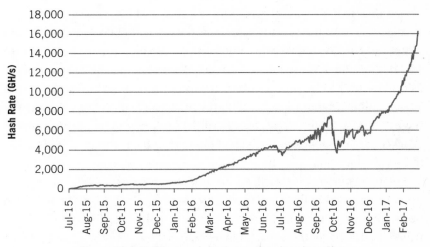

Figure 13.2 ■ Ethereum's hash rate rise since inception

Data sourced from Etherscan.io

As of March 2017, Bitcoin's hash rate had increased 3-fold over March 2016, while Ethereum's hash rate had increased 10-fold. While Ethereum is experiencing faster growth, which could be taken as a sign that more miners are enthusiastic about their potential profits from supporting Ethereum, it is also growing off a smaller initial hash rate than Bitcoin.

At the risk of being repetitive, more hash rate signifies more computers are being added to support the network, which signifies greater security. This typically only happens if the value of the cryptoasset and its associated transactions are increasing, because miners are profit-driven individuals. While hash rate often follows price, sometimes price can follow hash rate. This happens in situations where miners expect good things of the asset in the future, and therefore proactively connect machines to help secure the network. This instills confidence, and perhaps the expected good news has also traveled to the market, so the price starts going up.

Once it's been ascertained that the hash rate is growing, often the best way to compare the relative security of cryptoassets is through a calculation of the equipment securing the network. Using a dollar value is helpful because it gives us an idea of how much a bad actor would have to spend to re-create the network, which is what the actor would need to launch a 51 percent attack.

As of March 2017, a Bitcoin mining machine that produced 14 terahash per second (TH/s) could be bought for $2,300. The idea of TH/s can be thought of as similar to a personal computer's clock speed, which is often measured in gigahertz (GHz), and similarly represents the number of times a machine can execute instructions per second. It would take 286,000 of the aforementioned 14 TH/s machines to produce 4,000,000 TH/s, which was the hash rate of the Bitcoin network at the time. Hence, Bitcoin's network could be re-created with a $660 million spend, which would give an attacker control of 50 percent of the network. Yes, 50 percent, because if the hash rate started at 100, and an attacker bought enough to re-create it (100), then the hash rate would double to 200, at which point the attacker has a 50 percent share.

Ethereum's mining network, on the other hand, is less built out because it's a younger ecosystem that stores less value. As of March 2017, a 230 megahash per second (MH/s) mining machine could be purchased for $4,195,[3] and it would take 70,000 of these machines to recreate Ethereum's hash rate, totaling $294 million in value. Also, because Ethereum is supported by GPUs and not ASICs, the machines can more easily be constructed piecemeal by a hobbyist on a budget.

Using $660 million for Bitcoin and $294 million for Ethereum, while the network values for the two cryptocurrencies are respectively US$17.1 billion and $4.7 billion, we get a range of 3.9 cents to 6.3 cents of capital expenditure per dollar secured by the network. This range is a good baseline for the innovative investor to use for other cryptoassets to ensure they are secured with a similar level of capital spend as Bitcoin and Ethereum, which are the two best secured assets in the blockchain ecosystem.

BE CAREFUL WHEN DIRECTLY COMPARING
HASH RATES BETWEEN CRYPTOASSETS

While it may initially seem logical to do, it's often not appropriate to directly compare the hash rate of different cryptoassets to judge relative security, because the type of machines providing the hash rate can vary among different blockchains, as can their cost. As we covered in Chapters 4 and 5, different blockchain architectures use different hash functions in the consensus process. Different hash functions are suitable for different kinds of chips, be they CPUs, GPUs, or ASICs, and these chips come in computers that vary in cost. For example, Bitcoin is mined with ASICs, which yield the greatest hash rate per dollar spent, while Ethereum is mined mostly with GPUs. Therefore, $1,000 will purchase more hash rate for a Bitcoin computer than an Ethereum computer, and it is this dollar value that's most important in deterring attackers from attempting to recreate the network. Hence, while as of March 2017 Bitcoin's hash rate of 4,000,000 TH/s was technically 250,000-fold higher than Ethereum's 16,000 GH/s, this does not mean Bitcoin was 250,000 times more secure than Ethereum.

Decentralized Assets Should Have Decentralized Miners

Overall, hash rate is important, but so too is its decentralization. After all, if the hash rate is extremely high but 75 percent of it is controlled by a single entity, then that is not a decentralized system. It is actually a highly centralized system and therefore vulnerable to the whims of that one entity. If a cryptoasset is vulnerable to the whims of a single entity or small oligarchy, then that person or small group could choose to perform a 51 percent attack at some point, either to crush the value of the asset (a malicious kamikaze attack), or to try to profit from spending money they don't have. Such a risk must be considered and avoided.

Figures 13.3, 13.4, and 13.5 are charts showing the hash rate distribution among miners for Ethereum, Litecoin, and Bitcoin as of March 2017.

It's apparent that Litecoin is the most centralized, while Bitcoin is the most decentralized. A way to quantify the decentralization is the Herfindahl-Hirschman Index (HHI), which is a metric to measure competition and market concentration.[4] For example, the U.S. Department of Justice uses the HHI when examining potential mergers and acquisitions, to assess how they may

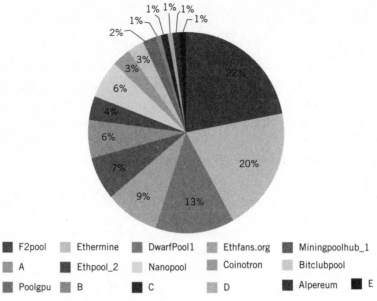

Figure 13.3 ■ Ethereum's hash rate distribution

Data sourced from Etherscan.io

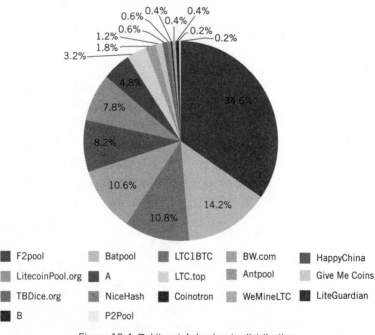

Figure 13.4 ■ Litecoin's hash rate distribution

Data sourced from https://www.litecoinpool.org/pools

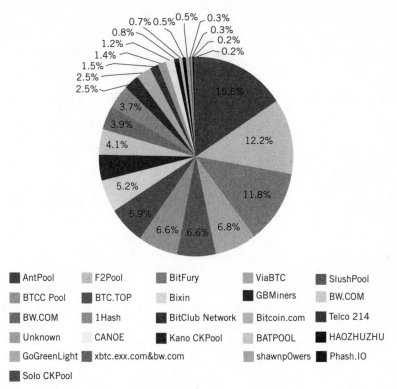

Figure 13.5 ■ Bitcoin's hash rate distribution

Data sourced from https://blockchain.info/pools

influence the centralization of the industry.[5] The metric is calculated by taking the percent market share of each entity, squaring each market share, and summing these squares before multiplying by 10,000.

For example, a system that has two players with 50 percent market share apiece would have an HHI of 5,000, because $(0.5^2) + (.5^2) = 0.5$, and $0.5 \times 10,000 = 5,000$. For the HHI, anything less than 1,500 qualifies as a competitive marketplace, anything between 1,500 to 2,500 is a moderately concentrated marketplace, and anything greater than 2,500 is a highly concentrated marketplace.[6]

Blockchain networks should never classify as a highly concentrated marketplace, and ideally, should always fall into the competitive marketplace category. The more concentrated a marketplace is, the closer a single entity can be to gaining majority share of the compute power and performing a 51 percent attack. Figure 13.6 shows that both Bitcoin and Ethereum qualify as competitive marketplaces, while Litecoin is a moderately concentrated marketplace.[7]

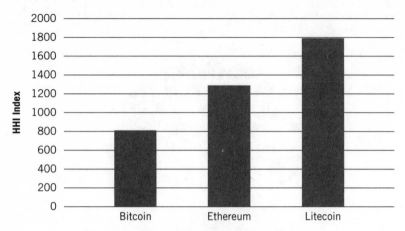

Figure 13.6 ■ The health of Bitcoin, Ethereum,
and Litecoin's mining ecosystems based on the HHI
Data sourced from Etherscan.io, litecoinpool.org, and Blockchain.info

The centralization of miners in different blockchain networks varies over time depending on how much growth the cryptoasset experiences and the evolution of the compute infrastructure to support it. For example, Figure 13.7 is a graph of Bitcoin's HHI index over time.

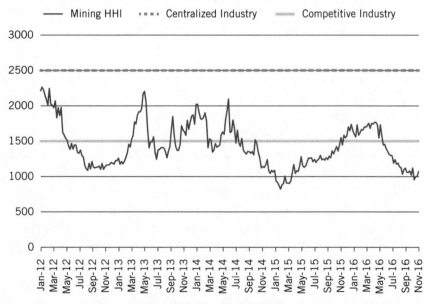

Figure 13.7 ■ Bitcoin's HHI over time
Data sourced from Andrew Geyl

At times, Bitcoin has been a moderately concentrated marketplace, just as Litecoin mining is currently a moderately concentrated marketplace. Litecoin recognizes the impact that large mining pools can have on the health of its ecosystem and the quality of its coin. To that point, Litecoin developers have instituted an awareness campaign called "Spread the Hashes" for those mining litecoin to consider spreading out their mining activities.[8] The campaign recommends that litecoin computers mine with a variety of mining pools rather than concentrating solely in one.

Geographic Distribution of Miners

Beyond hash rate and the percent distribution of hash rate ownership, it's also important to know how geographically distributed the computers are that are maintaining a cryptoasset's blockchain. After all, if the miners for a cryptoasset are all in a single country, then that cryptoasset could be at the mercy of that nation's government. This provides a macroeconomic view that should be incorporated into our fundamental analysis of these assets.

Much has been made about how many of the largest mining firms have facilities in China or Iceland[9] where the cost of electricity is low. However, by looking at all the Bitcoin nodes (a location where the Bitcoin software has been downloaded and Bitcoin's blockchain is being maintained), locating where the overall activity is concentrated becomes clearer. Figure 13.8 shows the distribution of bitcoin nodes[10] on a global basis.

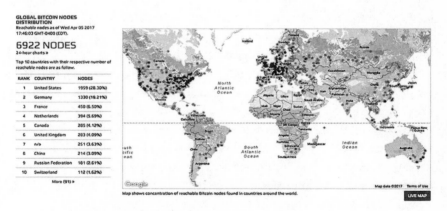

Figure 13.8 ■ Bitcoin node distribution as of April 2017

Source: https://bitnodes.21.co/

People are often confused when they see Figure 13.8 as the United States and Germany have the most Bitcoin nodes, while China is lower in the list, which at face value seems to contradict the idea that most miners are in China. Not all nodes are made equal. A single node could have a large number of mining computers behind it, hence capturing a large percentage of the overall network's hash rate, while another node could have a single mining computer supporting it, amounting to a tiny fraction of Bitcoin's hash rate. A node is merely a point of connection to the network, and they differ drastically in the compute power they contribute. Hence, the combination of geographic node distribution and hash rate concentration amongst the nodes gives a fuller picture of the decentralization of hardware supporting a cryptoasset.

SOFTWARE DEVELOPERS

William Mougayar, author of *The Business Blockchain*, has written extensively about how to identify and evaluate new blockchain ventures and sums up the importance of developers succinctly: "Before users can trust the protocol, they need to trust the people who created it."[11] As we touched upon in the prior chapter, investigate the prior qualifications of lead developers for a protocol as much as possible.

While the initial pedigree of developers is important, so too is their long-term commitment. Developers shouldn't create a protocol and simply walk away. These systems are made of open-source software, which must evolve over time to stay secure and relevant. If no one is maintaining the software, then two things will happen: One, bugs will be found and exploited by bad actors. Two, without enough developers, the software will stagnate, ultimately losing out to more compelling projects.

Developers have their own network effect: the more smart developers there are working on a project, the more useful and intriguing that project becomes to other developers. These developers are then drawn to the project, and a positively reinforcing flywheel is created. On the other hand, if developers are exiting a project, then it quickly becomes less and less interesting to other developers, ultimately leaving no one to captain the software ship. With no one at the helm, then the companies and users relying upon it will ultimately defect as well, all of which will drop the value of the cryptoasset.

While developer activity is incredibly important, it is also notoriously hard to quantify with accuracy. Most cryptoasset projects are stored and orchestrated through GitHub, which has its own set of graphs of developer activity. Graphs include categories like contributors, commits, code frequency, punch card, and network, though many of them lack meaningful data. For example, while a graph can be seen on contributions, sometimes more contributions can be a negative factor if it was associated with a major bug being found in the software and developers rushing to fix it. Furthermore, each cryptoasset is composed of many different projects, which makes getting a broad view on GitHub hard to do.

As a solution, CryptoCompare has sought to amalgamate developer activity and metrics to make it easier to compare the different cryptoassets. Figure 13.9 is a graph with a metric CryptoCompare has created called *Code Repository Points*,[12] which they explain as follows: "Code Repository points are awarded as follows: 1 for a star, 2 for a fork (somebody trying to create a copy or just play with the code), and 3 for each subscriber."

A star is when someone stars code on GitHub, which users do to bookmark the code and show appreciation for it.[13] We explained forks in detail in Chapter 5 around the DAOsaster, but in this instance, a fork is a good thing. It refers to a situation where new developers forked the code of the cryptoasset to experiment with it. Recall that this is how Litecoin, Dash, and Zcash were created from Bitcoin: developers forked Bitcoin's code, modified it, and then re-released the software with different functionality. Subscribers refer to people wanting to stay actively involved with the code. In short, the more code repository points, the more developer activity has occurred around the cryptoasset's code.

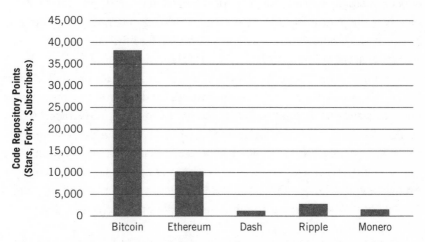

Figure 13.9 ■ Code repository points for different cryptoassets (March 29, 2017)
Data sourced from CryptoCompare

However, what's unfair about this metric is that bitcoin has been around for over eight years, while other cryptoassets have been around for a fraction of that time. Standardizing for the amount of time the cryptoassets have been under construction yields the graph in Figure 13.10.[14]

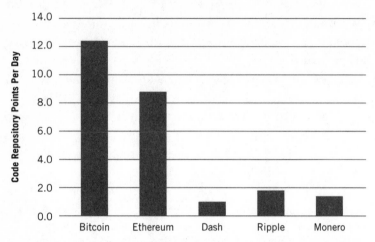

Figure 13.10 ∎ Frequency of developer activity for different cryptoassets (March 29, 2017)

Data sourced from CryptoCompare

Using this standardized measure for developer activity, it's clear Bitcoin and Ethereum are two standout projects. With Dash as the baseline, Ripple developers are 80 percent more active and Monero developers 40 percent more. However, the phrase "You get what you pay for" comes to mind. With network values of $17.1 billion for Bitcoin and $4.7 billion for Ethereum, it makes sense that their developers are so active. Their activity has clearly built a valuable platform that many people are drawn to use. With Dash, Ripple, and Monero at network values of $600 million, $360 million, and $280 million respectively, it's understandable that they don't have as wide and active a developer base.

To calibrate for network value, in Figure 13.11 we take the total network value of a cryptoasset and divide it by the cumulative repository points, the idea being that a certain amount of work has gone into creating each cryptoasset, begging the question, "What is the dollar value per repository point?" The higher this number, the dearer each repository point is valued, and potentially overvalued.

Using this methodology, as of March 2017 Dash was the cryptoasset architecture most valued by the market, as people were paying roughly $500,000 per

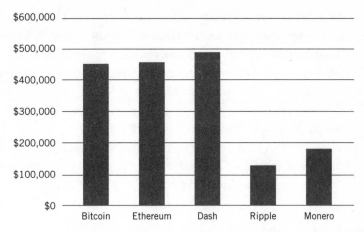

Figure 13.11 ■ Dollar value per code repository point for different cryptoassets
(March 29, 2017)
Data sourced from CryptoCompare

repository point, though this does not mean it will stay that way. Interestingly, Bitcoin and Ethereum are very close, while Ripple and Monero seemingly have the most undervalued developers.

Another good site for monitoring overall developer activity is OpenHub.[15] For example, OpenHub shows the number of lines of code that have been written for a project, as shown in Figure 13.12.

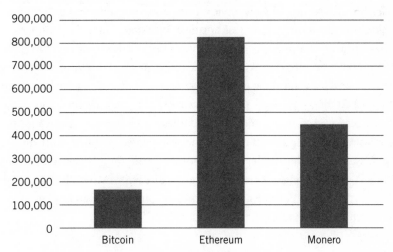

Figure 13.12 ■ Lines of code written for Bitcoin, Ethereum,
and Monero as shown by OpenHub
Data sourced from OpenHub

Possessing more lines of code is not necessarily better for an asset. Sometimes the opposite is true, and less is more because a great developer can write the same program in half the number of lines as a mediocre developer. Bitcoin, Ethereum, and Monero are quite different, so it's hard to compare them directly. Bitcoin aims to be minimalist, while Monero has added privacy functionality, and Ethereum is the most expansive in scope. Most important, all three rank as *Very High Activity* on OpenHub's activity meter.

While these metrics of developer activity are by no means authoritative, they give some idea of what to look for when exploring the commitment and activity of the developers behind a cryptoasset.

COMPANY SUPPORT

Similar in difficulty to assessing developer support is assessing company support for a cryptoasset. Websites like SpendBitcoins.com[16] inform visitors how many places accept a specific cryptoasset; a metric important for cryptocurrencies but not so much for cryptocommodities and cryptotokens.

A different approach is to monitor the number of companies supporting a cryptoasset, which can be done by tracking venture capital investments. CoinDesk provides some of this information as seen in Figure 13.13. Though, as we will address in Chapter 16 on ICOs, the trend in this space is moving away from venture funding and toward crowdfunding.

Getting a longitudinal view on how companies are supporting a cryptoasset over time is more important than a single snapshot. One of the best metrics we have found as a proxy for company support is the number of exchanges that support a cryptoasset. As a cryptoasset gains greater legitimacy and support, an increasing number of exchanges carry it. As mentioned in Chapter 9, the last exchanges to add a cryptoasset are the most regulated exchanges, such as Bitstamp, GDAX, and Gemini. These exchanges have strong brands and relations with regulators that they need to protect, so they won't support a cryptoasset until it has undergone thorough technological and market-based vetting. A simple Google search is enough to discern which exchanges support which cryptoassets. Volume aggregators like CoinMarketCap also give insight into which exchanges support which currencies.[17]

Blockchain Venture Capital						
Bitcoin Venture Investments: Coin Desk						
Close Date	Company	Classification	Round Size ($m)	Cumulative Funding ($m)	Round	Investors
9-Feb-2017	Coinfirm	"RegTech" (Regulation Technology)	0.7	0.7	Seed	Luma Ventures
7-Feb-2017	Hashed Health	Infrastructure	1.85	1.85	N/A	Martin Ventures, Fenbushi Capital
31-Jan-2017	Storj	Infrastructure	0.1	0.1	Seed	Utah Governor's Office of Economic Development (GOED)
30-Jan-2017	Bitfury	Infrastructure	30	90	Series D	Credit China FinTech Holdings
30-Jan-2017	Bitpesa	Payment Processor	2.5	3.6	Series A	Draper VC, Greycroft LLC, Digital Currency Group, Pantera Capital Management, Blockchain Capital, Zephyr Acorn, FuturePerfectVC and BnkToTheFuture
24-Jan-2017	Cambridge Blockchain	Infrastructure	2	2	Seed	Partech Ventures, Digital Currency Group
19-Jan-2017	CoolBitX	Wallet	0.2	0.2	Seed	Midana Capital
17-Jan-2017	SatoshiPay	Financial Services	0.68	1.07	N/A	Blue Star Capital
17-Jan-2017	NeuFund	Venture Capital	2	2	Series A	Atlantic Labs, Klaas Kersting
11-Jan-2017	Qtum	Financial Services	1	1	Seed	Anthony Di Iorio, Star Xu, Xiaolai Li, Bo Shen
4-Jan-2017	Blockstack	Infrastructure	4	5.3	Series A	Union Sqauare Ventures, Lux Capital, Naval Ravikant, Digital Currency Group, Compound, Version One, Kal Vepuri and Rising Tide
3-Jan-2017	Bitpagos	Financial Services	1.9	0.9	Series A	Huiyin Blockchain Ventures Boost VC, Digital Currency Group and Draper VC

Figure 13.13 ■ Blockchain venture capital investments as tracked through CoinDesk
Source: CoinDesk

Another good proxy for the increased acceptance of a cryptoasset and its growing offering by highly regulated exchanges is the amount of fiat currency used to purchase it. As also mentioned in Chapter 9, in the early days of a cryptoasset listing, the majority of the volume often goes through bitcoin, meaning that buys and sells are done in bitcoin, not dollars or euros. As cryptoassets grow in diversity, so too do their trading pairs with fiat currencies, as shown with Ethereum's ether in Figure 13.14.

In the one-year period from March 2016 to March 2017, ether went from being traded 12 percent of the time with fiat currency to 50 percent of the time. This is a good sign of the maturation of an asset, and shows it is gaining wider recognition and acceptance.

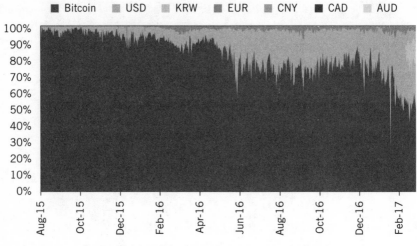

Figure 13.14 ■ Ether's growing currency pair diversity

Data sourced from CryptoCompare

USER ADOPTION

A number of metrics can assess the state and rate of mainstream adoption. We will focus on those that display the traction of people using the cryptoasset for its core utility. The basic metrics are:

- Number of users
- Number of transactions propagated on the blockchain
- Dollar value of those transactions
- Valuation metric, which is the network value of a cryptoasset divided by its daily dollar transaction volume

We include examples of these metrics for Bitcoin and Ethereum. It should be noted that many of these numbers are not easily accessible for the other crypto-assets because they are still in their very early days, and thus data has not been extracted and presented in an easily digestible manner. Even for Ethereum, certain metrics are not as easily accessible as they are for Bitcoin. Two of the best data resources for Bitcoin and Ethereum respectively are Blockchain.info's charts section[18] and Etherscan's charts section,[19] and we posit that other cryptoassets will have similar services built to extract and visualize data from their blockchains.

Number of Users

Figure 13.15 shows the number of wallet users for Blockchain.info, a leading bitcoin wallet provider (a wallet is where bitcoin users store the keys to access their bitcoin). Clearly, having more users with wallets that can hold a crypto-asset is good for that asset: more users, more usage, more acceptance. While the chart shows an exponential trend, there are a few drawbacks to this metric. For one, it only shows the growth of Blockchain.info's wallet users, but many other wallet providers exist. For example, as of March 2017, Coinbase had 14.2 million wallets, on par with Blockchain.info. Second, an individual can have more than one wallet, so some of these numbers could be due to users creating many wallets, a flaw which extends to other wallet providers and their metrics as well.

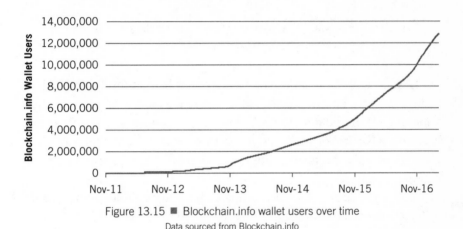

Figure 13.15 ■ Blockchain.info wallet users over time
Data sourced from Blockchain.info

Willy Woo, a Coindesk.com contributor, utilized Google Trends to evaluate the searches done on Google for the term "BTC USD." He wanted to do this as "an effective proxy for the growth and engagement of bitcoin over time."[20] In other words, he wanted to use this metric to determine the growth of bitcoin users. Figure 13.16 shows the trend of this search term over time. Woo indicates that the peaks "are in line with price bubbles, periods where more users head online to check the value of their wealth." Woo makes the leap that an active bitcoin user checks the price every day, so he believes the chart helps to identify the number of bitcoin users.

If we assume this to be true, then Woo's analysis indicates a doubling in bitcoin users every year and an order of magnitude growth every 3.375 years. He calls this Woo's Law in honor of Moore's Law[21] (which is famous for predicting that the manufacturing density of transistors per square inch would double every eighteen months). It will be interesting to see how Woo's Law holds up over time.

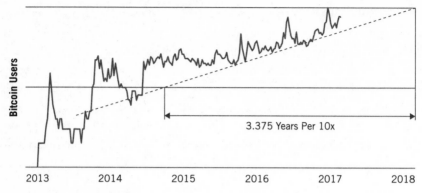

Figure 13.16 ■ Woo's Law in Action: Bitcoin users double every 12 months

Source: http://www.coindesk.com/using-google-trends-estimate-bitcoins-user-growth/

Consider too, the number of addresses on a blockchain. For Bitcoin, an address is where bitcoin is sent, and therefore the more addresses, the more locations that are holding bitcoin. However, a company like Coinbase may have only a handful of addresses, which serve to store bitcoin for millions of users. Thus, while this metric shows a nice up-and-to-the-right trend, it's only part of the picture.

Figure 13.17 shows the hyper growth of Ethereum's unique address count. With Ethereum, an address can either store a balance of ether, like Bitcoin, or it can store a smart contract. Either denotes an increase in use.

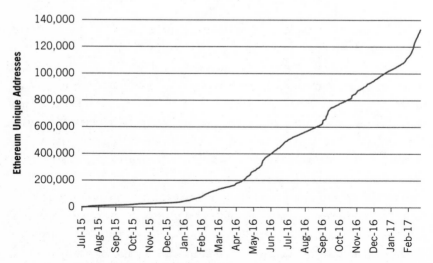

Figure 13.17 ■ The growth of Ethereum's unique addresses

Data sourced from Etherscan.io

Number of Transactions

Figures 13.18 and 13.19 show the number of transactions using Bitcoin and Ethereum's blockchains respectively. The rising numbers are healthy signs for each of the blockchains and their associated cryptoassets. This information for bitcoin can be accessed on Blockchain.info[22] and for ether at Etherscan.[23]

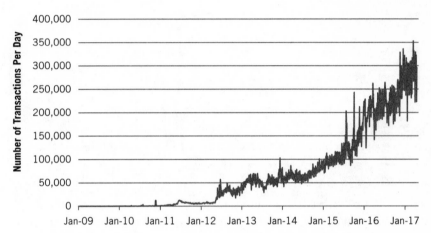

Figure 13.18 ■ Number of transactions per day using Bitcoin's blockchain
Data sourced from Blockchain.info

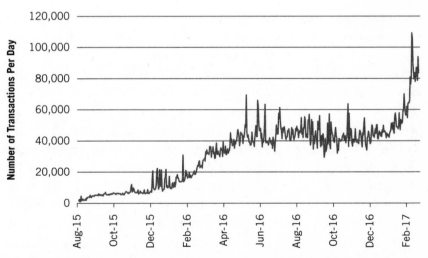

Figure 13.19 ■ Number of transactions per day using Ethereum's blockchain
Data sourced from Etherscan.io

Dollar Value of Transactions

While the number of transactions is an important metric, it says nothing about the monetary value of those transactions. Figure 13.20 shows the numbers for bitcoin. In the first quarter of 2017, Bitcoin was processing over $270 million per day, which translates to $188,000 per minute or $3,100 per second.[24]

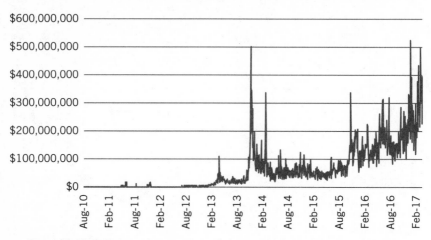

Figure 13.20 ■ Estimated transaction volume per day using Bitcoin's blockchain
Data sourced from Blockchain.info

A Potential Valuation Method

Just as valuation methods for equities have evolved over the years, so too will methods to value cryptoassets grow over time. One valuation method we're considering is to calibrate how much the market is willing to pay for the transactional utility of a blockchain. To gain this information, we divide the network value of a cryptoasset by its daily transaction volume. If the network value has outpaced the transactional volume of that asset, then this ratio will grow larger, which could imply the price of the asset has outpaced its utility. We call this the crypto "PE ratio," taking inspiration from the common ratio used for equities. For cryptoassets we put forth that the denominator of valuation should be transaction volumes, not earnings, as these are not companies with cash flows.

One would assume that an efficient price for an asset would indicate a steadiness of network value to the transaction volume of the asset. Increasing transactional volume of an asset should be met by a similar increase in the value of that asset. Upside swings in pricing without similar swings in transaction volume could indicate an overheating of the market and thus, overvaluation of an asset.

Over time, the market will likely find a happy medium for this ratio, just as equity markets find a happy medium for price to sales or price to earnings ratios. Cryptoassets, including bitcoin, are still too young with too little market data to claim exactly where this equilibrium ratio will stabilize. That said, looking at Figure 13.21, it appears that bitcoin has a comfortable base when its network value is 50 times its daily transactional volume. Maintaining a price that keeps the ratio near 50 could indicate that the asset is being fairly priced, and wide swings beyond that range can signal bearish or bullish trends.

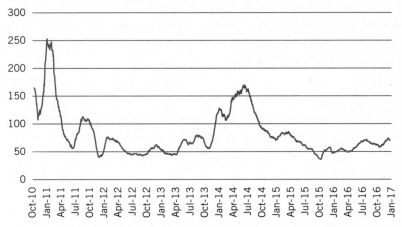

Figure 13.21 ■ Bitcoin's network value divided by estimated
transaction volume (30-day rolling average)
Data sourced from Blockchain.info

SUMMARY ON OPERATING FUNDAMENTALS

The process of performing fundamental analysis on a new asset class such as cryptoassets is in its early stages. As much as possible we've tried to utilize the rigor and depth available through many of the tools equity analysts have used over the years to come up with the useful metrics we've provided in these two chapters. Obviously, the study of equities and cryptoassets are fundamentally different. Yet we've tried to create resources and approaches for this type of analysis that can hold up over time as cryptoassets continue to grow and mature. We also know that as more data is created, as new trends are identified, and as more analysts enter the cryptoasset space, many of the resources we've utilized here may be superseded by even more elaborate and exact tools.

It's our hope that we have provided innovative investors with tools to do the necessary research and evaluation of these assets, as they would do with any other investment in their portfolio. Just as this chapter will help arm the innovative investor, we'd like to see it provide future cryptoasset analysts with the tools to continue to build more robust fundamental analysis models for these assets.

TECHNICAL ANALYSIS OF CRYPTOASSETS

Technical analysis comes with its own tools and metrics. Although fundamental analysis differs between cryptoassets and other asset classes, technical analysis is largely the same. Technical analysis is simply the evaluation of the price and volume movements of an asset over time to help time buys and sells. Of course, it's not a guaranteed method for finding the exact "right time" to buy or sell, but technical analysis has become a powerful tool that bitcoin and other cryptoasset traders use to understand market timing. Technical analysis is best used in conjunction with fundamental analysis to identify appropriate investments and when to make them. Here we provide some basic charts and considerations that the innovative investor can use.

Support and Resistance

Charting the support and resistance lines of an asset's price movement over time is a tried and tested tool for technical analysis. Figure 13.22 shows bitcoin's price movement through the year 2015, a period where it oscillated within a predictable *trading range*. In Figure 13.22 the top line is called the resistance line, indicating a price that bitcoin is having trouble breaking through. Often these lines can be numbers of psychological weight, in this case the $300 mark. When the price of bitcoin hits $300 it shows a tendency to bounce back into its trading range. On the flip side of resistance is support, which shows a price that bitcoin doesn't want to violate, in this case $200. Each time bitcoin nears the support line it bounces back into its trading range, and the one time that it breaks through this support it quickly climbs above it again.

Note that while this range can be a helpful guide, an asset doesn't always remain range-bound. For example, at the end of the depicted range the price seems to be breaking out to potentially form a new higher price and new trading range. For many technical analysts, such a breakout accompanied by high trading volume is a buy signal as it signifies something notable has happened to push the market to value the asset more richly. Often, previous resistance lines will become support lines if the asset has broken through a resistance line convincingly and stays elevated. Similarly, a prior line of support can become a point of resistance if the asset crashes through its prior support and stays beneath that line.

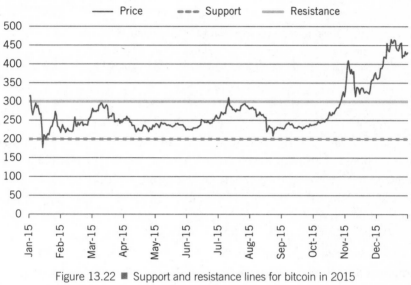

Figure 13.22 ■ Support and resistance lines for bitcoin in 2015

Data sourced from CoinDesk

This simple illustration of support and resistance lines is expanded on within detailed technical analysis resources available online, including the work of Brian Beamish of The Rational Investor,[25] among others.

Simple Moving Average

One of the most common tools for technical analysts is the simple moving average, or SMA, which smooths out the price trend of an asset over a period of time.

SMAs are provided by most online charting sites and, as the name implies, the calculation is simple. It merely plots the average price of an asset over a period of time, and that period can be days, weeks, or months. It's called a moving average because with each new day there is a new average, which includes the price on the newest day, while dropping the price of the oldest day. Hence, the average moves over time. Common averages include 50-day,

100-day, and 200-day moving averages, as well as longer term averages, like the 200-week moving average to observe trends on larger time scales. SMAs can indicate points of support and resistance and when used together can indicate changes in momentum. Cryptocompare.com makes the point:

> Often simple moving averages are used in conjunction with each other to spot trend reversals and shifts in momentum. For example when a short term SMA is below a longer term one and then crosses it—you have indicated an upward shift in momentum that is a buy signal.[26]

Figure 13.23 shows bitcoin's price from the launch of Mt. Gox in July 2010 through the end of 2012, along with its 50- and 200-day SMAs. Note that an average doesn't begin until enough days have passed for the first point to be plotted. To CryptoCompare's point, in the spring of 2012 the 50-day SMA punched through the 200-day SMA, and stayed above it, indicating upward momentum. Inversely, if a short term average crashes beneath a long term average, that is a bearish signal as the price of the asset is falling quickly and is commonly referred to as a *death cross*. Such behavior can be seen in the fall of 2011 when the 50-day moving average fell beneath the 200-day moving average.

Figure 13.23 ■ Simple Moving Averages in the early days of bitcoin
Data sourced from CoinDesk

Pay Attention to Volume

Because of the varying levels of trading that occur with cryptoassets, it's important for the innovative investor to pay close attention to the trading volume of an asset. For a young cryptoasset, it's not unusual to see price increases or decreases along with low volume. This indicates that the trading book is thin and thus the asset is susceptible to wild swings in price. By including an analysis of volume, these swings in price can indicate a sustained trend or a temporary movement. As Charles Bovaird points out in his piece on Technical Analysis for Coindesk.com,

> Bitcoin traders should keep in mind that volume plays an important role in evaluating price trends. High volume points to strong price trends, while low volume indicates weaker trends. Generally, rising prices coincide with increasing volume. If bitcoin prices enjoy an uptrend, but the currency's upward movements take place amid weak volume, this could mean that the trend is running out of gas and could soon be over.[27]

Similarly, a falling price with increasingly strong volume indicates capitulation as traders are rushing for the exits, whereas a falling price on low volume is of less concern.

Remember, most cryptoassets are still in an early stage, and as such, technical charts for these assets will lack the history of longer term assets such as bitcoin. You'll find many instances of newer cryptoassets experiencing wild price swings after their creation, but over time these younger assets begin to follow the rules of technical analysis. This is a sign that these assets are maturing, and as such, are being followed by a broader group of traders. This indicates they can be more fully analyzed and evaluated using technical analysis, allowing the innovative investor to better time the market and identify buy and sell opportunities.

• • •

Innovative investors must independently examine bitcoin and other cryptoassets, avoiding the temptation to buy or sell simply because everyone else is doing so. There's a growing wealth of information and data online on each of these assets, and if investors can't find enough data on an asset to perform the necessary analysis, that's probably a sign that it should be avoided as an investment. Let's call that the Burniske-Tatar Law.

Once the innovative investor has performed the necessary fundamental and technical analysis, the next step is to pull the trigger and actually make the investment. In the next few chapters we'll present the wide, and still growing, range of opportunities for investors to gain access to bitcoin and other cryptoassets.

Chapter 14

Investing Directly in Cryptoassets: Mining, Exchanges, and Wallets

Today, investors have many avenues for purchasing bitcoin and other cryptoassets. Options will continue to evolve, but broadly there are two main considerations: how to acquire cryptoassets and how to store them. Since cryptoassets are digital bearer instruments, they are unlike many other investments that are held by a centralized custodian. For example, regardless of which platform an investor uses to buy stocks, there is a centralized custodian who is "housing" the assets and keeping track of the investor's balance.[1] With cryptoassets, the innovative investor can opt for a similar situation or can have full autonomy and control in storage. The avenue chosen depends on what the innovative investor most values, and as with much of life, there are always trade-offs.

MINING

A brief history of the evolution of mining is needed so that the innovative investor can better understand the current state of affairs for bitcoin and other cryptoassets. From there, it is easier to decide if this avenue of acquisition is appropriate. Even for those who have no interest in mining themselves, it's valuable to have a deeper understanding because for many cryptoassets mining is the means of new supply issuance and the security system underpinning transactions.

When Bitcoin's network was launched in January 2009, mining was the only method of acquiring bitcoin, and Satoshi Nakamoto and Hal Finney were the two main miners.[2] As we've discussed, new bitcoin is minted through the process of verifying and confirming transactions in Bitcoin's blockchain, the orchestration of which is a large part of the software that Satoshi created. In this way, it ensures the decentralized creation of the currency in controlled amounts, which prior to bitcoin had not been accomplished on a global scale.

The mining process for bitcoin is a continual cycle of hashing a few pieces of data together in pursuit of an output that meets a predetermined difficulty level, mainly the number of 0s that the output starts with. We call this output the *golden hash*. Recall that a hash function takes data—for example the text in this sentence—and hashes it into a fixed-length string of alphanumeric digits. While the output of a hash function is always of fixed length, the characters within it are unpredictable, and therefore changing one piece of data in the input can drastically change the output. It's called a golden hash because it bestows the privilege of that miner's block of transactions being appended to Bitcoin's blockchain. As a reward, that miner gets paid in a coinbase transaction, which is the first transaction in the block. Currently, that transaction delivers 12.5 bitcoin to the lucky miner.

The computers involved in Bitcoin's mining process take four pieces of data: a hash of the transactions for that block, the hash (identifier) of the previous block,[3] the time, and a random number called the *nonce*. Different computers on the network take these four variables and increment the nonce, perhaps starting with a nonce equal to 0, then going to 1, then to 2, hoping that by changing this one variable the hash output will meet the necessary requirement of the number of starting zeros. The more nonces the miner can test, the more chances the miner will find a golden hash that meets the requirement. The rate at which new nonces can be tested is called the *hash rate*; it is the number of times per second a computer can run these four variables through a hash function and derive a new hash.

Anyone with a computer can connect to Bitcoin's network, download past blocks, keep track of new transactions, and crunch the necessary data in pursuit of the golden hash. Such open architecture is one of Bitcoin's strongest points. While that might sound like an easy way to earn bitcoin, it is now incredibly difficult. Since the launch of Bitcoin, not only have the number of computers mining it increased, but the types of computers used have evolved significantly.

Initially, computers on the network crunched through hashes using their central processing unit (CPU), which is the primary chip responsible for the functioning of our computers. Mining with this method hogged the resources of the computer. And although a CPU is a good multitasker, it's not the most efficient chip for doing the same task over and over, which is exactly what searching for the golden hash involved.

Theoretically, a better chip for mining is the graphical processing unit (GPU). As its name implies, GPUs are used to generate the graphics that appear on screens, but they are now also widely used for machine learning applications. GPUs are massively parallel processing units, meaning they can run similar calculations in parallel because they have hundreds or thousands of mini-processing units, as opposed to CPUs that have just a handful of processing units.[4]

While the little units within a GPU cannot perform the wide range of abstract operations that a CPU can, they are good enough for hashing together data. Since there are thousands or more of these cores, in aggregate a GPU chip can make many more attempts at the golden hash per second than a CPU chip can.

However, to use GPUs a new version of the Bitcoin software needed to be created that could instruct a GPU how to go about the process, and writing that code took time. It was finally released in the summer of 2010, after Jeff Garzik offered a reward of 10,000 bitcoin to the originators—a mining operation known as puddinpop—to open source the software for all to use.[5] While he may not have expected the price to rise so much in the coming years, Garzik's donation now totals more than $10 million.

While GPUs were a vast improvement over CPUs, two more iterations of technology occurred to produce a more efficient chip for faster guessing of golden hashes. First came field-programmable gate arrays (FPGA), an interim chip, before the granddaddy of them all appeared: application-specific integrated circuits (ASICs). As the name implies, ASICs are application-specific, meaning that the physical hardware must be designed and manufactured with the application in mind. CPUs, GPUs, and FPGAs can all be bought generically and, with proper engineering, be applied to a specific purpose after the purchase. The physical layout of ASICs, on the other hand, needs to be etched into the chip at the semiconductor fabrication factory.

Designing and manufacturing such a specific chip requires a significant initial investment, and it was only when Bitcoin's network became big enough and bitcoin worth enough that a company could fully pursue this opportunity. The first computer—or mining rig—with ASIC chips that were specifically manufactured for the process was connected in January 2013.[6] Currently, top-of-the-line ASICs have a hash rate of 14 TH/s, meaning these machines crunch data and output a hash 14 trillion times a second.[7]

Collectively, the more computers attached to the Bitcoin network, the higher the odds of one of them discovering a golden hash. Without any adjustment, more computers would increase the supply rate of new bitcoin, leading to runaway supply inflation. For that reason, Satoshi built into Bitcoin's software the rule that as more compute power is added to the network, the network makes it harder to find the golden hash by increasing the number of zeros the hash is required to start with. This adjustment is made every 2,018 blocks, or every two weeks, with the target of miners finding a golden hash every 10 minutes, and thereby controlling the rate at which new bitcoin is minted. As a result, more and more people are competing for a smaller and smaller prize, which while still profitable for professional miners is largely out of reach of Bitcoin hobbyists. For perspective, the combined compute power of Bitcoin's network is over 100,000 times faster than the top 500 supercomputers in the world combined.[8]

Mining Beyond Bitcoin

While the strength of Bitcoin's mining network is legendary, most other cryptoassets are less daunting. If so inclined, mining within networks such as Ethereum, Zcash, and others is still open to enthusiastic and dedicated hobbyists, and none of these networks is dominated by ASICs (yet).[9] In fact, recall that one of the frequent adjustments subsequent assets made was to the block hashing algorithm to fight against centralization of miners. For that reason, ether, zcash, and many other cryptoassets are mostly mined wtih GPUs. As these assets grow in value, though, their mining networks become more competitive because the potential profit of getting paid in the native asset becomes more desirable. Conceptually, mining networks are a perfect competition, and thus as margins increase, new participants will flood in until economic equilibrium is once again achieved. Thus, the greater the value of the asset, the more money miners make, which draws new miners into the ecosystem, thereby increasing the security of the network. It's a virtuous cycle that ensures the bigger the network value of a cryptoasset, the more security there is to support it.

Whether it be Bitcoin, Ethereum, or Zcash, many miners join mining pools, which means they connect with other miners and collectively the pool contributes their hash power to finding golden hashes. The pool then shares in the profits, with different models for how the profits are split.[10] A single miner might find only a block once a month, or worse. By being part of a pool, miners get a more predictable revenue stream.

There are a few major costs to mining: equipment, physical space necessary for the machines, electricity, and labor. For Bitcoin, dedicated mining devices are available, such as those from Antminer and Avalon, and the key metric to look for is the efficiency of the machine. In other words, how many hashes are generated for a certain amount of power, expressed in the ratio watts per gigahash (W/GH). To help better understand these cost calculations, refer to mining profitability calculation websites, such as CoinWarz.[11]

Cloud-Based Mining Pools

Innovative investors may consider a cloud-based *mining pool* service. Here, an investor buys into an existing mining pool and shares in the rewards from its mining efforts. There's no need for owning and maintaining dedicated hardware, just as cloud-based software such as Salesforce doesn't require maintaining all the back-end hardware. Investors simply buy a share of the processing power provided by mining efforts performed in a remote data center.

Thorough due diligence and research are needed before buying into a cloud-based mining pool service because a fair share of fraud and scams have occurred. A study of Bitcoin-based scams by Professors Marie Vasek and Tyler Moore from SMU included findings that several cloud-based mining operations were Ponzi schemes that "take payments from 'investors' but never deliver product." Their research even identified specific mining scams. "Active Mining and Ice Drill are operations that raised money to purportedly make ASICs and share the profits but never delivered. AsicMiningEquipment.com and Dragon-Miner.com are fraudulent mining e-commerce websites."[12]

Before investing in a cloud-based mining pool, conduct research on the potential investment. If it sounds too good to be true, it probably is. Verify that the operation has a physical location, a listing of existing equipment, and a track record of past projects. Genesis Mining is one of the largest cloud-based bitcoin mining pool services.[13] It's been in business since 2013 and offers mining in bitcoin, litecoin, zcash, and ether.[14] On its website it shows photos and videos of its data centers; many are in Iceland where electricity costs are low due to its geothermal power.

Proof-of-Stake

Outside of proof-of-work, other consensus mechanisms exist, such as *proof-of-stake (PoS)*. Proof-of-stake can be thought of as an alternative form of mining, one that doesn't require lots of hardware and electricity, but instead requires people to put their reputation and assets at risk to help validate transactions. Logistically, proof-of-stake requires transaction validators to "stake" a balance of the cryptoasset and then attest to the validity of transactions in blocks. If validators are lying or otherwise deceiving the network, they will lose their staked assets. As the name implies, in "proving they have something at stake," the validators are incentivized to be honest.

Often these systems provide an interest rate, like 5 percent, that rewards the validators who have staked their assets to help in the transaction validation process. There are also hybrid proof-of-work, proof-of-stake mining ecosystems and other variations, but proof-of-work is the most well-proven consensus mechanism, and the majority of cryptoassets use it. However, Ethereum will potentially switch to proof-of-stake early in 2018, as it is more efficient from an energy perspective, and therefore many claim is more scalable. When Ethereum switches from proof-of-work to proof-of-stake, it will be a major proving point for the viability of this consensus mechanism to secure large-scale cryptoasset networks.

CRYPTOASSET EXCHANGES AND OTC DESKS

Once bitcoin and other cryptoassets are minted, miners can exchange them for other cryptoassets or the fiat currency of their choice. To do so, the miner must sell the cryptoasset to someone else, either over-the-counter (OTC) or through an exchange.

Many miners, and large investors, choose OTC services like those provided by Cumberland Mining, Genesis Trading, or itBit. OTC is not quite an exchange because the buy and sell orders are not out in the open. Instead, an entity like the aforementioned services matches large buys with large sells, which allows big trades to be made without moving the order books within an exchange. OTC is a potential path for accredited innovative investors that want to deploy large amounts of capital.

Most investors, however, acquire cryptoassets through an exchange. Depending on the exchange, they can connect their bank account, credit card, or deposit bitcoin. Trading in the more novel cryptoassets most often requires that the investor already has bitcoin, as the exchanges that offer these crypto-assets often don't have fiat currency onramps.

During the tumultuous beginning of bitcoin, when it was the only crypto-asset in existence, numerous exchanges opened and subsequently closed, and the reasons often weren't pretty: financial difficulties, hacks, criminal activities, and actions of various regulatory authorities, to name a few.[15] It's important to recognize that in the early days of bitcoin, there was no exchange infrastructure, and since bitcoin was still in its infancy, people attempting to provide exchange services were often not equipped to do so.

The first exchange on record was seeded with a transfer of 5,050 bitcoin for $5.02, and actually ended up shutting down a few months later due to a lack of interest.[16] Mt. Gox was the first *mainstream* exchange, but it took two weeks for a customer's account to be cleared, and initially fiat currency had to be wired to Japan. However, as the assets and underlying technology have matured, so too have the means of buying and selling them. To this end, today numerous quality exchanges are available to investors looking to gain and transact the more than 800 cryptoassets that currently exist.[17]

Some of the most popular Western exchanges include Bitstamp, Bittrex, Global Digital Asset Exchange (GDAX), Gemini, itBit, Kraken, and Poloniex. BTCC, OKCoin, and Huobi dominate China, but also offer services in other geographic locations. There are country-specific exchanges, such as Bitso in Mexico, Unocoin in India, and BitBay in Poland.[18]

When deciding which exchange to use, a key trade-off needs to be considered: security versus access. Security is self-explanatory. By access we refer to the diversity of cryptoassets on offer. The most regulated exchanges, such as Bitstamp, GDAX, and Gemini, offer the fewest cryptoassets because they wait to ensure an asset is past a certain level of maturity before adding it to their platform. Other exchanges, such as Poloniex or Bittrex, add assets much earlier in their lives, so more aggressive or adventurous traders tend to use these platforms. Not only do these exchanges not have the same consumer protections in place, but the assets they offer are much more prone to wild price swings. Exchanges such as Bitfinex and Kraken provide a mix of security, regulatory adherence, and access. We are not discouraging use of any of these exchanges. It all depends on the balance of security and access the innovative investor is looking for.

To better understand some of the paranoia around exchange security and reliability, it's important to know that over time exchanges have been a weak point because they are centralized repositories of cryptoassets, which makes them targets for hacking. Unlike a bank heist which requires physical force and puts the thieves' lives at risk, thefts of cryptoassets from an exchange can be accomplished with (relatively) clean hands from anywhere in the world. Beyond the ability to steal assets from afar, the irreversible nature of cryptoasset transactions makes them even more enticing to hackers. If someone steals a credit card or hacks into a bank account, the associated institution can reverse the transactions. With cryptoassets, there is no centralized intermediary to come to the rescue.

THE HIDDEN COST OF CHARGEBACKS

Chargebacks occur when a customer disputes a credit card charge and that charge is reversed. Often, when the charge is reversed, it is the merchant that takes the loss. Processing and investigating these chargebacks incur a cost for the credit card company, which are then often levied as fees against the merchant. Due to these extra costs, merchants may need to adjust prices to protect themselves from both legitimate and illegitimate disputed charges.

Cryptoasset transactions are irreversible; therefore chargebacks are impossible. While an irreversible transaction may sound scary, it actually benefits the efficiency of the overall system. With credit card chargebacks, everyone has to bear the cost, whereas with cryptoassets only those who are careless bear the cost.

Many claim that hacked exchanges are proof that cryptoassets are insecure, but this displays a fundamental misunderstanding of the software architecture. Recall the four layers of any blockchain ecosystem that we discussed in Chapter 2: decentralized hardware, cryptoasset software, applications, and users. It is the third layer, applications, that are targeted in the majority of hacks. Thus, an exchange, which is an application that runs on top of the cryptoasset software, gets hacked. The underlying blockchain performs its job perfectly and remains uncompromised. The same analogy can be applied to applications that run on Apple's operating systems. Just because one of the apps is hacked doesn't mean Apple's underlying operating system or hardware is insecure.

Understanding that it's the applications and exchanges that use and trade cryptoassets that are most susceptible to hacks, it's all the more important for the innovative investor to be diligent when deciding which exchange to use. The following should be taken into consideration.

What Is the Reputation of the Exchange?

The best way to ascertain reputation is to investigate the management, venture capital investors, and regulatory approvals. Search reputable online sites to see what others are saying about the exchanges. Are there frequent customer complaints? In particular, look for whether an exchange has experienced a hack or had business problems in the past. This can be as easy as just typing the name of the exchange and the word "hack" into Google. For instance, "Bitfinex hack." While having been hacked can be a concern, consider what changes the exchanges have made since any security breach. One other good thing to note is where the exchange is physically headquartered. If that information isn't available, it's probably best to avoid the exchange.

What Cryptoassets Are Available for Trading?

For investors seeking specific assets, make sure the exchange offers trading in the desired cryptoasset. It's critical to understand that exchanges with a large number of cryptoassets are at greater operational risk. They typically perform less due diligence on those assets, which then passes that risk and responsibility on to the investor.

Are Extra Capabilities Offered, Like Derivatives or Margin Trading?

As with the variety of cryptoassets, exchanges also differ in the capabilities they offer. Some provide derivatives products such as futures contracts, while others specialize in boutique derivatives. For example, a boutique derivative offering by BitMEX was an option on whether the Winklevoss ETF would be approved by the SEC in March 2017. Similarly, margin trading is another functionality to investigate, and not all margin trading is made equal. Some exchanges offer extreme levels of margin trading, like 30 to 1, while others are much more reserved, like 3 to 1. Also referred to as leverage, 30 to 1 margin trading means an investor only has to put down $1,000 to trade with $30,000 of money. While gains can be astronomical, so can losses, and the same applies to derivatives. Some exchanges "socialize losses" for leverage gone wrong because there is no other way the products can be offered.[19] Socializing losses means that all investors on the exchange take a loss for a few investors' foolhardiness.

What Funding Mechanisms Are Available to Open an Account?

Funding mechanisms will dictate whether the innovative investor can use the service to begin with. Investors who already own bitcoin have more options because exchanges will accept a direct transfer of bitcoin that will allow for immediate trading of the cryptoassets offered on the platform. Funding an account with fiat currency typically requires links to bank accounts or credit cards. They will require a more extensive account opening process that may extend over several days and run into local restrictions. When providing bank account information to an exchange, it's especially important to have done the research on that entity to ensure security. Providing bank account information to any financial entity online is not to be taken lightly.

Is the Service Geographically Constrained?

Some exchanges are restricted by geography, and thus will require an address for access to certain aspects of their services. This is particularly relevant for New York residents, where the BitLicense has made it considerably harder for cryptoasset startups to operate. The BitLicense was a piece of regulation put in place in 2015 that required companies interfacing with cryptoassets to go through a lengthy and expensive regulatory process to operate in New York, which led the majority of cryptoasset startups to cease operations in the state.

What Are the KYC and AML Requirements?

Know your customer (KYC) and anti-money laundering (AML) regulations are increasingly mandatory for cryptoasset exchanges in the United States and are designed to protect against illegal and/or fraudulent activity. In opening an account, consider the amount of personal information required. Exchanges such as Bitstamp, GDAX, and Gemini have been proactive in working with regulators to require more detailed information on customers signing up for an account. Such information can delay the opening of an account, often by a couple of days. Those who feel that privacy is a benefit to cryptoassets, which are supranational by nature, might avoid exchanges that require this level of documentation. In general, a higher level of regulation may benefit the consumer protections of the investor and ensure the stability of an exchange.[20]

Does the Exchange Provide Insurance?

As the use of bitcoin and cryptoasset exchanges have grown, there has also been the growth of insurance plans for exchanges. One such insurer is Mitsui Sumitomo Insurance, which offers loss protection to a number of exchanges.[21] Other insurers are planning to enter this space as well, and it's beneficial for innovative investors to research whether the exchange they choose has this insurance. Coinbase was one of the first companies to offer insurance for its clients' bitcoin holdings, which includes the bitcoin in GDAX, the exchange it operates.[22] In part, Coinbase is able to insure its clients' bitcoin because it keeps less than 2 percent of customer funds online; the rest is in highly secure offline storage.[23]

HOT WALLET VERSUS COLD STORAGE

Let's turn to the distinction between hot wallets and cold storage, and why it's important to understand both. The acquisition and storage of cryptoassets are two separate considerations. While exchanges, by default, will store the assets they trade, that is not always the safest place to store the asset long-term.

Cryptoassets are stored in either a hot wallet or cold storage. The *hot* in hot wallet refers to the connection to the Internet. A wallet is hot when it can be directly accessed through the Internet or is on a machine that has an Internet connection. If the innovative investor can access his or her cryptoassets directly through a web browser, or through a desktop or mobile application on a machine where that machine is connected to the Internet, then it's a hot wallet.

Cold storage, on the other hand, means the machine that stores the crypto-asset is not connected to the Internet. In this case, a hacker would have to physically steal the machine to gain access to the cryptoassets. Some methods require that the machine storing the cryptoasset has never touched the Internet. Not once. While that sounds extreme, it is a best practice for firms that store large amounts of cryptoassets. It is not necessary for all but the most security-conscious investor.

What does it even mean to store a cryptoasset? This refers to storage of the private key that allows the holder to send the cryptoasset to another holder of a private key. A private key is just a string of digits that unlocks a digital safe. The private key allows for the holder of that key to mathematically prove to the network that the holder is the owner of the cryptoasset and can do with it as he or she likes.[24] That digital key can be placed in a hot wallet or in cold storage, and there are a variety of services that provide for such storage.

For both hot and cold storage, there are two options for controlling the private key that the innovative investor can choose from, creating a quadrant of four options in total (Figure 14.1). Most exchanges, for example, take care of the private key for the customer, so that all the customer has to do is log into the exchange as with any typical website. These exchanges qualify as a hot wallet where a third party controls the private key. Services such as Coinbase provide cold storage where a third party still controls the private key. In situations where a third party controls the private key, often the service doesn't have a private key for each customer's assets. Instead, the service will have a few private keys that secure a large number of clients' assets, and those keys are guarded very carefully.

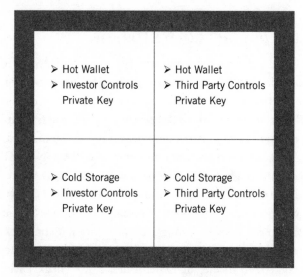

Figure 14.1 ■ The four quadrants of securing cryptoassets

If the innovative investor is reluctant to trust a third party, the other option is to take control of the private keys directly. While this comes with its own risks, like losing the private key, if the proper precautions are taken, it ensures autonomy and puts security directly in the owner's hands.

CUSTODY VIA EXCHANGES

By default, exchanges must store a customer's cryptoassets, most commonly done by handling the private keys. We'll repeat, many exchanges don't even have separate private keys for different customers. The exchange has its own private keys to the cryptoassets it is responsible for on the respective blockchain and then has internal books that record the customer balances. Depending on the exchange, there are varying levels of security hygiene and different proportions of the exchange's assets that are kept in hot or cold storage. Over time, these security distinctions have proven critical. For a clearer understanding, we'll cover a few big hacks that occurred on bitcoin exchanges that stored 100 percent of their bitcoin in hot wallets.

Let's begin with the infamous Mt. Gox. While this exchange did much to expand the usage and recognition of bitcoin throughout the world, it met its end in early 2014[25] when the company declared bankruptcy after over $450 million[26] of client bitcoin holdings went missing. Although the company was a pioneer in providing investors and enthusiasts the opportunity to gain access more easily to bitcoin, Mt. Gox also had weak management involved in an asset class that was still in its infancy—never a good combination.

Jed McCaleb was the original owner of Mt. Gox. Early on he learned that matching buyers and sellers of bitcoin was more than he bargained for when wires for tens of thousands of dollars started to pour in. McCaleb sold the site, and its growing activity, to Mark Karpeles, who was known in chat rooms as MagicalTux and enjoyed posting kitten videos online. To his credit, Karpeles rewrote the site to address the increased interest and activity, and he survived through the early days when other bitcoin exchanges quickly folded.[27]

Although he exhibited a level of coding competence, Karpeles soon found himself out of his league when it came to business. He was not investing in his company's growth, and his coding expertise soon showed cracks as well. A more experienced technology shop would have implemented a test environment and version control software for its code, which was the backbone of Mt. Gox's operation. Karpeles didn't do either, and all code changes were routed through him directly, which created bottlenecks when changes were needed quickly.

While Karpeles may have been negligent in many facets of the Mt. Gox business, he did understand the difference between hot and cold storage of bitcoin. He put himself in charge of all the private keys for the bitcoin the exchange stored. After a hack in 2011, Karpeles decided to move the majority of bitcoin offline into cold storage, which required him to write down the private keys and place them in safety deposit boxes throughout Tokyo, where the company was located. This required a huge amount of paperwork and accounting, which was clearly not a strong point for Karpeles.[28] While the keys were in cold storage, Karpeles claims that a hacker manipulated him through a transaction malleability bug in the core Bitcoin software.[29] While Karpeles's claims have been called into question by many in the bitcoin community, there's no denying that the major reason for this hack was due to poor security hygiene with weak operational protocols put into place by the company for the movement of bitcoin. Such negligence cost investors $450 million in bitcoin.

More recently, a hack of Bitfinex's exchange cost investors $72 million.[30] The hack was a result of Bitfinex storing 100 percent of its client assets in hot wallets. There is debate on why Bitfinex did this. Possibly it was for purposes of liquidity, as Bitfinex is one of the most liquid and active exchanges, or it could have been a result of regulations put in place. Prior to the hack, Bitfinex had settled with the CFTC for $75,000 primarily because its cold storage of bitcoin ran afoul of CFTC regulations. The move to place all clients' assets into hot wallets is cited by many as due to the fine and CFTC regulations.[31] Either way, this hack proved that no matter the security protocols put in place, hot wallets are always more insecure than properly executed cold storage because the hot wallet can be accessed from afar by anyone with an Internet connection. Only a physical break-in would allow a thief to gain access to assets in cold storage.

At the time of the Mt. Gox hack, bitcoin and its underlying technology was still in its infancy and experiencing growing pains, like any other new technology. Famous venture capitalist Fred Wilson wrote soon after the incident, "We are witnessing the maturation of a sector and part of that will inevitably be failures, crashes, and other messes. Almost every technology that I've watched come into a mass adoption has gone through these sorts of growing pains."[32] Innovators and early adopters of any new technology are taking risks, but the exchanges are professionalizing over time. Mt. Gox is no more; Bitfinex has restructured itself and is humming along. These hacks have taught lessons not only to existing and new cryptoasset exchanges, but to clients as well.

The exchanges that run the highest risk of being hacked are those that have the largest amount of assets in hot wallets. Cold storage might impact the ability to access assets quickly, but what you lose in accessibility you gain in security.

THE WORLD OF CRYPTOASSET WALLETS

Storing cryptoassets on an exchange may not always be the safest option. The risk is lower for those exchanges that have insurance, keep the majority of their assets in cold storage, and employ other best-in-class security measures like penetration testing and regular audits. For other exchanges, the risk should only be tolerated if the innovative investor is trading regularly and making use of the exchange's capabilities, such as offering newer cryptoassets. If not trading regularly, investors should consider one of the following wallet options to store their assets safely.

Broadly speaking, there are five kinds of wallets: web (cloud), desktop, mobile, hardware, and paper. For the sake of brevity, we use bitcoin to illustrate these examples as it provides the scaffolding necessary to investigate similar options for other cryptoassets.

The best resource for learning more about different kinds of bitcoin wallets is bitcoin.org,[33] and we include additional information sources in the Resources section of this book. Recognize that as interest and access to more cryptoassets continues to grow, the list of wallets to secure these assets will grow, too.

Web Wallets

Most web wallets are not much different from exchanges. The keys are often outside the investor's control and in the hands of a centralized third party. If the third party doesn't employ the proper security techniques, then the cryptoassets may be at risk. As with an exchange, the web wallet can be accessed from anywhere, which is one of the main benefits. Popular web wallets include Blockchain.info and Coinbase. Some web wallets do provide the option of controlling the private key, which makes them like a lightweight desktop wallet (covered below) that can be accessed remotely.

An increasingly prevalent feature in web wallets is *vaulting*. A vault delays the withdrawal process of any cryptoasset so that the holder has time to negate any attempted withdrawal. This is primarily a tactic to thwart hackers who may have compromised the user's password and are trying to move cryptoassets to another address. Coinbase has the most well-known vaulting service within its web wallet.

CRYPTOASSET VAULTS

One of the nice features of Coinbase is that it allows a customer to maintain an easily accessible balance of bitcoin, as well as a more illiquid but highly secure form of storage known as its Vault. Although placing bitcoin balances into the Vault enhances security, it does require two-factor authentication and time delays before withdrawal. This means that moving funds from the Vault takes 48 hours. Coinbase's dual functionality is like having a checking and a savings account at a bank. Bitcoin that investors need to access quickly can be kept in a regular Coinbase account (the checking account), and for added security additional bitcoin can be held in a Vault account (the savings account).

Desktop Wallets

With a desktop wallet, the private keys are stored directly on the computer where the software is downloaded. The user has full control, and no one else can lose, spend, or send his or her bitcoin. There are two kinds of desktop wallets: a *full client* and a *lightweight client*. When we say client, it simply refers to the functionality of the software application that is running on the computer. A full client is a much more intensive software application, whereas a lightweight client provides a more hassle-free approach to storing bitcoin.

In the early days of Bitcoin, there was only the wallet associated with Satoshi's software, which is now referred to as Bitcoin Core. This wallet is a full client, meaning it requires a full download of Bitcoin's blockchain and therefore substantial bandwidth and storage space. When a computer is running this software, it is counted as a *full node* in Bitcoin's network, meaning it has a record of every single Bitcoin transaction. Full nodes are great for security and autonomy and are the backbone of propagating and verifying bitcoin transactions, but the hardware requirements are only for the most hardcore of hobbyists.[34]

Lightweight clients, also referred to as thin clients, don't download Bitcoin's entire blockchain, nor do they propagate or verify new transactions being passed through the network. Instead, they rely on full nodes for complete information on Bitcoin's blockchain, and are primarily focused on providing transactional information involving only the user's bitcoin. A lightweight wallet is much more practical for the average user who doesn't have the means to deal with running a full client. With these wallets, the private key(s) are on the computer on which the software is downloaded. Popular lightweight clients include Coinomi, Electrum, and Jaxx.

Mobile Wallets

Technically, we are referring to mobile wallets that store the private keys on the device, as opposed to a third party's servers. Mobile wallets are similar to lightweight clients in that they don't download Bitcoin's blockchain (it would break the smartphone). Innovative investors can use them on the go should they need to transfer bitcoin to friends to pay for dinner at the local bar that accepts bitcoin for beers.

Numerous wallets appear on app stores as mobile applications but are not technically mobile wallets. They are web wallets that provide access through a mobile application. The distinction boils down to who is storing the private keys. If a third party is storing the private keys and the wallet is accessing that information through the Internet, then that is a web wallet even if it's in the form of a mobile application.[35] If the private keys are stored on the smartphone, then that mobile application is a mobile wallet, as is the case for mobile wallets such as Airbitz and Breadwallet.

Hardware Wallets

As bitcoin has become more popular and widely used, companies have sprung up that create dedicated hardware for storing private keys, and thereby storing and sending bitcoin or cryptoassets to others. Several hardware wallets provide a variety of functionality. Some offer a full suite of key generation, storage, and sending capabilities; others are simply used as an extra layer of transaction confirmation security; others still need to be plugged into a computer to work. A few of the more popular wallets are as follows:[36]

- **Trezor.** This is one of the more secure ways to store bitcoin, as it generates private keys that never leave the device. This protects the data from viruses and malware that may impact other devices or online storage.
- **Ledger Nano S.** This device plugs into a USB port and allows for the storage of bitcoin, ether, and other altcoins. It has a neat OLED display on what looks like a flash drive that provides confirmation when a transaction takes place on the device.
- **KeepKey.** This USB device not only securely stores bitcoin but also provides information on transactions and confirmations on its OLED display. It is also PIN-protected.

While a hardware wallet can always be misplaced, all is not necessarily lost if that happens. During the initialization stage of setting up the hardware wallet there is a *seed*, which is like a backup password. That seed needs to be stored in an extremely secure place because if the hardware wallet ever goes missing, the seed will regenerate the private keys that were on the hardware wallet and enable access to the bitcoin again.

Since hardware wallets require specific hardware engineering and associated software engineering, they often don't support a wide array of cryptoassets. Most hardware wallets support bitcoin. The Ledger Nano S provides support to some cryptoassets beyond bitcoin, and KeepKey is now integrating with ShapeShift to support additional cryptocurrencies beyond bitcoin.[37] We're sure to see this space grow over the next few years as more hardware wallets expand their capabilities to support various cryptoassets.

Paper Wallets

One of the simplest ways of storing private keys is also one of the most secure, if done properly. Welcome to the *paper wallet*, which involves writing the long alphanumeric string that is the public-private key pair on a piece of paper. A paper wallet qualifies as a form of cold storage. The paper wallet can be locked away in a safe for decades, and so long as the specific asset's blockchain continues to exist, that private key can be used to access it. Paper wallets support all cryptoassets because all they require are pen and paper. Many store these in a fireproof safe deposit box or an equally secure location.

MANY CHOICES, SAME DISCIPLINES

With all the available choices, it's vital that investors do their due diligence when choosing the wallets and exchanges that best suit their needs. The basic progression will be "how to acquire" and "how to store" the cryptoasset, and while the same service can provide both functions, it's useful to consider what is most important before making a decision. Just as an investor would take the time to consider which financial advisor to use, the innovative investor must take time to investigate which cryptoasset "acquirer and storer" to use.

We recognize that the world of cryptoassets requires new habit patterns, an often uncomfortable process, especially when money (in any form, digital or paper) is at stake. As the visibility and marketplace grows for cryptoassets, options will materialize that don't require new habit patterns because they will incorporate cryptoassets into the investment systems and vehicles with which the investor is already familiar. We're seeing money managers, investment firms, and other capital market players step into the fray to investigate and create investment vehicles that fit the mold of capital market assets and can be housed in brokerage accounts, and potentially even 401(k) plans.

In the next chapter, we explore the growing capital market investment choices available to investors. These still require due diligence, discipline, and research, but they do away with the potentially scary components of private key storage and setting up new accounts with startups.

Chapter 15

"Where's the Bitcoin ETF?"

B uying cryptoassets through a dedicated cryptoasset exchange is a direct avenue for investors to gain access to this new asset class, but it does require orienting with a new application and user interface, as well as trusting in what might be a young business.

There is a benefit to incorporating cryptoassets directly into the interface you use to manage a preexisting investment portfolio, where prices can be tracked easily, asset allocation models can be more carefully monitored, and tax benefits can be leveraged. In this chapter, we discuss various capital market vehicles that can give the innovative investor access to cryptoassets through established investment channels, as well as what may be available in the future. We also discuss what the innovative investor should expect from financial advisors as this space continues to grow.

BITCOIN INVESTMENT TRUST

Grayscale Investments offers the largest capital markets vehicle with bitcoin exposure, clocking in at north of $200 million or roughly 1 percent of all bitcoin outstanding as of March 2017. Grayscale was established in 2013 by its parent company, Digital Currency Group (DCG). Founded by Barry Silbert, a serial entrepreneur and influential figure in the Bitcoin community, some would say that DCG is in the early stages of becoming the Berkshire Hathaway of Bitcoin.[1] Grayscale's focus within DCG's portfolio of operating companies is to provide digital currency investing options to the capital markets. Currently, it has the Bitcoin Investment Trust (BIT), the Ethereum Classic (ETC) Investment Trust, and a potential bitcoin ETF (exchange traded fund) in filing with the SEC.

The BIT was the first product that Grayscale brought to market and upon launch was only available to accredited investors. The BIT was structured to acquire and secure bitcoin in a trust and then provide shares in the trust to investors, with each share representing approximately 1/10 the value of a single bitcoin. In theory, investors could assume that every 10 shares would be backed by a single bitcoin.[2] No hedging or leverage is used in the trust; it simply holds bitcoin and allows investors to gain access to its price fluctuations without having to deal with the underlying asset. The bitcoin itself is stored with Xapo, a firm that specializes in the secure custody of large amounts of bitcoin.[3] On its website, Grayscale advertises the following about the BIT:[4]

- Titled, auditable ownership through a traditional investment vehicle
- Eligibility for tax-advantaged accounts
- Publicly quoted
- Supported by a network of trusted service providers
- Robust security and storage

These services come with a management fee of 2 percent annually. After a holding period of one year, investors can sell their shares in the OTCQX markets under the symbol GBTC.[5] Through this process, accredited investors can exit their initial investment, realizing any profits or losses, and in so doing give all levels of investors access to their liquidated shares of the BIT. Other investors can buy GBTC through their stockbroker of choice, whether that be Fidelity or other firms.

SELF-DIRECTED IRA

One of the lesser-known options for investors seeking retirement-based investments is the self-directed IRA. While it has been in place since the creation of IRAs in 1974, what distinguishes it from the traditional IRA is the variety of investment options available. Most people use an IRA to invest in equities, bonds, mutual funds, and cash equivalents such as money market instruments. With a self-directed IRA, an investor can go beyond these investments to include such assets as real estate and gold. This structure provides a level of flexibility for investors that allows for the inclusion of various alternative, often riskier, assets into an investment account. This flexibility requires numerous additional rules. One such rule is that any investment in this account can't benefit the account owner "indirectly." For example, an indirectly beneficial investment in a self-directed IRA would be the use of funds to buy a vacation home or other piece of real estate that the account owner would use personally.[6] These accounts often come with costly maintenance and management fees, so while they are useful, they require proper due diligence and care.

The second leg of the BIT wasn't always available. In early May 2015, the Financial Industry Regulatory Authority (FINRA) gave Grayscale the regulatory approval needed to allow the BIT to become a publicly traded vehicle on OTCQX.[7] On May 4, 2015, the very first accredited investors who had bought into the BIT were given the option to sell their shares of GBTC in the OTCQX market.[8] The first trade was for 2 shares of GBTC at $44/share. Through the entire day there were just 765 shares traded, or just over 75 bitcoin. Admittedly a thin market, but this day in May was the first time a bitcoin vehicle was traded on a regulated U.S. capital market.

Through the first quarter of 2017, there is plenty of reason to be excited about the BIT and GBTC,[9] but they are far from perfect vehicles. Grayscale's creativity in allowing accredited investors to buy into a one-year lockup before selling in public markets does have a drawback. Unlike ETFs or mutual funds, which can issue more shares to meet market demand, Grayscale is not able to issue more shares of GBTC to meet investor demand. Instead, the creation of new units of GBTC is entirely dependent on accredited investors being willing to sell their shares, which they can only do after one year. Furthermore, now that Grayscale has an S-1 filing under review with the SEC they are not able to create more shares of the BIT for accredited investors that would like to buy into the private placement.

Meanwhile, the price of GBTC can be bid up or down, depending on what people were willing to pay for access to these shares. The first trade for GBTC was at $44/share, and each share maps to roughly 1/10 of a bitcoin. So $44/share would imply that bitcoin was in the $440 range. Instead, at the time of the trade for $44/share, bitcoin was in the low $200s. Someone was willing to pay nearly a 100 percent premium to get access to bitcoin as an investment

Figure 15.1 ■ GBTC's NAV compared to its price

Source: https://grayscale.co/bitcoin-investment-trust/#market-performance

without having to deal with all the nitty-gritty explained in the prior chapter. Figure 15.1 shows how GBTC has differed from its net asset value (NAV) over time. (NAV is the true value of the bitcoin underlying the shares. Anytime the gray line is above the black line means that GBTC is trading at a premium to the underlying value of the shares.)

It's clear that GBTC has traded well above its net asset value for much of its short life. Different explanations exist for this, such as that GBTC now allows everyday investors to put bitcoin exposure directly into their traditional portfolios or retirement accounts, and institutional investors can also easily buy GBTC. Whatever the reason, it is a sign that investors are interested in gaining bitcoin exposure in their portfolios. As of March 2017, the most common method to do this through a capital market vehicle is with GBTC, and therefore the premium is the price one must pay for such access. Additionally, some argue the premium is worth the ability to enjoy the benefits of bitcoin's price appreciation while providing tax reporting flexibility. However, at its core, GBTC has a supply-demand problem. New units of freely traded GBTC can only be created when accredited investors choose to exit their initial investment in the BIT, and there is no requirement to ever do so. Thus, as demand builds, the supply to match the demand isn't always there.

Some may initially see GBTC as an ETF, and therefore wonder why so much drama has unfolded around a "bitcoin ETF." However, the BIT and GBTC are a far cry from an ETF, both in the regulatory approval they have been granted and in the operational complexity. ETFs are constructed so that the value of the shares stay close to the net asset value. Keeping shares close to NAV avoids the sizeable premiums like those which GBTC investors must endure. Furthermore, an ETF requires sign-off from the SEC. While the BIT is a step in the right direction, many steps remain before an SEC-approved ETF will be available to investors.

THE WINKLEVOSS TWINS AND THE BITCOIN ETF RACE

Upon inception of the BIT, Grayscale was the only provider of a bitcoin-based capital market investment vehicle in the United States, but others were interested in getting a piece of the action. Little did Grayscale know it would have competition from former Olympic rowers and near-founders of Facebook. Perhaps best known for their involvement with the latter, Cameron and Tyler Winklevoss are two well-to-do investors. They claimed to be the originators of the idea for Facebook, which led to a $60-million settlement with Mark Zuckerberg. Since much of that settlement was in shares, its present-day equivalent is in the hundreds of millions.

However, the twins were not about to disappear into oblivion with their millions; they had tasted greatness and were not the kind of figures who easily faded from the limelight. Eager for new ventures, Bitcoin provided just the opportunity. They were introduced to the idea of Bitcoin in 2012 by David Azar while vacationing in Ibiza,[10] putting them well ahead of the informational curve. The twins were smitten with the concept and started buying the currency hand over fist, including investing in bitcoin-based startups.

At one point in 2013, they reported owning about 1 percent of all bitcoin in existence (at the time, well over 100,000 bitcoin).[11] Cameron has been credited with buying the bitcoin that first pushed the currency's total network value over $1 billion.[12] Seeing the opportunity, he placed a bid for bitcoin at $91.26 or above on Mt. Gox, the precise price that would make bitcoin's total network value greater than $1 billion.

The twins weren't satisfied with being passive investors; they wanted to bring products to market. To that end, in July 2013, they filed an SEC Form S-1 for the Winklevoss Bitcoin Trust, which they intended to list as an ETF under the ticker COIN.[13] Typical S-1s are often 100 pages or more and cover every imaginable detail of a product. By writing an S-1 for a bitcoin product, the Winkelvoss twins signaled their seriousness.

An ETF is arguably the best investment vehicle to house bitcoin. It has a transparent and low fee schedule and has an internal structure that keeps the

ETF close to the net asset value, while providing an investor with an easy way to trade it during the market day. Furthermore, the twins saw the SEC approval as the holy grail for winning investor confidence, and thereby taking bitcoin to the mainstream. While an admirable idea, they would soon find this path was longer than they likely expected.

By the start of 2017, the Winkelvoss twins were still waiting to get an ETF approved. In the interim, they had made amendment after amendment to their S-1, consulted with too many lawyers to count, and even started their own cryptoasset exchange, known as Gemini.

GEMINI EXCHANGE

Creating an ETF was not the only bitcoin product the Winklevoss brothers were working on. In 2015, they launched their own cryptoasset exchange called Gemini. The twins followed the proper regulatory path and worked to secure licensing from the New York Department of Financial Services. Although a lengthy process, as of March 2017 their exchange was one of two companies in the space that was a *limited liability trust company*, making it regulated similarly to a bank. The twins were inspired to create this exchange in response to concerns from the SEC over the lack of regulated exchanges.

Approaching March 10, 2017, all eyes were on the Winkelvoss ETF, as the SEC was required to make a decision on a 19b-4 filing the twins had submitted, which was a necessary step to listing an ETF. The prospect of a bitcoin ETF being approved gripped the cryptoasset community. An approval would not only be one of the greatest regulatory wins for the budding asset class, but would also require a large amount of bitcoin to be sourced to meet the demand of capital market investors buying the ETF.[14] In a research report published early in January 2017, analyst Spencer Bogart, at the time with Needham & Company, wrote, "We think the listing of a bitcoin ETF would have a profound effect on the price of bitcoin. Conservatively, we estimate that a bitcoin ETF could attract $300 million in assets in its first week and the resulting effort to source the underlying bitcoin for the Trust would likely drive the price of bitcoin up significantly."[15]

Prior to the decision, the price of bitcoin rose in anticipation of this surge in demand. Although those with the greatest understanding of cryptoassets and the capital markets doubted the product would get approved,[16] the price of bitcoin hit a new high before the decision. On March 10, at an SEC event totally unrelated to Bitcoin known as the Evidence Summit, an SEC employee made a public comment: "I will say that, for people that are emailing in, we have nothing to say about bitcoin, so please stop asking."[17] Clearly, the entire community was hungry for news on this decision.

Later that day, the SEC denied approval to the Winklevoss ETF.[18] Following is the key part of that ruling:

> The Commission is disapproving this proposed rule change because it does not find the proposal to be consistent with Section 6(b)(5) of the Exchange Act, which requires, among other things, that the rules of a national securities exchange be designed to prevent fraudulent and manipulative acts and practices and to protect investors and the public interest. The Commission believes that, in order to meet this standard, an exchange that lists and trades shares of commodity-trust exchange-traded products ("ETPs") must, in addition to other applicable requirements, satisfy two requirements that are dispositive in this matter. First, the exchange must have surveillance-sharing agreements with significant markets for trading the underlying commodity or derivatives on that commodity. And second, those markets must be regulated.
>
> Based on the record before it, the Commission believes that the significant markets for bitcoin are unregulated. Therefore, as the Exchange has not entered into, and would currently be unable to enter into, the type of surveillance-sharing agreement that has been in place with respect to all previously approved commodity-trust ETPs—agreements that help address concerns about the potential for fraudulent or manipulative acts and practices in this market—the Commission does not find the proposed rule change to be consistent with the Exchange Act.

The two big takeaways were that the SEC decided the markets for bitcoin were "unregulated" and that there were not sufficient "surveillance-sharing agreements" between Bats Exchange—the exchange where the bitcoin ETF would list—and the cryptoasset exchanges where bitcoin for the ETF would be sourced.

Regardless of what people expected going into the SEC decision, most everyone was taken aback by the rigidity of the SEC's rejection. Notably, the SEC didn't spend much time on the specifics of the Winkelvoss ETF but focused more on the overarching nature of the bitcoin markets. Saying that these markets were unregulated was an extra slap to the Winkelvosses, who had spent significant time and money on setting up the stringently regulated Gemini exchange. In focusing on the bitcoin markets at large, the rejection implied that an ETF will not happen in the United States for some time.

Immediately following the SEC decision not to approve the ETF, which was released just after 4 p.m. EST on a Friday, bitcoin dropped from $1,250 to below $1,000, an over 20 percent drop in a matter of minutes. It quickly rallied back toward $1,100. The incident allowed the naysayers to write their "I told you so" and "Bitcoin is dead" commentaries once again. The *Wall Street Journal* decided to enlighten its readers over the weekend with an article on the SEC decision titled, "Let's Be Real: Bitcoin Is a Useless Investment."[19]

When these bloggers and commentators returned to their desks on Monday, they found that investors on the 24/7 cryptoasset exchanges had been working over the weekend. On Monday, naysarers were faced with the reality that bitcoin was once again back over $1,200, and the network value for all cryptoassets had increased $4 billion since the SEC decision. Yes, $4 billion in three days.

The Winkelvoss ETF was not the first bitcoin ETF the SEC rejected. In July 2016, SolidX Partners filed with the SEC for the SolidX Bitcoin Trust ETF, with the intention of listing it on the NYSE under the ticker XBTC.[20] A major difference between SolidX and the Winkelvoss product was that SolidX aimed to insure its trust for up to $125 million against any theft or hack of bitcoin. In March 2017, the SEC rejected the SolidX ETF.

ARK INVEST AND BITCOIN EXPOSURE IN ETFS

As of March 2017 there were two ETFs that offered bitcoin exposure, ARK Invest's Next Generation Internet ETF (ARKW) as well as its overall Innovation ETF (ARKK). Both combine bitcoin exposure with a portfolio of growth stocks, and have been some of the highest performing ETFs in the market. Using Grayscale's BIT, ARK Invest became the first public fund manager to invest in bitcoin in September of 2015, and as of this writing still has the only ETFs on the market with bitcoin exposure. Given ARK's focus on fast-moving technologies like machine learning, autonomous vehicles, and genomics, investing in bitcoin was a natural fit for the firm.

THE ETN OPTION

Outside of the United States, more options for capital market-based bitcoin products exist, such as two exchange traded notes (ETN) offered by XBT Provider on Nasdaq Nordic in Stockholm, Sweden. Nasdaq Nordic is a regulated exchange system that is a subsidiary of the well-known Nasdaq in the United States. To list on Nasdaq Nordic, these products had to surmount a significant number of regulatory hurdles. Notably, these ETNs had been approved by Sweden's Financial Supervisory Authority (FSA), a government agency overseeing financial regulation in Sweden.

While ETNs are exchange traded, just as ETFs are, one is a *note* and the other is a *fund*. The easiest way to sum up the difference is that an ETN gives the investor a digital note that promises the investor will get paid depending on the asset's performance, while an ETF actually holds the assets and thereby tracks its value on the market.

In technical terms, ETNs are senior unsecured debt instruments that track a market index or benchmark. An ETN provides investors with exposure to an asset without the issuers of the ETN having to own the assets. Since an ETN is a debt instrument, investors are then subject to the credit quality of the issuer. If the issuer goes bankrupt, then investors in the ETN may get only a fraction of what they invested in the ETN, whereas with an ETF the fund holds the underlying assets. Therefore, investors in an ETN must have faith in the issuer's ability to continue to operate, as well as the issuer's ability to track an index without necessarily owning the basket of assets that make up the index.

Issuers of ETNs are usually a bank or financial firm that backs the instrument with its credibility and serves to quell concerns regarding the financial strength of the issuer. Morgan Stanley was the initial issuer of this type of security, and Barclays is also a frequent issuer, both well-diversified international banks with solid ratings. However, as we learned from the crisis of 2008, recognizing and evaluating the underwriting firm is critical, and not always so easy to do.[21] As a debt instrument, the health and well-being of the underlying issuer is the added risk that the innovative investor possesses when owning an ETN.

As with ETFs, ETNs allow investors to integrate exposure of an asset into their portfolio without having to deal with the messy details of acquiring and securing that asset. For instance, if an investor believes in commodity futures like live cattle, but doesn't want to get involved with trading the actual futures contracts, he or she can invest in an ETN that tracks that futures index. The issuer of that ETN is responsible for delivering the value of that index (minus fees) to the investor upon maturity or *early repurchase*. Because the ETN trades on an exchange, it's susceptible to market forces and can trade at a premium or discount to its underlying value.[22] Trading on an exchange also allows for liquidity, so an investor can easily buy or sell. ETNs can also be held in standard brokerage or custodial accounts.

In October 2015, XBT Provider issued *Bitcoin Tracker One* (COINXBT) to track the USD price of bitcoin.[23] Bitcoin Tracker One takes the average USD exchange rate of bitcoin from the Bitfinex, Bitstamp, and GDAX exchanges to determine the underlying value of bitcoin for the investment.[24] The following year, XBT Provider issued the *Bitcoin Tracker Euro*. Both investments were made available through the Interactive Brokers platform, a discount broker service available to investors.[25]

For these products, XBT Provider charges a 2.5 percent management fee, 25 percent higher than the fee Grayscale charges. Perhaps most important for the innovative investor, unlike many ETNs, XBT Provider is at all times fully hedged, meaning it holds the underlying bitcoin equal to the value of the ETN. This can significantly reduce reliance on XBT Provider's credit quality because even if the company goes bankrupt there should still be the underlying bitcoin in place to reimburse investors. As stated on the website, "XBT Provider do[es] not have any market risk. The company always holds bitcoins equivalent to the value of ETNs issued."[26]

In mid-2016, XBT Provider was purchased by Global Advisors (Jersey) Limited (GABI) after XBT Provider's main stockholder, KnCMiner, declared bankruptcy. KnCMiner had long been a bitcoin mining company and producer of bitcoin mining rigs. With an ETN the credibility of the underlying issuer is paramount, and GABI recognized that as well. Following KnC's bankruptcy, trading of XBT Provider's two ETNs temporarily paused as a new guarantor was pursued, with GABI ultimately coming to the rescue.[27]

The GABI team is led by Jean-Marie Mognetti and Daniel Masters, who cut their teeth as commodities traders at Lehman Brothers and JPMorgan respectively. They bring considerable capital markets experience to the bitcoin space. Prior to purchasing XBT Provider, GABI had created a bitcoin fund intended for institutional investors called the GABI.[28] The fund is domiciled in Jersey, United Kingdom, an area known for its innovative approach to regulation, similar to the Cayman Islands. By purchasing XBT Provider, GABI strengthened the reliability of the counterparty to the bitcoin ETNs and added a nice asset to its growing bitcoin investing platform for institutions. The rationale was summed up by Masters: "Global Advisors Bitcoin Investment Fund (GABI) is the only fully regulated Bitcoin investment fund targeting institutions and in adding XBT we are addressing the online retail and professional markets."[29]

THE ETI OPTION

Another bitcoin investment vehicle for investors is the *exchange traded instrument* (ETI). ETIs are similar to ETFs in that they are asset-backed securities, whereas an ETN doesn't have to be backed by the underlying asset. However, ETIs are much less common and are primarily intended to house alternative investments such as futures or options.[30]

In July 2016, a bitcoin ETI was listed on the Gibraltar Stock Exchange under the symbol BTCETI.[31] It charges a 1.75 percent management fee, placing it below both Grayscale and XBT Provider, and custodies its assets with Coinbase. While the sponsor and arranger of the ETI—Revoltura and Argentarius ETI Management Limited—are not well known, what is notable is the involvement of the government of Gibraltar and Gibraltar's regulator, the Financial Services Commission.

It is clear that Gibraltar sees an opportunity and is making a play for itself as a virtual currency hub. Albert Isola, Gibraltar's Minister for Financial Services and Gaming, said, "We continue to work with the private sector and our regulator on an appropriate regulatory environment for operators in the digital currency space, and the launch of this ETI on our stock exchange demonstrates our ability to be innovative and deliver speed to market."[32]

In the same month as Gibraltar's bitcoin ETI announcement, a Swiss issuer called Vontobel announced a tracker certificate for bitcoin that appears to operate like an ETN, though the details are sparse. July 2016 was a busy month for capital markets-focused bitcoin products, but represents only the beginning of what we expect to see as the years roll on.

CAN AN INVESTOR FEEL COMFORTABLE WITH THE PRICING OF CRYPTOASSETS?

As the innovative investor may have noticed, many of the exchange-traded products listed above rely on price indices. While a price index sounds simple, it can be a complex mathematical process to assess the exact price the market is offering, especially for cryptoassets that trade globally and can be purchased through a wide array of fiat currencies and cryptoassets. However, pricing is important for the future growth of capital market vehicles holding cryptoassets, so it is an area of development that the innovative investor should watch.

The pricing problem is particularly acute for bitcoin that trades in different geographies and with different fiat currency pairs. Currently, the operations of different cryptoasset exchanges can be thought of as isolated liquidity pools, so if one exchange is experiencing significantly stronger demand than other exchanges, the bitcoin on that exchange may trade at a premium to other exchanges. In the equities markets, such differences in price would quickly be solved by arbitrage, but due to time delays in moving bitcoin between different exchanges, not to mention fiat currency capital controls, these pricing discrepancies persist.

The combination of growing interest in bitcoin and recognition of the need for robust and regulated bitcoin indices has led two major investment markets, the NYSE and the Chicago Mercantile Exchange (CME), to implement their own bitcoin indices. The NYSE launched its bitcoin pricing index, NYXBT, in May 2015.[33] At the time, the president of the NYSE, Thomas Farley, said, "Bitcoin values are quickly becoming a data point that our customers want to follow as they consider transacting, trading, or investing with this emerging asset class. As a global index leader and administrator of ICE LIBOR, ICE Futures U.S. Dollar Index, and many other notable benchmarks, we are pleased to bring transparency to this market."[34]

The NYBXT methodology utilizes data-based rules that produce what they feel is an "objective and fair value for one bitcoin." The index initially began by taking data from Coinbase, in which the NYSE had a minority investment,[35] though it has since branched out to include other exchanges.

In the latter part of 2016, the CME Group also launched its own bitcoin price indices with the CME CF Bitcoin Reference Rate and the CME CF Bitcoin Real Time Index.[36] It also created an independent advisory committee, including bitcoin evangelist Andreas Antonopoulos to oversee its pricing model, which utilized prices from various exchanges throughout the world.[37] Many have speculated that this index could be the precursor to bitcoin futures and other derivatives products, which is CME Group's specialty.

We commonly use the Tradeblock index, XBX, which is a leading bitcoin index for institutional traders of bitcoin to get the most accurate price of the asset throughout a trading day.[38] Intended for institutional investor use, the index derives a price for bitcoin using algorithms that account for market liquidity, manipulation attempts, and other anomalies that occur throughout the global exchanges.[39]

While all of the aforementioned indices are bitcoin-focused, we expect to see many indices focused on other maturing cryptoassets appear. This will foreshadow more capital market vehicles to come.

TALKING TO A FINANCIAL ADVISOR ABOUT CRYPTOASSETS

David Berger, creator of the Digital Currency Council, believes the time has come for financial advisors to be able to discuss bitcoin and cryptoassets as they relate to their clients' portfolios. "Advisers need to understand the technological underpinnings of Bitcoin, as well as how to hold, securely store, and utilize it. Advisers also need to understand the digital-currency ecosystem and the ways to evaluate risk and invest wisely within that ecosystem. They should familiarize themselves with the financial and tax implications, as well as the legal and regulatory issues—all of which are developing daily."[40]

Currently, GBTC is available for typical investors through brokerage firms. With an online and self-directed investment account, investors should be able to get a quote on GBTC and buy the asset for their accounts.

For investors with an advisor at a wealth management firm, placing the order for GBTC may require interfacing with your advisor so the firm can make the purchase. It won't be uncommon to get some pushback due to a lack of awareness related to this investment vehicle from financial advisors, whether they're independent or from a wirehouse. At this point, innovative investors should recognize that bitcoin and other cryptoassets can have a positive impact on their investment portfolios. Financial advisors and investment firms would be well served to be knowledgeable, informed, and open to discuss these investment vehicles appropriately with clients.

Fortunately, the financial services industry is warming to these investments and the need to bring advisors up to speed. In 2014, the Financial Planning Association (FPA) produced a report clearly detailing its take on the matter titled, "The Value of Bitcoin in Enhancing the Efficiency of an Investor's Portfolio."[41] The FPA supports financial advisors and others associated with the Certified Financial Planner™ (CFP™) certification. In the report it asserted that, for many investors, bitcoin could provide a potential opportunity to diversify and boost their portfolios.

Although we expect that advisors will increasingly become aware of and knowledgeable about bitcoin and cryptoasset investments, the innovative investor may encounter an immediate dismissal, a sense of curiosity, some level of knowledge, or perhaps just a chuckle from his or her advisor on the topic. Given this, here are some points to consider:

1. A good advisor is truly looking out for his or her clients. Bitcoin and cryptoassets are new and have short and volatile track records, so the adviser's immediate negative reaction or dismissal shouldn't be a refutation of his or her quality as an advisor.
2. Investors should be prepared to provide links and resources to educate the advisor. The Resources section in the back of this book can be a big help.
3. Remind the advisor that it's not about putting everything in these investments, and his or her advice can help identify where these assets may appropriately fit in the asset allocation model the advisor has built. (If there's no asset allocation model or financial plan the advisor can reference, that should be a red flag for the investor.)
4. If the advisor doesn't believe in these assets, or refuses to invest in them on the innovative investor's behalf, the asset can be purchased directly as outlined in Chapter 14 or by purchasing GBTC through a self-directed account. If the investor takes this route, we highly recommend informing the advisor of this investment so the advisor can include it in his or her records as reference for the advisor's asset allocation plans. Good advisors should be open to keeping records of client assets held away from their firm.
5. If the financial advisor is a deer in the headlights on the topic, hand him or her a copy of this book.

INDEPENDENT FINANCIAL ADVISORS VERSUS WIREHOUSE ADVISORS

Ric Edelman, one of America's top financial advisors, agrees with Berger. Edelman is an author and speaker, and has been named America's top independent financial advisor three times by *Barron's* magazine. Now we can add bitcoin believer to the list. "It's important that investors stay aware and knowledgeable about bitcoin," Edelman says. Beyond bitcoin, Edelman sees great potential in blockchain technology as a solution for many businesses that he believes "can benefit from advancements made in this technology."[42]

Edelman's attitude as an adviser may be unique, and one reason may be because he's an independent financial advisor, which is different from a wirehouse-based financial advisor who works at Wells Fargo, Morgan Stanley, or Merrill Lynch. Wirehouse advisors may have more constraints on their ability to recommend investment vehicles related to bitcoin or cryptoassets. This may be due to those firms having internal policies that keep their advisors from recommending products that haven't been fully evaluated by their own internal research teams or simply by a lack of knowledge and interest in these assets as investment vehicles.

WHAT'S NEXT?

We believe that cryptoasset investment vehicles will continue to proliferate, broadening exposure to even the most conservative investors who will eventually realize the uncorrelated value add of this new asset class. Even though the SEC didn't approve the Winklevoss or SolidX ETFs, we believe international regulators will continue to explore this innovative new asset class, which ultimately may help to raise the SEC's comfort level with bitcoin and cryptoassets. That said, the SEC's priority is consumer protection, and if it feels there are still not enough consumer protections in place for bitcoin and other cryptoassets, then it has no obligation to approve any exchange-traded products.

Globally, securitization efforts will continue around bitcoin, which will open the door for other cryptoassets that hold true merit, like ether, to be incorporated into capital market vehicles. Grayscale has moved forward with the Ethereum Classic (ETC) Investment Trust, which operates similarly to the BIT but holds ether classic, not to be confused with the much larger asset, ether.

Ultimately, we see a future in which there will be numerous options to invest in capital market vehicles that securitize cryptoassets. For example, we expect there to be multiasset mutual funds with cryptoassets used for diversification. Similar to REX Share's S&P 500 gold-hedged ETF, we may someday have a S&P 500 bitcoin-hedged ETF. Similarly, we will likely have funds of cryptoassets based on their functionality, such as a cryptocommodity fund, or perhaps a fund of the privacy focused cryptocurrencies like monero, dash, and zcash. Lastly, given the growing trend of indexation, as the cryptoasset space matures significantly, we could see network value weighted cryptoasset ETFs, including potentially a basket of the top 5, 10, or 20 cryptoassets.

In the last two chapters, we discussed how the innovative investor can gain access to bitcoin and cryptoassets from a wide range of vehicles, including mining, direct purchases from exchanges, and capital market investments like GBTC and its kin. Another exciting part of the cryptoasset world for the innovative investor includes the ability to get involved directly with the developer teams, launching cryptoassets from the beginning. In the past, this world was open only to the wealthy, but with new trends such as crowdfunding, token launches, and innovative regulation via the JOBS Act, opportunities exist for innovative investors of all shapes and sizes to get involved.

Chapter 16

The Wild World of ICOs

D uring the early tech days, innovators such as Steve Jobs, Bill Gates, and Michael Dell became iconic figures who had turned ideas into multibillion-dollar businesses. Over the last decade, we've seen visionaries such as Elon Musk, Peter Thiel, and Mark Zuckerberg do the same. These innovators changed the world because people believed in their visions, and these early believers invested money to turn their ideas into reality. While these investments brought great benefit, they were not based on altruism; initial investors were looking to get a sizable return on their risky investments.

Investing in early stage, private companies is most often referred to as *venture capital*. The term itself conveys the risk involved. After all, *venture* as a verb conveys a journey into the unknown, and *capital* refers to wealth and resources. Venture capital is just that: risking the unknown in the pursuit of outsized rewards, but knowing all along that the probability of failure is high.

Venture capital is a relatively young industry, intimately entwined with Silicon Valley. While Silicon Valley made venture capital the famous industry it is today, venture capital made Silicon Valley. One of the earliest and most widely recognized companies that helped jump-start the venture capital industry was Intel, which today produces the chips in most of our computers. The company was started in Santa Clara, California, by well-known and highly regarded scientists, Gordon E. Moore (famous for creating "Moore's Law"[1]) and Robert Noyce (cocreator of the integrated circuit), but they were hard-pressed to raise money for their new company. Ultimately, Intel found a benefactor in Arthur Rock—an American financier who coined the term *venture capitalist*[2]—who helped them raise $2.5 million in convertible debentures that included $10,000 from his own pocket.[3] The company went public two years later in 1970, raising $6.8 million and providing significant rewards to Rock and those who bought the debentures. Intel was one of the first companies to utilize venture capital as a method of funding its startup, and due to its success, helped pioneer the concept in Silicon Valley.

Despite the relative youth of venture capital, many cryptoasset firms are now turning the model on its head. The disruptors are in danger of being disrupted. For the innovative investor, it's key to realize that cryptoassets are not only making it easier for driven entrepreneurs to raise money, they're also creating opportunities for the average investor to get into the earliest rounds of what could be the next Facebook or Uber. Welcome to the colliding worlds of crowdfunding and cryptoassets.

THE OLD METHOD: THE INVESTOR'S PERSPECTIVE

Up until recently, the first opportunity the average investor had to invest in a company was upon its initial public offering (IPO), when the company's shares began trading on a well-known exchange like the Nasdaq or NYSE. However, leading up to an IPO, the company had likely gone through numerous rounds of private funding. As a private company grows, there are different names for each investing round, starting with a seed round before moving to a Series A, B, C, D, and so on. In each of these rounds, when investors put money into the company, they typically receive a percentage of that company, which is expressed in shares. Such funding is usually open only to venture capitalists, other private equity investors, or wealthy individuals. An IPO converts those private shares into public shares, which are then traded on a public exchange that the everyday investor can get access to.

As the innovative investor can probably infer, the earliest rounds, when the risks are highest, are often the most profitable rounds for an investor if the company succeeds. On one hand, keeping these rounds shielded from the public protects the average citizen from the inherent risks of these early stages of investing, but on the other, it also excludes them from the opportunity. Compounding the issue, over the last decade companies have been waiting longer and longer to go public, which places more and more of the returns in the private markets.

Ben Evans, an analyst at Andreessen Horowitz—one of the most famous venture capital firms in the world—published a report in 2015 that clearly laid out the value shift toward private markets. The median time for a tech company to IPO in 1999 was four years, whereas in 2014 it was 11 years,[4] meaning the average investor now has to wait nearly three times as long to get access to company shares. Although there's less enthusiasm for IPOs than there was during the tech boom, much of the delay is due to regulatory changes as a result of that tech and telecom boom, as well as the financial crisis of 2008. In the late 1990s, companies used to IPO with $20 million in annual revenue, whereas in 2014, the median annual revenue was just shy of $100 million, which had come down from a peak of nearly $200 million during the financial crisis.[5] While this trend has resulted in more stable IPOs and reduced risk for capital market investors, with less risk, there's often less reward.

As Ben Evans wrote in his report, "Almost all the returns are now private. Old world tech giants returned plenty in public markets—new ones have not." By old world tech giants, he's referring to companies such as Microsoft, Oracle, and even Amazon, all of which have provided much more value creation for public markets than private markets. Meanwhile, with companies like LinkedIn, Yelp, Facebook, and Twitter, the clear majority of returns have gone to private investors. For example, while Microsoft grew private money 20,000 percent, it grew public money 60,000 percent. Compare that to Facebook, which grew private money 80,000 percent, and public money under 1,000 percent. As Ben Evans put in his slides, "For Facebook to match Microsoft's public market returns, it would need to be worth $45 trillion," which is two and half times the GDP of the United States.[6]

THE OLD METHOD: THE COMPANY'S PERSPECTIVE

While it may seem like the average investor has been excluded somewhat over the last decade, they haven't been the only ones. Most companies are also locked out of the funding model described above because securing venture capital is an extremely competitive process, and the path to the public market is even more rigorous. For first-time founders who want to approach venture capitalists for an investment, often they must know someone-who-knows-someone. Having such a connection allows for a warm introduction as opposed to being among the hundreds of cold calls that venture capitalists inevitably receive. To know someone-who-knows-someone requires already being in the know, which creates a catch-22.

Turning to the public markets from inception for funding is also rarely possible, as an IPO is a laborious and expensive process. An IPO requires management to file an S-1 with the Securities and Exchange Commission (SEC), go on a road show to make investors aware of their offering, pay expensive investment bankers to properly price the public shares, and so on.

Due to the laboriousness of going public, only the largest and most successful companies typically pursue this funding path. They do so once they have matured and want access to the even bigger capital pool provided by the public markets. Furthermore, going public allows them to reward their early, private investors, who after the IPO can sell their shares in the more liquid public markets.

Without access to venture capitalists or the public markets, the preferred method for most startups to raise funding involves family and friends, credit card debt, and a healthy dose of faith. The good news is that the Internet boom has spawned a stream of aspiring entrepreneurs, and regulations are adapting to allow the innovative investor and innovative entrepreneur to unite around new ideas.

A NEW METHOD OF FUNDING STARTUPS

During the financial crisis of 2008, debt markets froze and stock markets crashed, causing major, and in many cases catastrophic, losses for the individual investor. To protect investors from similar experiences in the future, new regulations were put into place. Many of these targeted banks and their involvement in the crisis, which ultimately affected the ability of startups to gain access to the capital markets and other traditional funding methods, including loans and borrowing. In part, these regulations are why we have seen an increase in the amount of time it takes for companies to get to an IPO.

However, some leaders recognized that the world needed to spur more innovation and not strangle it.[7] They began to question the regulations and used famous Internet company founders, such as Steve Jobs, Bill Gates, and Michael Dell, as examples of how American innovation has made the country great. These leaders understood that if starting a company and securing funding was made more difficult, America would suffer.

Simultaneously, a funding shift was occurring, as many entrepreneurs realized they didn't have to rely on venture capital, family, debt, or the capital markets to raise seed money: the Internet had become a major force in connecting entrepreneurs to investors through the process of *crowdfunding*. It allowed individuals and businesses with an idea and plan to seek out other individuals who were willing to invest. What grew out of the inability of entrepreneurs of small or obscure projects to gain access to the more traditional methods of raising capital was a new method for connecting them to all levels of investors.

Crowdfunding sites such as Kickstarter, Indiegogo, and others positioned themselves online as a way for connecting entrepreneurs and investors. In exchange for investors pledging money, the project or company promised to return the fruits of its labor, depending on the amount a specific investor pledged. Recognizing that this platform was a fertile ground for scams, the sites implemented policies and procedures to protect investors. For instance, Kickstarter maintains investor funds in escrow until a project is funded to a sufficiently high level. If not enough people invest, then funding stops and investors get their money back.

Many projects have been funded by investors who simply wanted to see it become a reality, while others funded projects to receive the product. To get a feel for what Kickstarter can provide to investors interested in the bitcoin and blockchain space, simply type those terms into the search box on the Kickstarter site.[8] Opportunities for investing in documentaries, books, games, and application development can be found. Fund a documentary on Bitcoin, for example, and on completion investors receive a DVD of that documentary.

One of the most compelling aspects of crowdfunding was that it not only allowed dreamers to build their product or business, it allowed investors of all levels to participate in seeing these dreams come true. Prior to crowdfunding, in those cases where investors wanted to share in the equity opportunities provided by a startup, they still had to be an accredited investor. While the intention of requiring investors at this stage to be accredited is good, it has the side effect of locking the average investor out of some of the earliest stage investments with the highest returns.

In 2012, the phenomenon of crowdfunding came to the forefront of government regulator attention. Fortunately, rather than killing the concept, the government decided to create policies around it and market it to assist startups. The Jumpstart Our Business Startups (JOBS) Act was signed into law on April 5, 2012.[9] It was an acknowledgment of the potential of crowdfunding to provide alternative financing methods for startups. Additionally, the act sought to provide equity-based opportunities to a wide range of investors, including nonaccredited ones.[10]

CROWDFUNDING PORTALS FOR ALL INVESTORS

The ability of the JOBS Act to open the door to venture capital for non-accredited investors, including crowdfunding and ICO investments, has been a great step forward in increasing the number of people who may be included in these opportunities. One of the provisions of the JOBS Act will be the implementation of portals—online platforms on which investors can find investment opportunities. These portals must be approved by both the SEC and FINRA.[11] Although there aren't currently many such portals (Wefunder is one), over time, the number will increase and provide even more opportunities for investors and entrepreneurs.[12] Additionally, we expect that portals will soon be set up by broker-dealers to provide a combination of investment opportunities with advice and access.

The JOBS Act gave nonaccredited investors their first opportunity in 80 years[13] to invest privately in startups and receive equity compensation. Although the act was signed into law in 2012, Title III of the act, which allows for nonaccredited investors, was only put in place in May 2016.[14] Much of this delay had to do with the need for the SEC to be involved and adopt "final rules to permit companies to offer and sell securities through crowdfunding."[15] Some of the policies put in place with Title III included restrictions on the length of fundraising efforts, the amount that an investor could invest, and that investments must take place within an SEC-regulated intermediary, either through a broker-dealer or a funding portal.[16]

It's expected that even with these restrictions, investors will have more opportunities to gain equity-based compensation for investments in new businesses, including cryptoasset-based investments. The barn door of alternative financing methods for startups is wide open, and those involved with cryptoasset-based projects have already begun using their technologies to find ways to raise capital.

THE DIFFERENCE BETWEEN A CRYPTOASSET AND A STARTUP

Before we dive into the specifics of how a cryptoasset offering is carried out, the innovative investor needs to understand that the model of crowdfunding cryptoassets is doubly disruptive. By leveraging crowdfunding, cryptoasset offerings are creating room for the average investor to stand alongside venture capitalists, and the crowdfunding structure is potentially obviating the need for venture capitalists and the capital markets entirely. The second aspect is what makes the integration of crowdfunding with cryptoassets doubly disruptive, and puts cryptoasset offerings in another league entirely separate from Kickstarter. Joel Monegro, cofounder of Placeholder Ventures and former blockchain lead at Union Square Ventures (USV), was the first to encapsulate this idea cleanly in a blog titled, "Fat Protocols."

Monegro's thesis is as follows: The Web is supported by protocols like the transmission control protocol/Internet protocol (TCP/IP), the hypertext transfer protocol (HTTP), and simple mail transfer protocol (SMTP), all of which have become standards for routing information around the Internet. However, these protocols are commoditized, in that while they form the backbone of our Internet, they are poorly monetized. Instead, what is monetized is the applications on top of the protocols. These applications have turned into mega-corporations, such as Facebook and Amazon, which rely on the base protocols of the Web and yet capture the vast majority of the value. The construction of the Web as we currently know it is shown in Figure 16.1 from USV with "Value Captured" on the y-axis.

Contrast this model with that of cryptoassets, where the protocol layer must be directly monetized for the applications on it to work. Bitcoin is a good example. The protocol is Bitcoin itself, which is monetized via the native asset of bitcoin. All the applications like Coinbase, OpenBazaar, and Purse.io rely on Bitcoin, which drives up the value of bitcoin. In other words, within a blockchain ecosystem, for the applications to have any value, the protocol needs to store value, so the more that applications derive value from the protocol, the more the value of the protocol layer grows. Given many applications will be built on these protocols, a protocol should grow to be larger in monetary value than any single application atop it, which is the inverse of the value creation of the Internet. See Figure 16.2 for a depiction of how value is captured within blockchain architectures.

The Web

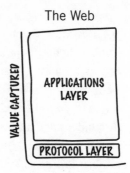

Figure 16.1 ▪ Thin protocols and fat applications:
how value is captured within the Web
Source: www.usv.com/blog/fat-protocols

Blockchain

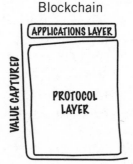

Figure 16.2 ▪ Fat protocols and thin applications:
how value is captured within blockchains
Source: www.usv.com/blog/fat-protocols

Interestingly, once these blockchain protocols are released, they take on lives of their own. While some are supported by foundations, like the Ethereum Foundation or Zcash Foundation, the protocols themselves are not companies. They don't have income statements, cash flows, or shareholders they report to. The creation of these foundations is intended to help the protocol by providing some level of structure and organization, but the protocol's value does not depend on the foundation. Furthermore, as open-source software projects, anyone with the proper merits can join the protocol development team. These protocols have no need for the capital markets because they create self-reinforcing economic ecosystems. The more people use the protocol, the more valuable the native assets within it become, drawing more people to use the protocol, creating a self-reinforcing positive feedback loop. Often, core protocol developers will also work for a company that provides application(s) that use the protocol, and that is a way for the protocol developers to get paid over the long term. They can also benefit from holding the native asset since inception.

LAUNCHING A NEW CRYPTOASSET WITH AN ICO

Initial coin offering (ICO) is the term most commonly used to describe crowd-funding the launch of a new cryptoasset. We'd like to expand this term to refer to *initial cryptoasset offering*, as the specific use of the term "coin" implies that these are currencies, which as we covered in Chapter 4, is most certainly not the case for all cryptoassets. Our definition is more expansive, as many new ICOs relate to the creation of new cryptotokens and cryptocommodities.

To get an idea of the growth of ICOs over the last few years, see Figure 16.3. In this chart, note two of the major ICOs that occurred during this period: the successful Ethereum launch in 2014 and the infamous launch of The DAO in 2016. For a few months after the DAOsaster there was a significant drop-off in ICOs, but by the end of 2016, cumulative ICO funding was $236 million for the year, which was nearly 50 percent of the $496 million raised through traditional venture capital for blockchain projects in 2016.[17] Given the rate of growth in ICOs, 2017 may be the year where more money is raised through ICOs than through traditional venture capital.

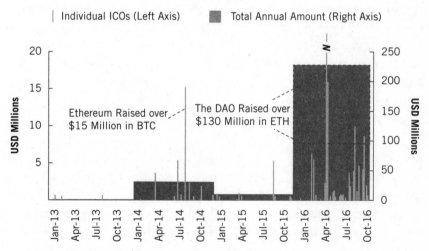

Figure 16.3 ■ ICOs since January 2013. (Light gray lines show individual ICOs and the amount they raised, while the dark gray bars show the cumulative amount raised via ICOs in a year.)

Source: https://www.smithandcrown.com/icos-crowdsale-history/

Announcing the ICO

The new cryptoasset can be announced any number of ways: a conference, on Twitter, Reddit, Medium, or Bitcointalk. It is important that the announcement is followed by a white paper containing details about the founders and advisory board, and that it clearly outlines the structure of the initial crowdsale. It should be easy to contact the founding team, whether through one of the aforementioned social media channels or a dedicated Slack or Telegram channel. If an ICO is scant on information, that is an immediate red flag.

The innovative investor should use the relevant aspects of the framework we detailed in Chapter 12 to investigate whether an ICO is a sound investment. That said, things are a little trickier with ICOs than with currently functioning cryptoassets. Since ICOs use the crowdfunding model to raise money to build a network, there often is no existing network up and running, thus no blockchain, hash rate, user base, or companies built on it. Everything is an idea at this stage. As a result, the integrity and prior history of the founding and advisory team are all the more important, as is the thematic investigation of whether this ICO is filling a marketplace and business need.

Structuring and Timing of the ICO

ICOs have a fixed start and end date, and often there is a bonus structure involved with investing earlier. For instance, investing at an early stage may get an investor 10 to 20 percent more of a cryptoasset. The bonus structure is meant to incentivize people to buy in early, which helps to assure that the ICO will hit its target offering. There's nothing like bonuses followed by scarcity to drive people to buy.

It's best practice that an ICO also have a minimum and maximum amount that it plans to raise. The minimum is to ensure the development team will have enough to make a viable product, and the maximum is to keep the speculation of crowds in check. For example, the infamous DAO ICO didn't set a maximum limit on the fundraising amount, which led to rampant speculation.

The offering should lay out how the new asset will be distributed, and how the funds that are raised will be used. Often the founding team will keep some of the assets for themselves, which is similar to when a founding team of a startup keeps a percentage of the company. What's important is that these terms are fair and accompanied by reasonable explanations.

Crowdsale Begins

Typically, the innovative investor will submit funds for an ICO by sending either bitcoin or ether to a special address the developer team provides. Just as one could send bitcoin or ether to an address to pay for an online purchase, innovative investors can send bitcoin or ether to an address to reserve their share of an ICO.

Depending on the intent of the ICO, investors may receive a cryptocurrency, cryptocommodity, or cryptotoken in return for their initial investment. How an investor receives the appropriate cryptoasset can differ, as some may require the creation of a wallet to store the asset prior to making them available for sale on an exchange (creating this wallet might be a more technical effort and could require following detailed instructions from the ICO provider); others will simply provide access to the asset that can be moved to an exchange (this can have an impact on the value of an asset if there's a large amount of early sales on exchanges soon after the closing of an ICO). Typically, information on the ICO will outline how the asset delivery process will work, and this should be read prior to making an investment so that there are no surprises for the investor.

Keeping Track of the ICOs

Numerous online sites list new ICOs and other resources to keep tabs on current and future ones.[18] Smith + Crown is a well-respected firm that's positioning itself as an information source for the ICO world. It provides an updated list of current, past, and upcoming ICO sales.[19] Other resources include ICO Countdown[20] and Cyber-Fund.[21] CoinFund also operates a great Slack community, with dozens of threads, many of which are dedicated to conversations about the specifics of upcoming ICOs.

Criticism of the ICO Model

Daniel Krawisz of the Satoshi Institute[22] considers ICOs "snake oil" and "pump and dump scams."[23] Pavel Kravchenko, founder of Distributed Lab, questions if we "really need all of these coins" and advises, "Let's think for a moment before participating in an ICO—could the same technology solve the same problems without the coin?"[24] While some ICOs can be from misleading asset issuers or seem "Ponzi-like," innovative investors have the resources provided in Chapter 11 to help them avoid such schemes. Others will scream that an ICO is a scam simply because they disagree with the funding model, as can be common with some Bitcoin Maximalists.

The ICO debate will continue, and it's prudent for the innovative investor to stay abreast of contemporary thinking around the benefits and drawbacks of ICOs.

The Howey Test for Discerning If an ICO Is a Security

The Howey Test is the result of the 1946 U.S. Supreme Court case, *SEC v Howey Co*, which investigated whether a convoluted scheme to sell and then lease tracts of land qualified as an "investment contract," also known as a security. The Howey Test determines whether something should be classified as a security, even if it is referred to differently in an offering to avoid regulatory action. If something classifies as a security, SEC oversight requires a long list of requirements to be met, which would likely dampen all but the most well-capitalized innovations in the exciting new world of cryptoasset offerings.

If an asset meets the following criteria, it will likely be considered a security:

1. It is an investment of money.[25]
2. The investment of money is in a common enterprise.
3. There is an expectation of profits from the investment.

For the most part, the teams behind ICOs want to avoid classification as a security because it will demand hefty legal fees, delay innovation, and require restructuring of the current cryptoasset landscape. While most ICOs meet the first two conditions, the third condition is up for interpretation. Do investors buy into an ICO as an "expectation of profit," or do they buy into an ICO to gain access to the ultimate utility that will be provided by the blockchain architecture? While the distinction may seem small, it can make all the difference.

A joint effort by Coinbase, Coin Center, ConsenSys, and Union Square Ventures, with the legal assistance of Debevoise & Plimpton LLP, produced a document called, "A Securities Law Framework for Blockchain Tokens."[26] It is especially important for the team behind an ICO to utilize this document in conjunction with a lawyer to determine if a cryptoasset sale falls under SEC jurisdiction. The SEC made it clear in July 2017 that some cryptoassets can be considered securities.[27]

The document includes a framework for scoring the ICO and identifying its applicability as a security, and thus its consideration in light of the regulations that go along with that classification. Innovative investors may also want to evaluate these criteria on their own in line with what they know about the ICO: if there's a belief by the investor that the offering should be considered an investment contract and the offering team is moving forward without that assumption, that could be a red flag about the legitimacy of an ICO. The SEC made it clear in July 2017 that some cryptoassets can be considered securities.[28]

The framework document is also helpful because it includes best practices for an ICO, which provides a good checklist for innovative investors. They are paraphrased below to provide context for what an investor should consider for any potential ICO investment (much of this overlaps with what has been stated already, but with ICOs, it's best to be doubly sure.) Note that in this context, cryptoasset is synonymous with token:

1. Is there a published white paper?
2. Is there a detailed development road map that includes a breakdown of all appropriate financials along the way?
3. Does it use an open, public blockchain, and is the code published?
4. Is there clear, logical, and fair pricing in the token sale?
5. Is it clear how much of the token has been assigned for the development team and how those tokens will be released? Releasing them over time keeps the developers engaged and protects against centralized control of the token.
6. Does the token sale tout itself as an investment? It should instead be promoted for its functionality and use case and include appropriate disclaimers that identify it as a product, not an investment.

ANGEL AND EARLY STAGE INVESTORS

One of the most exciting and potentially lucrative opportunities for an accredited investor is to be an *angel investor* with a startup. Angel investors can range from the family member who provides capital (or a credit card) to more formalized angel investors, who are either aligned with a venture capital firm or on their own seeking investment opportunities.

Angel investments can vary in size from the low thousands to much higher via early stage investment opportunities. If a venture moves on to more formalized funding after the angel stage, those who invested as angels may see the value of their investment increase, on paper at least. As a company grows and ultimately arrives at its exit strategy of an IPO or takeover, angel investors can achieve sizable gains from their initial investment.

The online site BnktotheFuture.com provides angel investing opportunities in cryptoassets and related companies to accredited investors. The site has provided opportunities to be angel and early stage investors in big names, such as Factom, BitPay, BitPesa, ShapeShift, Kraken, and even BnktotheFuture itself. It also provides access to mining pools for bitcoin and ether, in which investors can gain a daily dividend from the cryptoassets mined through those pools.

Angel investors may also join online communities such as AngelList[29] and Crunchbase[30] where accredited investors can connect with startups. Both have robust listings for blockchain related companies. In fact, AngelList has over 500 blockchain companies listed with an average $4 million valuation and a growing list of over 700 blockchain investors.[31] These sites are great ways to find information on existing startups and venture capitalists, and they can provide the accredited innovative investor with good information and background on the process of being an angel investor and the opportunities therein.

One of the oldest groups of angel investors in the blockchain and bitcoin space is called BitAngels.[32] Michael Terpin of BitAngels has been active in angel investing in blockchain companies for as long as the opportunities have existed. Terpin's annual conference, CoinAgenda, is one of the best opportunities for investors to see and hear management from blockchain startups present their ideas and business models. Each year, Terpin brings together the top startups in the space to present to varying levels of investors. In 2016, the company that won the conference's award for best of show[33] was Airbitz, which provides a single sign-on platform for blockchain apps. Soon after the conference, Airbitz raised over $700,000 on Bnktothefuture.com.[34]

• • •

Opportunities for the innovative investor to gain access to cryptoassets and the companies involved will continue to grow. We believe that these opportunities will not only impact the way people view their investing philosophy, but will also affect how they work with financial professionals who are involved in their investments, such as their financial advisors or accountants. The innovative investor can't lose sight of his or her financial goals and objectives. Chasing after what seem to be high-profit opportunities must be tempered by an understanding of the accompanying risk. Of all the chapters in our book, this chapter has covered material that is moving the most quickly. Therefore the innovative investor that wants to play in the world of ICOs will need to do ample due diligence beyond what he or she has read here, including staying abreast of statements from regulators on the classification of these assets.

We've shown the various, and still growing, ways investors can gain access to cryptoassets. Now that the innovative investor has come this far down the cryptoasset rabbit hole, it's time to revisit his or her current approach and investment portfolio in light of what has been learned.

Chapter 17

Preparing Current Portfolios for Blockchain Disruption

When Toffler stated in the 1970s that exponential change would cause millions of people to have an "abrupt collision with the future," it was issued as a warning. When considering investing in cryptoassets, innovative investors need to not only consider an individual investment (like bitcoin or ether) but also how this new asset class and the overall concept of blockchain technology could impact other assets within their portfolio. This chapter focuses on the importance of actively evaluating and potentially protecting one's portfolio in the face of exponential change.

When pondering the changes cryptoassets are bringing to the way we invest today, we must also recognize that the entire concept of blockchain technology heralds significant disruption to companies and industries. For most investors, these disruptions will affect investments that have already been made or are under consideration.

For instance, if Bitcoin influences how remittances are handled, what impact may that have on stocks like Western Union, a remittances kingpin? If Ethereum takes off as a decentralized world computer, will that have any effect on companies with cloud computing offerings, such as Amazon, Microsoft, and Google? If companies can get paid more quickly and with lower transaction fees using the latest cryptocurrency, will that have an impact on credit card providers like Visa and American Express?

EXPONENTIAL DISRUPTION

Clayton Christensen, a professor at Harvard Business School, wrote the seminal text on how large companies, often referred to as incumbents, struggle with maneuvering around exponential change. In *The Innovator's Dilemma: When New Technologies Cause Great Firms to Fail*, Christensen makes no qualms about how even the most well managed of firms can fail when confronted with a technology that threatens to disrupt their market. Broadly disruptive technologies lay the foundation for new growth, with the most influential blossoming into what are called general purpose technologies, which include electricity, the automobile, the Internet, and yes, blockchain technology. While such growth provides many opportunities, even if large companies recognize the potential of a technology, they are often handcuffed when they try to capitalize on it. The problem they face is threefold:

> First, disruptive products are simpler and cheaper; they generally promise lower margins, not greater profits. Second, disruptive technologies typically are first commercialized in emerging or insignificant markets. And third, leading firms' most profitable customers generally don't want, and indeed initially can't use, products based on disruptive technologies.[1]

Pursuing a product line in the new market is not additive to the incumbent's existing business because, as Christensen explains, disruptive products have lower margins, smaller markets, and target a customer base with whom the company is not familiar. Sometimes the new product line can even be subtractive from the company's existing business line—known as cannibalization— because it is superior to other products it already offers, and so customers start buying the new product as opposed to the more lucrative (for the company) older product. However, avoiding the new technology because of a fear of cannibalization can be the kiss of death. As Christensen points out,

> The fear of cannibalizing sales of existing products is often cited as a reason why established firms delay the introduction of new technologies. . . . But in disruptive situations, action must be taken before careful plans are made. Because much less can be known about what markets need or how large they can become, plans must serve a very different purpose: They must be plans for learning rather than plans for implementation.

Hence, the incumbent that avoids developing products that utilize the new technology may be maximizing short-term revenue, but is shooting itself in the foot over the long term. As Christensen notes, in the early stages of a disruptive technology, it is most important that the company learn and experiment. If the company doesn't experiment early on, then by the time the technology is inflecting in its growth—with a market that is sizeable enough to move the needle for the incumbent—it is too late. By that point, the smaller companies that took the time to master the new technology are much more nimble and experienced and will outcompete incumbents in what have become big growth markets.

If an incumbent misses enough of these growth opportunities, its offerings will become obsolete, its revenue will dwindle, its market capitalization will shrink, and it will become a dead-end investment. Often these are referred to as value-traps. As the innovative investor might expect, the fall of incumbents is happening at an accelerating rate, as is the rise of new winners. The disruption of incumbents can be quantified by how long the biggest companies stay in the S&P 500, or their average life span. The average life span for companies in the S&P 500 has fallen from 60 years in the 1960s to below 20 years of late.[2] This is clearly a sign that investors must not be complacent. One cannot assume that the companies succeeding today will continue to be the leading (and profitable) companies for decades to come.

Disruptive technologies are also being invented at an accelerating rate. The trend is one we have been witnessing for millennia. For example, between AD 900 and 1900, a new general purpose technology was invented roughly every 100 years, with notable examples including the steam engine, automobile, and electricity. In the twentieth century, a new general purpose technology came into existence every 15 years, with familiar examples like computers, the Internet, and biotechnology. In the twenty-first century, general purpose technologies have come into existence every 4 years, with autonomous robotics and blockchain technology as two of the more recent examples.[3]

While disruptive technologies tend to unseat incumbents, there are examples of companies that have managed to reinvent themselves continually for decades. Just as there is danger, there is also opportunity for incumbents to capitalize on exciting new growth markets, which can boost their revenue and market capitalizations. Discerning the difference between a value-trap and a reborn incumbent can make all the difference for the innovative investor.

BLOCKCHAIN TECHNOLOGY IN THE FINANCIAL SECTOR

In 2016, the father-son team of Don and Alex Tapscott published the book *Blockchain Revolution: How the Technology Behind Bitcoin Is Changing Money, Business, and the World,* and William Mougayar published the book, *The Business Blockchain: Promise, Practice, and Application of the Next Internet Technology.* As the titles imply, these books discuss the many ways in which blockchain technology is currently and will continue to disrupt how business is done worldwide. In this chapter, we investigate a few ways the financial sector may be upended by cryptoassets and how incumbents are responding. Using the financial sector as a leaping off point, investors can then apply their learnings to other industries.

The financial industry must slog through a swamp of regulation, sometimes making it slow to adapt to new technologies. Recently the industry has been showing its age with numerous data breaches, near-monopolistic structures, and continued use of tools and models developed decades ago that still run the inefficient money systems in place today. However, the Tapscotts believe the days of "Franken-finance"—that convoluted, contradictory, and often irrational system of finance we've lived under for so many years—are "numbered as blockchain technology promises to make the next decade one of great upheaval and dislocation but also immense opportunity for those who seize it."[4]

Recall from Chapter 2 that not all instances in which blockchain technology is used necessarily involve a cryptoasset (such as bitcoin or ether). In fact, thus far the majority of companies in the financial services space have opted for blockchain implementations void of cryptoassets. It is increasingly common for these implementations to be referred to as distributed ledger technology (DLT), which differentiates them from the blockchains of Bitcoin, Ethereum, and beyond. For companies pursuing a DLT strategy, they still utilize many of the innovations put forth by the developers of public blockchains, but they don't have to associate themselves with those groups or share their networks. They pick and choose the parts of the software they want to use and run it on their own hardware in their own networks, similar to intranets (earlier referred to as private, permissioned blockchains).

We see many DLT solutions as band-aids to the coming disruption. While DLT will help streamline existing processes—which will help profit margins in the short term—for the most part these solutions operate within what will become increasingly outdated business models. As we will cover with insurance, incumbents could use public blockchain architectures to provision similar services to what they do already, but it would cannibalize some of their revenue. Such cannibalization is admittedly painful, but as Christensen lays out, it is often necessary for long-term survival. Additionally, regulation can handcuff the incumbents, and in the financial services industry incumbents are particularly sensitive to regulatory rebukes after the financial crisis of 2008.

The incumbents protect themselves by dismissing cryptoassets, a popular example being JPMorgan's Jamie Dimon, who famously claimed bitcoin was "going to be stopped."[5] Mr. Dimon and other financial incumbents who dismiss cryptoassets are playing exactly to the precarious mold that Christensen outlines:

> Disruptive technologies bring to a market a very different value proposition than had been available previously. Generally, disruptive technologies underperform established products in mainstream markets. But they have other features that a few fringe (and generally new) customers value. Products based on disruptive technologies are typically cheaper, simpler, smaller, and, frequently, more convenient to use.

Disruptive technologies like cryptoassets initially gain traction because they're "cheaper, simpler, smaller." This early traction occurs on the fringe, not in the mainstream, which allows incumbents like Mr. Dimon to dismiss them. But cheaper, simpler, smaller things rarely stay on the fringe, and the shift to mainstream can be swift, catching the incumbents off guard.

Remittances and Blockchain Technology

One area long discussed as ripe for disruption is the personal remittances market, where individuals who work outside of their home countries send money back home to provide for their families. The market is massive, with the World Bank reporting worldwide remittance flows north of $600 billion, though it admits that the estimate is conservative: "The true size of remittances, including unrecorded flows through formal and informal channels, is believed to be significantly larger."[6]

Most remittances originate in high-income countries and are sent to individuals in developing countries, where the banking systems may not be easily accessible. As families in the receiving countries are typically unbanked—without access to a bank account or direct wire transfer capabilities—companies that provide a solution serve as a lifeline between the remitter and his or her family.[7] For many years companies such as Western Union and MoneyGram have used their lifeline position to levy high fees on these remitters, as they are among few options available and provide a mission critical service.

For example, toward the end of 2016 the global average fee for a remittance was just shy of 7.5 percent, with the weighted average coming in just under 6 percent.[8] These fees are decreasing, and rightfully so; in 2008, the average fee was nearly 10 percent, which meant that someone with $100 to send home only ending up giving $90 to his or her family, while the remitting company took the other $10.[9] It hardly seems fair; some call it exploitation.

As more competitors enter the market in the Internet era, people realize there is little reason for such high fees to be charged. While the term "wire money" may make it sound like the company providing the service is doing something sophisticated, in reality there's no wire. This is an outdated term from the days when Western Union was a telegraph company, literally using wires to send messages. Those wires are long gone. For the most part, all that happens in a remittance is a few centralized entities rebalance their books, debiting one account and crediting the other, after taking out a large chunk of the original amount, of course.

It's no stretch then to recognize that bitcoin, with its low cost, high speed, and a network that operates 24/7, could be the preferred currency for these types of international transactions. Of course, there are requirements to make this happen. The recipient needs to have a bitcoin wallet, or a business needs to serve as an intermediary, to ultimately get the funds to the recipient. While the latter option creates a new-age middleman—which potentially has its own set of problems—thus far these middlemen have proved to be much less costly than Western Union. The middleman can be a pawnshop owner with a cell phone, who receives the bitcoin and pays out local currency to the intended recipient.

In India, the largest receiver of remittances in the world with 12 percent of the global remittance total, a recent partnership between bitcoin exchanges is projected to bring the fee down to 0.5 percent for remittances into the country.[10] In Mexico, there's been a huge surge in volume at the country's bitcoin exchange, Bitso, where funds can be transferred for a similarly low fee.[11] All of these companies are eyeing the tens of billions of dollars the incumbents make from levying fat fees on vulnerable customers.

The impact of this major disruption in the remittance market should be recognized by the innovative investor not only because of the threat it creates to a publicly traded company like Western Union (WU) but for the opportunities it provides as well. For example, Bitso secured startup funding through the online investment service bnktothefuture.com, which, as we discussed in Chapter 16, connects investors with cryptoasset startups.[12]

Business-to-Business Payments and Blockchain Technology

Sending money internationally goes beyond citizens, as businesses also transmit large volumes to global business partners. While this industry is too large to dive into every detail, the same story laid out in remittances applies: fees are generally higher than they should be, and payments are slower than they should be. Visa, for example, has sensed the opportunity and is working with a startup called Chain to build a business-to-business payment solution using blockchain technology.[13] BitPesa is another company that leverages Bitcoin to help companies in Africa (currently Kenya, Nigeria, Tanzania, and Uganda) send and receive global payments.[14]

Ripple has been a popular startup for incumbents to work with, and some of them are creating projects that utilize its native asset, XRP. Incumbents such as Bank of America, RBC, Santander, BMO, CIBC, ATB Financial, and more use Ripple's blockchain-based technology to achieve faster and more secure financial transactions.[15] If realized, these efforts could not only reward the companies that utilize Ripple but also potentially benefit Ripple's own cryptoasset, XRP, which can be used as a bridge currency to help settlements on the Ripple network.[16]

The innovative investor will want to monitor how cheaper money flows may create opportunities for new and existing businesses in emerging markets. Capital fuels the growth of industries, and if money moves more freely between citizens and businesses, that may induce a significant economic boom in developing markets. This, too, may warrant an investigation of which geographies stand to benefit the most, as many ETFs and mutual funds can be purchased for exposure to targeted geographies. Geographic diversification can benefit a portfolio when isolated macroeconomic dislocations strike.

Insurance and Blockchain Technology

Thus far, most insurance companies have opted to investigate DLT implementations and have not ventured far into the world of cryptoassets. Large consulting firms are competing to be viewed as thought leaders on how distributed ledger technology will change the insurance industry, as these firms hope to win valuable contracts with deep-pocketed insurance companies that need help navigating the potential disruption. Deloitte believes that "a blockchain could allow the industry as a whole to streamline its processing and offer a better user experience for customers who have to make a claim. Simultaneously, storing claims and customer information on a blockchain would cut down fraudulent activity."[17]

Innovative investors can get a leg up on which insurance companies may be good short-term investment candidates and which to avoid, based on the action they take given the predictions of well-respected consulting firms. That said, as we have already mentioned, we view many of these DLT implementations as band-aids to prolong the life of systems that will fade into obsolescence over the coming decades. For the long term investor, careful analysis should be undertaken to understand if insurance companies are pursuing DLT use cases that will provide a lasting and meaningful solution. Lastly, some of the major consulting firms may be so entrenched in incumbent ideology that they too may be blind to the coming disruption.

Recall from Chapter 5 that there are already companies like Etherisc providing decentralized insurance policies. The disruption can go beyond the capital raising and claims management processes of insurance companies, and into the risk models themselves. For example, Augur's prediction platform built on Ethereum allows for markets to be created around the outcome of real-world events.[18] The predictive applications for this platform in the insurance area are varied and could have a direct impact on the actuarial industry, which is an integral part of the insurance industry and currently defines its pricing models.

Options exist for insurance companies to find a happy medium using the solutions provided by cryptoassets. For example, Factom has implemented a smart contract platform that allows for the creation of insurance policies with improved security and identification capabilities. Peter Kirby, the cofounder of Factom, points out that his platform can protect policyholders from fraud and identity theft, or at least provide them with the ability to track down the perpetrators of fraud and identity theft through the immutability provided by the blockchain technology that his platform is built on.[19] Cutting down on fraud and identity theft would help the bottom line of many insurance companies tremendously. Furthermore, operating in the transparency of public networks would do much to bolster trust in their operations, which could draw more customers.

DON'T REARRANGE THE DECK CHAIRS ON THE TITANIC

In the days immediately after the 2016 election of Donald Trump as U.S. president, the stocks of companies in the financial sector rallied in expectation of the new president's potential policy shifts from that of the prior administration.[20] During that time, investors benefited from having financial stocks in their portfolio, and perhaps, many more put these stocks into their portfolio after the election, either on the advice of advisors or as a reaction to the financial media claiming financial stocks were bound to benefit in the "age of Trump." However, focusing on these short-term trends is like rearranging the deck chairs on a sinking Titanic.

The innovative investor should ask if these gains were due to actual policies or the expectation of these policies, which hadn't yet been implemented. Policies can be temporarily effective at reinforcing the financial status quo but are only stopgaps in the face of long-term secular trends. It's important to recognize the disruption that bitcoin and cryptoassets can bring to the entire global financial system. Armed with this recognition, the innovative investor should consider the long-term investment prospects of financial companies clinging to their current operating models without consideration or recognition of the impending disruptions that these technologies will bring to the sector. The bottom line is that rather than fretting over where to position their deck chair, investors should consider if they should be long-term buyers of these existing banks and financial firms, given what they know about blockchain technology and the potential it brings to significantly change the banking industry.

THREE POTENTIAL STRATEGIES FOR SURVIVAL

We list three general strategies incumbents will likely use in their attempt to capitalize on the potential of blockchain technology.

If You Can't Beat 'Em, Buy 'Em

Toward the end of 2015 and through much of 2016, it seemed as if every single financial services firm was waking up to the potential of blockchain technology to disrupt its industry. When incumbents feel like they are late and being outmaneuvered by startups, they simply buy or invest in the startups. That is precisely what happened. The list of incumbents investing in bitcoin and blockchain startups accelerated to a frenzied pace starting in late 2015, and continued through the first half of 2016, including Citi, Visa, MasterCard, New York Life, Wells Fargo, Nasdaq, Transamerica, ABN AMRO, and Western Union.[21]

While the investing or takeover strategy has been a go-to for incumbents trying to avoid disruption, it is rarely as effective as hoped. Once the big company swallows the startup, or begins meddling, it is often hard for the startup to retain its fast-moving and flexible culture. Nimble cultures are key to succeeding in the early stages of a disruptive technology, and if the startup is tainted by corporate bureaucracy, then it will quickly lose its edge.

Circle the Wagons

Industry consortiums have been extremely popular among incumbents investigating how to apply distributed ledger technology to their industry. On one hand, a consortium makes perfect sense, as a distributed ledger needs to be shared among many parties for it to have any use. A collaborative consortium helps financial services companies—many of which have historically been competitors that keep their business processes close to their chest—learn how to share. On the other hand, these consortiums can hit snags if too many big names and big egos become involved.

One of the most famous consortiums is R3, which launched on September 15, 2015, with big names such as JPMorgan, Barclays, BBVA, Commonwealth Bank of Australia, Credit Suisse, Goldman Sachs, Royal Bank of Scotland, State Street, and UBS. By the end of September, 13 more financial companies had joined, including Bank of America, BNY Mellon, Citi, Deutsche Bank, Morgan Stanley, and Toronto-Dominion Bank. Before 2015 was over, 20 other financial companies joined R3. R3 consists of the leading financial companies in the world, many of which are held either in individual equity or bond positions in portfolios or are in managed money investments like mutual funds and ETFs.

Another consortium, The Hyperledger Project,[22] offers more open membership than R3. Remember, one of the strengths and defining aspects of an effective blockchain project is its open source ethos. The Hyperledger project was launched in December 2015 under the umbrella of the Linux Foundation to create a collaborative and open-source platform that could work with many industries, not just financial companies.[23] Companies currently supporting the project include Airbus, American Express, Daimler, IBM, and SAP.

The project states, "Hyperledger members and staff are committed to sharing best-practices and providing assistance with the use-case development, Proof-of-Concept (POC) testing, and adoption of Hyperledger."[24] Initial efforts undertaken by the group are in the finance and healthcare industries, with plans to build supply chain solutions as well. It will be interesting to see how this cross-industry collaborative and open source effort proceeds and what results come of it. An innovative investor will do well to follow the group's efforts to help identify specific companies that may benefit from the results.

One of the more interesting recent consortiums was the Enterprise Ethereum Alliance. It went public in late February 2017, and its founding members include Accenture, BNY Mellon, CME Group, JPMorgan, Microsoft, Thomson Reuters, and UBS.[25] What is most interesting about this alliance is that it aims to marry private industry and Ethereum's public blockchain. While the consortium will work on software outside of Ethereum's public blockchain, the intent is for all software to remain interoperable in case companies want to utilize Ethereum's open network in the future.

Create an Innovation Lab and Leave It Alone

The third strategy that an incumbent can follow is known as an *innovation lab*. Several universities, including Harvard, have set up innovation labs as a way to foster innovation through a collaborative effort between students and businesses. The corporate world has also jumped on this unique way of providing a forum for nurturing creative ideas with solid business skills. Often, these innovation labs are left alone, or largely untouched, by the incumbent parent, perhaps following Christensen's advice,

> With few exceptions, the only instances in which mainstream firms have successfully established a timely position in a disruptive technology were those in which the firms' managers set up an autonomous organization charged with building a new and independent business around the disruptive technology.

In the twenty-first century, the innovation lab concept has been embraced most famously by Google, which encourages creativity and innovation beyond an employee's current position. The company has created the Google Garage[26] as a (somewhat) formal structure in which employees can pursue innovations with others in the company. This has resulted in projects, such as its autonomous vehicles effort, that Google has grown organically in the hopes of providing additional future revenue.

A key feature that needs to be reinforced from Christensen's quote is the need to "set up an *autonomous* organization." Just setting up an innovation lab within a company is not a guarantee of success. These labs must be allowed to function as autonomous organizations, without the tunnel vision of existing business and profit models.

THE GREATEST OPPORTUNITY STILL AWAITS

We believe the greatest opportunities for investment growth are in public blockchains and their associated assets. It is the companies that stretch themselves to work with cryptoassets that will benefit the most over the long term. If instead a company pursues its own DLT solution, investors must decide if that solution will enhance the value of the company in the long term.

The opportunities are endless and will be only limited by the ingenuity of visionaries, developers, and business leaders. It will be an exciting time for innovation, and potentially, a rewarding time for those innovative investors who are equipped to recognize the opportunities that lie ahead.

TAX REPORTING OF CRYPTOASSET GAINS

Any financial professional or successful investor knows that managing an investment portfolio requires an understanding and approach to the tax ramifications (both on the gain and loss side) when making investment decisions. These types of strategies should also be part of innovative investors' approach to cryptoassets within their portfolio. While some decisions have been made related to the tax treatment of these assets, overall there's a lack of clarity, and even worse, a lack of understanding by the agencies providing tax guidance. As cryptoassets gain more publicity and acceptance, rest assured that government regulators and tax collectors will take more and more notice.

All cryptoassets have a value, and when bought or sold, can create a gain or loss for the innovative investor. It should come as no surprise that the Internal Revenue Service (IRS) of the United States has made clear its desire to get a cut of this digital pie. In 2014, the IRS decided it understood bitcoin and issued guidance on its tax treatment with IRS Notice 2014-21. Without detailing the fine print of the ruling,[27] the basic message was that although bitcoin may be called a virtual currency, for tax purposes the IRS would treat it as property. For example, stocks, bonds, and real estate are also considered property. The guidance stated, "General tax principles that apply to property transactions apply to transactions using virtual currency."[28]

Therefore, an investor, or even a casual user of bitcoin, must treat it for tax purposes the same way they would stocks, bonds, and real estate. A capital gain in any of these assets would warrant a taxable event. Accordingly, capital losses could be utilized as well. The bottom line with bitcoin, either for transactions or investing, is that the purchase and sale prices need to be tracked. The difference will be capital gains or losses, with appropriate tax treatment based on long- or short-term holds. The regulation also addresses income paid in bitcoin and even the mining of bitcoin, which are treated as immediate income at the market value of bitcoin at the time of possession.

The 2014 IRS guidance is interesting because, although it rules primarily on bitcoin, it refers to "virtual currency, such as bitcoin." Does this mean that the ruling includes all cryptoassets in the "virtual currency" classification?

Here's how the guidance defines what it means by virtual currency:

> In some environments, virtual currency operates like "real" currency—i.e., the coin and paper money of the United States or of any other country that is designated as legal tender, circulates, and is customarily used and accepted as a medium of exchange in the country of issuance—but it does not have legal tender status in any jurisdiction.

Looking at IRS Notice 2014-21, which provides a bit more information on tax guidance related to bitcoin and virtual currency, we find an attempt at further clarification:

> Virtual currency that has an equivalent value in real currency, or that acts as a substitute for real currency, is referred to as convertible virtual currency. Bitcoin is one example of a convertible virtual currency. Bitcoin can be digitally traded between users and can be purchased for, or exchanged into, U.S. dollars, Euros, and other real or virtual currencies.[29]

In this case, bitcoin is considered a "convertible" virtual currency. The ruling also refers the reader (who is by now rather confused) to a more "comprehensive description of convertible digital currencies" that was provided by the Financial Crimes Enforcement Network (FinCEN) back in 2013.[30] Although the FinCEN opinion has less to do with taxation and more to do with addressing the misuse of digital currencies for illegal activities, it reveals the fact that numerous regulatory agencies in the United States have been unable to provide clarity and a unified voice on how to classify bitcoin and cryptoassets.

The Commodity Futures Trading Commission (CFTC) also entered the fray when it charged a startup seeking to offer bitcoin-based options for not registering the product with it. This defined the asset as a commodity, not property, which would then be covered by the Commodity Exchange Act (CEA).[31]

The CFTC Director of Enforcement, Aitan Goelman, tried to clarify his opinion with this statement, "While there is a lot of excitement surrounding bitcoin and other virtual currencies, innovation does not excuse those acting in this space from following the same rules applicable to all participants in the commodity derivatives markets."[32] It is clearly confusing that the Director of Enforcement of the agency that ruled bitcoin a commodity also called it a "virtual currency."

If some cryptoassets are commodities, this could open them up to different tax treatment than if they were considered solely as property. Commodities fall under the 60/40 tax ruling, meaning 60 percent of the gains on a commodity transaction are treated as long-term capital gains and 40 percent are treated as short-term capital gains. This is different from taxing stocks where profitably selling an equity after 12 months is classified as a long-term capital gain with a current tax rate cap of 15 percent. Selling prior to 12 months would be considered a short-term gain with the tax ramification based on an investor's income bracket.

All cryptoassets are not alike. There needs to be further clarity and understanding of these assets by government agencies and potentially a new set of regulations (including tax treatments) that recognize these differences. For now, the IRS and the CFTC view these assets differently, and this will surely necessitate further clarifying rulings by the IRS to provide appropriate direction. Don't expect this to happen quickly; it took the IRS over 15 years to provide tax guidance on derivatives.[33]

For now, the course to take regarding tax treatment of these assets should rest with the investor and their accountant. The IRS considers them property, and therefore recording a gain or a loss in a similar manner to equities or bonds seems the prudent path to take.

Neither of us is an accountant, and we can't forecast how governmental regulators will ultimately reconcile the issues. Regarding taxes, the first thing investors should do is to discuss any bitcoin or cryptoasset activities with their accountant and lean on the accountant for information and advice. Second, and probably most important, is to keep records of all activities with these assets (this should include not only buys and sells, but if an asset was used to purchase a good or service).[34] It can be as simple as maintaining a paper-based or Excel spreadsheet that tracks the date and price of an asset when acquired and the same information when sold or when purchases are made with that asset. In time, more detailed reporting tools and resources will be available from the more reputable exchanges and from startups creating tools to track, record, and provide resources for blockchain tax reporting.

Even though the rules regarding taxation of these assets may change, one thing is clear: as with any other asset, the IRS is watching.

Chapter 18

The Future of Investing Is Here

Throughout this book, we've tried to provide historical context on investing and cryptoassets. Hopefully at this point, there's a clear recognition that cryptoassets should be evaluated alongside other traditional and alternative asset classes. Just as with any other asset class, there are good cryptoasset investments and there are bad ones. Considering these investments requires the same level of due diligence and research as does any other potential investment.

Although investment opportunities in cryptoassets are growing, currently most access is available through the purchase and trading in individual cryptoassets on exchanges. As we outlined in Chapter 15, some capital market investments currently exist and more will come to market in the future. What form these investments will take is yet to be seen. Will they be mutual funds made up of various cryptoassets? Perhaps an ETF that invests in an index of a specific slice of cryptoassets, like a focused privacy portfolio of monero, dash, and zcash? Already opportunities for investors to gain access to hedge funds that actively manage different cryptoassets, including the latest ICOs, are arising. But maybe the hedge fund structure will largely become a relic of the past, with asset management infrastructure decentralized through platforms like Melonport. The potential products and vehicles are endless and provide investors and money managers with great opportunities for profit.

Will individual money managers become famous for their expertise and active management of these assets, or will passive investments consisting of rules-based categories of cryptoassets become the vehicle of choice?

In the 1980s, Fidelity's Magellan Fund was where investors wanted to place their money, and it was all because of one person: Peter Lynch. During Lynch's time, the fund grew from $20 million to $14 billion, and he beat the S&P 500 index 11 out of 13 years. It was a heyday for active managers and for mutual funds in general, and investors chased money managers, not stocks. This enthusiasm for specific money managers wasn't isolated to equities in the eighties. As recently as 2015, much was made about bond guru Bill Gross's departure from Pimco to Janus, as Pimco found that 21 percent of its total assets left when Gross did.[1]

Twenty-five years after Peter Lynch left Fidelity, many financial pundits and writers have criticized his techniques, specifically his "buy what you know" advice. This was a cornerstone of his philosophy, as he bought stocks based on products he used as a customer, experiencing the company's business model in the flesh. In clarifying his famous comment in the face of criticism for active management, Lynch stressed the need for fundamental analysis of any investment. "People buy a stock and they know nothing about it," Lynch said. "That's gambling, and it's not good."[2]

For the innovative investor, recognizing that no investment should be made with little to no knowledge is not only sage advice but common sense. Here's another Burniske-Tatar Rule: Don't invest in bitcoin, ether, or any other cryptoasset just because it's doubled or tripled in the last week. Before investing, be able to explain the basics of the asset to a friend and ascertain if it fits well given the risk profile and goals of your investment portfolio.

The Millennial Age of Investing

We've provided a substantial amount of historical context in this book as it relates to investing in cryptoassets. Many longtime investors may regard this information as a reminder of how they've formed their own investing approaches and strategies, often having learned the hard way. For these investors, taking the step to considering and potentially investing in cryptoassets may be an evolution in their own investing strategy as they become innovative investors. However, a segment of millennials recognizes these opportunities and are becoming newly minted investors through their forays into cryptoassets.

Much has been written and hypothesized about millennials, or those that entered adulthood around the turn of the century. Millennials have an entirely different approach to banking and investing than baby boomers who invested through the dot-com crash and the financial crisis of 2008.

Having come of age through market crises, millennials are surprisingly conscious of their financial well-being. A recent study conducted through Facebook found millennials are highly educated, and perhaps due to the student loans required to gain this status, their financial situation is an important consideration in their life. In fact, 86 percent of millennials put money away each month.[3] Equally interesting, according to a Goldman Sachs survey, 33 percent of millennials think they won't need a bank by 2020.[4]

Seeing these statistics, it's no wonder that many financial institutions are seeking ways to engage the millennial banking and investing client. The problem is that the business models of many wealth managers are not positioned to cater to millennials. Over the last two decades, wealth management firms have encouraged their financial advisors to sign up only investors with $250,000 in assets and move away from servicing all levels of investors.[5] The reasoning has been to allow advisors to provide better service to a smaller base of clients, which is also good for profit margins. However, this means that their client base is aging. Because of these business policies, they are now less able to acquire and support young investors who are perhaps most in need of their assistance.

Perhaps, when wealth management firms were shifting millennials to online investing sites, rather than providing them access to personal financial advisors, they were doing this to address the disruptions that millennials were bringing to their model. From a business perspective, it was a more cost-effective way to support this demographic. However, this approach *addressed* rather than *engaged* the demographic. Further research is making it clear that millennials are concerned enough to talk about their financial futures, sometimes more so than their baby boomer parents. A study from Transamerica reports the following:

> Three out of four (76 percent) Millennial workers are discussing saving, investing, and planning for retirement with family and friends. Surprisingly, Millennials (18 percent) are twice as likely to "frequently" discuss the topic compared to Baby Boomers (9 percent).[6]

This from a generation that watched their parents significantly impacted by the Great Recession, either through downsizings or losses in investment portfolios. Many of them consider the stock markets akin to gambling casinos. However, they also recognize the value of saving, investing, and planning for the future. Wealth management firms that believe online investing sites will placate millennials until they get older and wealthier (and reach the minimum for a financial advisor relationship) are missing the point of disruption. As many of the wealth management firms have ignored them, millennials may be turning their backs on these firms as well, and not surprisingly, they're looking for investment vehicles and firms they can feel comfortable with. In fact, a digital native generation likely has little problem accepting the value of a digital native asset. A recent article in *Huffington Post* had this to say:

> Millennials, assisted by a cadre of impressively socially awkward Bitcoin startup VC types, are piling intellectual and financial capital into this whole cryptocurrency idea—Bitcoin, Ethereum, all of it. What "e-" in front of any noun did for techie investor excitement in the 1990s, "crypto" and "blockchain" seems to be doing today.[7]

Are millennials turning to bitcoin and cryptoassets for their investments? Is a Vanguard fund or a small investment in Apple any better? Whereas the Vanguard fund has a minimum investment amount and buying an equity will require a commission, millennials see cryptoasset markets as a way to begin investing with a modest amount of money and in small increments, which is often not possible with stocks or funds.[8]

The important point is that at least they're doing something to invest their funds and build the groundwork for a healthy financial future. We have seen firsthand millennials who have learned about investing from buying cryptoassets and have implemented investing approaches, such as taking profits at certain price points, seeking diversification into multiple assets, and so on. A local bitcoin meetup will include not only computer nerds discussing hash rates and the virtues of proof-of-work vs. proof-of-stake, but also deep and financially sound discussions among participants of various ages about recent cryptoasset investments.

GOLDILOCKS YEARS OF CRYPTOASSETS?

We may be at a point where millennials recognize the opportunity that crypto-assets provide, while most of Wall Street, including the typical investor, financial advisors, and the majority of large institutional investors haven't jumped on the cryptoassets bandwagon. But they are watching. Certain large investors are even dipping their toes in, implying an increase in investment vehicles could be around the corner.

Institutional money managers stepping up to cryptoassets and creating investment vehicles will have a huge impact on the awareness of these assets within a wider population of investors. The need to fund these investment vehicles will also impact the demand for cryptoassets, potentially putting significant upward price pressure on the associated markets. The benefits to the innovative investor who is already well positioned with a cryptoasset portfolio could be substantial. It should be noted that when more institutions become involved, and more information outlets come to life, the cryptoasset markets will become more competitive. Right now, a well-educated and astute innovative investor still has an edge in the cryptoasset markets. That may not always be the case.

We're in a Goldilocks period for cryptoassets, where the infrastructure and regulation has matured considerably, but most of Wall Street and institutional investors have yet to enter the fray. Therefore, there's still an informational and trading edge for the astute innovative investor who enters these markets now. This is a chance to get onboard before the entirety of the investing world wakes up to this opportunity. Taking the step forward with the knowledge we've provided and a firm grasp on one's financial plans, goals, and objectives will be what separates an innovative investor from the typical investor.

BEING AN INNOVATIVE AND EVER-LEARNING INVESTOR

Along with skyrocketing all-time highs, the number of cryptoassets available has surged. The growth of ICOs, and resultant proliferation, has gone beyond what any reporter or follower of this industry can keep up with. Cryptoassets are a moving target. While this is true for any asset class and any investment, the cryptoasset target moves faster than most. That's why we've armed the innovative investor with the ability to understand and evaluate these assets through historical context and time-tested investment tools and techniques, such as modern portfolio theory and asset allocation.

Innovative investors are active participants in their financial future, but this doesn't mean they must be alone on that journey. Relying on the advice of financial professionals can be effective because they can provide research and direction. Yet while innovative investors may take advice from experienced professionals, the final decisions are their own. They adapt their investing approach, strategies, and even selections based on what is occurring around them. This is especially vital in the age of exponential change that we're living in.

Buy and hold works, until it doesn't. Investing for the long term works until there's a need for income in retirement. Times change. The markets go up and the markets go down, sometimes in drastic ways. Situations change. A sick relative or job loss can create havoc with any financial plan.

Innovative investors are all about choosing their own investing philosophy, their own investing approach, and having their own viewpoint on what is a suitable investment for their own situation. It's not about dismissing the opinions of others; rather it's about evaluating the advice of others from a solid, educated, and informed base of knowledge.

We've taken the innovative investor on a trip through the world of cryptoassets and its colorful history, one that's still being written. It's a fascinating world to be a part of, and for those new to it, we hope that we've provided a good entry point. For those already part of this world, we hope we've expanded the view. We're excited about the opportunity it provides not only for investors but for the larger community as well.

We believe that when Satoshi was creating Bitcoin, he was also creating a view of the future. We hope that with this book we've been able to elucidate that future just a little more and provide you a means to be part of it—because that future is here.

Chris and Jack's Go-to Crypto Resources

Bitcoin Magazine: https://bitcoinmagazine.com/
This is our go-to resource for long-form articles that dive deep into critical developments in the cryptoasset space. While there is day-to-day coverage, we rely on it mostly for deep dives into complex topics.

BitInfoCharts: https://bitinfocharts.com/
While the user interface has historically been an eyesore, don't judge a book by its cover. The site is a data trove for information that's hard to find elsewhere, such as transaction characteristics, hash rate, rich lists, and so on for most all of the notable cryptoassets.

Blockchain.info: https://blockchain.info/charts
The best place for charts and easily downloadable CSV files of Bitcoin network statistics.

BraveNewCoin: https://bravenewcoin.com/
A bevy of resources from analysis, to APIs, to carefully crafted indices, BraveNewCoin is focused on providing professional-grade resources.

CoinCap: https://coincap.io/

One of the best mobile apps for getting a quick view of the latest market action on all the cryptoassets. It also has a website, but in our opinion the mobile app is the gem, and even includes a feature for tracking your customized crypto-asset portfolio.

CoinDance: https://coin.dance/

Touting itself as "community-driven Bitcoin statistics and services," CoinDance is loaded with unique Bitcoin charts, including statistics on LocalBitcoins trading volumes, node activity, sentiment polls, user demographics, and more.

CoinDesk: http://www.coindesk.com/

The ledger of record for the latest bitcoin, blockchain, and cryptoasset news. If you want to know what's happened over the last 24 hours, a skim of CoinDesk is your best bet.

CoinMarketCap: https://coinmarketcap.com/

Provides pricing and trading volumes for all cryptoasset markets, as well as charts for aggregate cryptoasset action. One of the sites we visit most frequently during the day when the markets are hot.

CryptoCompare: https://www.cryptocompare.com/

The site where we consistently download the most data on the widest array of cryptoassets, CryptoCompare not only gives great (free) data on trading and volume patterns, but also technical indicators, social media stats, developer activity, and more.

Education: https://www.coursera.org/learn/cryptocurrency

There are a growing number of quality courses available online that provide a deep understanding of bitcoin and cryptoassets. One of our favorites is the "Bitcoin and Cryptocurrency Technologies" course provided by Princeton University via Coursera.

Etherscan: https://etherscan.io/charts

The best place for charts and easily downloadable CSV files of Ethereum network statistics, as well as insight into the cryptotokens operating on top of Ethereum.

Exchange War: https://exchangewar.info/

An all-encompassing website to track the activity of different cryptoasset exchanges globally and their respective share in different trading pairs.

Google Alerts: https://www.google.com/alerts

To keep abreast of the latest news around bitcoin and cryptoassets, use the Google Alerts function to get an e-mail (usually daily) listing the latest news stories around your favorite keywords.

Smith + Crown: https://www.smithandcrown.com/

The most complete website for all things ICO, including past, present, and future sales, with a fair amount of research interspersed throughout the site.

TradeBlock: https://tradeblock.com/markets/

As of writing, TradeBlock provides the most "Bloomberg-feeling" user interface for investigating cross-exchange action of BTC, ETH, ETC, and LTC.

Beyond these websites, we rely on Twitter most heavily for information, followed by a mix of focused Reddit, Slack, and Telegram groups. Our Twitter accounts are:

 @cburniske

 @JackTatar

For more resources, please visit: http://www.BitcoinandBeyond.com.

Notes

Introduction

1. http://www.worldwidewebsize.com/.
2. Paul Baran, *On Distributed Communications: I. Introduction to Distributed Communications Networks* (Santa Monica, CA: RAND Corporation, 1964), http://www.rand.org/pubs/research_memoranda/RM3420.html.
3. http://www.Internetsociety.org/Internet/what-Internet/history-Internet/brief-history -Internet.
4. http://www.Internetlivestats.com/google-search-statistics/.
5. https://www.textrequest.com/blog/texting-statistics-answer-questions/.
6. https://www.lifewire.com/how-many-emails-are-sent-every-day-1171210.
7. https://hbr.org/2016/05/the-impact-of-the-blockchain-goes-beyond-financial-services.
8. https://dailyfintech.com/2014/08/28/hey-banks-your-fat-margin-is-my-opportunity/.
9. http://www.coindesk.com/microsoft-blockchain-azure-marley-gray/.
10. http://fortune.com/2016/08/19/10-stocks-beaten-googles-1780-gain/.
11. https://en.wikipedia.org/wiki/Dot-com_bubble#cite_note-40.
12. https://coinmarketcap.com/historical/20161225/.
13. https://www.fool.com/investing/general/2013/12/25/buffettbooks.aspx.

Chapter 1

1. https://www.stlouisfed.org/financial-crisis/full-timeline; http://historyofbitcoin.org/.
2. http://www.gao.gov/assets/660/651322.pdf.
3. http://wayback.archive.org/web/20120529203623/http://p2pfoundation.ning.com/profile/ SatoshiNakamoto.

289

4. http://observer.com/2011/10/did-the-new-yorkers-joshua-davis-nail-the-identity-of
    -bitcoin-creator-satoshi-nakamoto/.

5. https://en.wikipedia.org/wiki/Satoshi_Nakamoto#cite_note-betabeat-12.

6. http://www.economist.com/news/business-and-finance/21698060-craig-wright-reveals
    -himself-as-satoshi-nakamoto.

7. https://www.wired.com/2016/05/craig-wright-privately-proved-hes-bitcoins-creator/.

8. http://www.economist.com/news/finance-and-economics/21698294-quest-find-satoshi
    -nakamoto-continues-wrightu2019s-wrongs.

9. http://www.nytimes.com/2008/03/17/business/17bear.html?_r=0.

10. https://www.federalreserve.gov/newsevents/reform_bearstearns.htm.

11. http://www.wsj.com/articles/SB123051066413538349.

12. The situation was even worse, as CMOs were not the only culprit. More complex
    instruments like collateralized debt obligations (CDOs) made the situation even stickier.

13. http://www.wsj.com/articles/SB123051066413538349.

14. http://historyofbitcoin.org/.

15. http://blogs.wsj.com/deals/2008/09/10/live-blogging-the-lehman-conference-call/.

16. http://www.nytimes.com/2008/09/10/business/10place.html?_r=1&hp&oref=slogin;
    http://old.seattletimes.com/html/businesstechnology/2008171076_weblehman10.html.

17. http://www.wsj.com/articles/SB123051066413538349.

18. http://som.yale.edu/sites/default/files/files/001-2014-3A-V1-LehmanBrothers-A-REVA.pdf.

19. https://www.stlouisfed.org/financial-crisis/full-timeline.

20. https://bitcoin.org/bitcoin.pdf.

21. http://www.mail-archive.com/cryptography@metzdowd.com/msg09980.html.

22. https://www.fdic.gov/news/news/press/2006/pr06086b.pdf.

23. http://www.mail-archive.com/cryptography@metzdowd.com/msg09959.html.

24. http://www.mail-archive.com/cryptography@metzdowd.com/msg09971.html.

25. http://www.mail-archive.com/cryptography@metzdowd.com/msg10006.html.

26. http://www.nytimes.com/packages/html/national/200904_CREDITCRISIS/recipients.html.

27. https://en.bitcoin.it/wiki/Genesis_block.

28. http://www.thetimes.co.uk/tto/business/industries/banking/article2160028.ece.

29. http://historyofbitcoin.org/.

30. http://p2pfoundation.ning.com/forum/topics/bitcoin-open-source?xg_source=activity.

31. http://archive.is/Gvonb#selection-3137.0-3145.230.

32. http://www.nytimes.com/interactive/2009/02/04/business/20090205-bailout-totals
    -graphic.html?_r=0.

Chapter 2

1. https://papers.ssrn.com/sol3/papers.cfm?abstract_id=2808762.

2. https://99bitcoins.com/bitcoinobituaries/.

3. Simon Singh, *The Code Book* (Anchor, 2000).

4. This quote (or maxim) is often credited to the great Mark Twain, but as with many great quotes the actual author of it is unclear. See http://quoteinvestigator.com/2014/01/12/history-rhymes/.

5. https://www.bloomberg.com/view/articles/2016-09-01/maybe-blockchain-really-does-have-magical-powers.

6. https://www.cbinsights.com/blog/industries-disrupted-blockchain/.

7. http://www.washington.edu/news/2015/09/17/a-q-a-with-pedro-domingos-author-of-the-master-algorithm/.

Chapter 3

1. http://gawker.com/the-underground-website-where-you-can-buy-any-drug-imag-30818160.

2. CoinDesk BPI.

3. https://www.bloomberg.com/news/articles/2013-03-28/bitcoin-may-be-the-global-economys-last-safe-haven.

4. http://money.cnn.com/2013/11/27/investing/bitcoin-1000/; http://money.cnn.com/2013/11/18/technology/bitcoin-regulation/?iid=EL.

5. http://www.nytimes.com/2013/12/06/business/international/china-bars-banks-from-using-bitcoin.html.

6. https://www.fbi.gov/contact-us/field-offices/newyork/news/press-releases/ross-ulbricht-aka-dread-pirate-roberts-sentenced-in-manhattan-federal-court-to-life-in-prison.

7. https://www.theguardian.com/money/us-money-blog/2014/feb/25/bitcoin-mt-gox-scandal-reputation-crime.

8. http://www.bbc.com/news/technology-24371894.

9. Bitcoiner refers to an advocate of Bitcoin.

10. We'll describe wallets in detail in Chapter 14.

11. http://www.bankofengland.co.uk/publications/Documents/quarterlybulletin/2014/qb14q3digitalcurrenciesbitcoin1.pdf.

12. http://insidebitcoins.com/new-york/2015.

13. https://www.bloomberg.com/news/features/2015-09-01/blythe-masters-tells-banks-the-blockchain-changes-everything.

14. http://www.economist.com/news/leaders/21677198-technology-behind-bitcoin-could-transform-how-economy-works-trust-machine.

15. The computers are not technically miners because they are not minting any new assets and they are not paid directly for their work.

16. http://www.nyu.edu/econ/user/jovanovi/JovRousseauGPT.pdf.

17. http://www.gartner.com/newsroom/id/3412017.

18. http://www.gartner.com/technology/research/methodologies/hype-cycle.jsp.

Chapter 4

1. Network value = (units of the asset outstanding) × ($ value per asset). This is often referred to as the market capitalization of an asset on many current resources, but the authors prefer this term as more accurately conveying the total value of a cryptoasset.

2. https://coinmarketcap.com/.

3. http://cryptome.org/jya/digicrash.htm.

4. Ibid.

5. Ibid.

6. https://bitcoinmagazine.com/articles/quick-history-cryptocurrencies-bbtc-bitcoin-1397682630/.

7. http://karmakoin.com/how_it_works.

8. MoIP is a riff off the term "VoIP," which stands for Voice-over-Internet-Protocol. Skype, FaceTime, and Google Hangouts are all examples of VoIP.

9. Remember that a coinbase transaction goes to the miner that discovered the block through the proof-of-work process.

10. As more machines are dedicated to mine on the network, there are more "guesses" at the solution to the PoW puzzle, which means the solution will be guessed more quickly if the difficulty of the problem is not increased. Keeping a steady cadence of 10 minutes for blocks means that transactions will be incorporated into Bitcoin's blockchain in a timely manner, and it also mathematically meters the supply issuance of bitcoin.

11. Here the term refers to the transaction in a block that pays the miner, whereas it is most commonly associated with a company called Coinbase.

12. Astute investors may realize that the halving doesn't happen exactly every four years. The reason for this is because if lots of machines are being added to the mining network, then block times will average faster than 10 minutes before the difficulty is reset again. This speeds up the time between every 210,000 blocks.

13. https://blockchain.info/charts/total-bitcoins.

14. The term was even used for one of the first books written about Bitcoin, *Digital Gold: Bitcoin and the Inside Story of the Misfits and Millionaires Trying to Reinvent Money*, by Nathaniel Popper, Harper Collins, 2015.

15. https://namecoin.org/.

16. https://bit.namecoin.org/.

17. https://bitcointalk.org/index.php?topic=1790.0.

18. https://litecoin.info/History_of_cryptocurrency.

19. https://litecoin.info/Comparison_between_Litecoin_and_Bitcoin/Alternative_work_in_progress_version.

20. https://coinmarketcap.com/historical/20170101/.

21. http://ryanfugger.com/.

22. https://www.americanbanker.com/news/disruptor-chris-larsen-returns-with-a-bitcoin-like-payment-system.

23. Ibid.

24. https://bitcointalk.org/index.php?topic=128413.0.

25. http://www.marketwired.com/press-release/opencoin-developer-ripple-protocol-closes-funding-from-andreessen-horowitz-ff-angel-1777707.htm.

26. https://bitcoinmagazine.com/articles/introducing-ripple-1361931577/.

27. https://charts.ripple.com/#/.

28. https://coincap.io/.

29. https://ripple.com/.

30. https://bitcointalk.org/index.php?topic=361813.0.

31. What's a meme? https://www.merriam-webster.com/dictionary/meme.

32. https://www.wired.com/2013/12/best-memes-2013/.

33. http://www.businessinsider.com/what-is-dogecoin-2013-12.

34. Ibid.

35. https://github.com/dogecoin/dogecoin/issues/23.

36. http://www.businessinsider.com/what-is-dogecoin-2013-12.

37. http://www.financemagnates.com/cryptocurrency/education-centre/what-is-dogecoin/.

38. http://www.abc.net.au/pm/content/2013/s3931812.htm.

39. https://99bitcoins.com/price-chart-history/.

40. https://motherboard.vice.com/en_us/article/worth-1-billion-icelands-cryptocurrency-is -the-third-largest-in-the-world.

41. https://coinmarketcap.com/currencies/auroracoin/.

42. https://medium.com/the-nordic-web/the-failed-crypto-currency-experiment-in-iceland -251e28df2c54#.retvu6wp2.

43. https://www.reddit.com/r/auroracoin/comments/223vhq/someone_just_bought_a_pint _of_beer_for_1/.

44. https://www.nytimes.com/2016/04/06/world/europe/panama-papers-iceland.html.

45. https://pirateparty.org.au/wiki/Policies/Distributed_Digital_Currencies_and_Economies.

46. https://news.bitcoin.com/polls-iceland-pro-bitcoin-pirate-party/.

47. http://bitcoinist.com/iceland-election-interest-auroracoin/.

48. https://cryptonote.org/inside.php#equal-proof-of-work.

49. https://cryptonote.org/.

50. https://twitter.com/adam3us/status/447105453634641921.

51. https://bitcointalk.org/index.php?topic=512747.msg5661039#msg5661039.

52. https://bitcointalk.org/index.php?topic=512747.msg6123624#msg6123624.

53. https://bitcointalk.org/index.php?topic=512747.msg6126012#msg6126012.

54. https://bitcointalk.org/index.php?topic=563821.0.

55. https://lab.getmonero.org/pubs/MRL-0003.pdf.

56. https://cryptonote.org/inside#untraceable-payments.

57. https://www.reddit.com/r/Monero/comments/3rya3e/what_are_the_basic_parameter scharacteristics_of/cwsv64j/.

58. https://imgur.com/a/De0G2.

59. https://www.dash.org/wp-content/uploads/2015/04/Dash-WhitepaperV1.pdf.

60. https://dashdot.io/alpha/index_118.html?page_id=118.

61. https://www.coindesk.com/what-is-the-value-zcash-market-searches-answers/.

Chapter 5

1. https://bitcoinmagazine.com/articles/smart-contracts-described-by-nick-szabo-years-ago -now-becoming-reality-1461693751/.

2. Dmitry Buterin is also very much involved in the cryptoasset world as cofounder of Blockgeeks and other influential startups.

3. http://fortune.com/ethereum-blockchain-vitalik-buterin/.

4. http://www.ioi2012.org/competition/results-2/.

5. https://backchannel.com/the-uncanny-mind-that-built-ethereum-9b448dc9d14f#.4yr8yhfp8.

6. https://blog.ethereum.org/2014/01/23/ethereum-now-going-public/.

7. http://counterparty.io/platform/.

8. https://steemit.com/ethereum/@najoh/beyond-bitcoin-and-crypto-currency-ethereum.

9. https://blog.ethereum.org/2014/01/23/ethereum-now-going-public/.

10. https://github.com/ethereum/wiki/wiki/white-paper.

11. *Turing complete* refers to a system that is effectively capable of the full functionality of a general purpose computer. Bitcoin was intentionally constructed not to be Turing complete to constrain complexity and prioritize security.

12. https://ethereum.org/ether.

13. Nathaniel Popper, *Digital Gold: Bitcoin and the Inside Story of the Misfits and Millionaires Trying to Reinvent Monday*, Harper, 2015.

14. http://www.coindesk.com/peter-thiel-fellowship-ethereum-vitalik-buterin/.

15. http://www.wtn.net/summit-2014/2014-world-technology-awards-winners.

16. http://ether.fund/market.

17. https://www.ethereum.org/foundation.

18. https://blog.ethereum.org/2015/03/14/ethereum-the-first-year/.

19. http://ethdocs.org/en/latest/introduction/history-of-ethereum.html.

20. http://ether.fund/market.

21. http://ethdocs.org/en/latest/introduction/history-of-ethereum.html.

22. Ibid.

23. https://medium.com/the-future-requires-more/flight-delay-dapp-lessons-learned-a59e4e39a8d1.

24. https://www.wired.com/2016/06/biggest-crowdfunding-project-ever-dao-mess/.

25. https://www.nytimes.com/2016/05/28/business/dealbook/paper-points-up-flaws-in-venture-fund-based-on-virtual-money.html.

26. https://docs.google.com/document/d/10kTyCmGPhvZy94F7VWyS-dQ4lsBacR2dUg GTtV98C40/edit#heading=h.e437su2ytbf9.

27. https://github.com/TheDAO.

28. https://bitcoinmagazine.com/articles/the-ethereum-community-debates-soft-fork-to-blacklist-funds-in-wake-of-m-dao-heist-1466193335/.

29. http://www.forbes.com/sites/francescoppola/2016/07/21/a-painful-lesson-for-the-ethereum-community/#724124515714.

30. https://forum.daohub.org/t/hard-fork-implementation-update/6026.

31. https://twitter.com/Poloniex/status/757068619234803712.

32. https://blog.lawnmower.io/in-the-aftermath-of-the-ethereum-hard-fork-prompted-by-the-dao-hack-the-outvoted-15-are-rising-up-ea408a5eaaba#.baachmi2w.

33. https://ethereumclassic.github.io/.

34. https://youtu.be/yegyih591Jo.

35. http://blog.augur.net/guide-to-augurs-rep/.

36. https://twitter.com/search?q=%40brian_armstrong%20augur&src=typ.

37. https://twitter.com/vitalikbuterin/status/649698251197804545.

38. https://www.smithandcrown.com/rootstock-raises-1-million-bring-ethereum-like-smart -contracts-bitcoin/.

Chapter 6

1. http://www.marketwatch.com/story/do-bitcoins-belong-in-your-retirement-portfolio-2013 -08-29.

2. Eric has since become a cryptoasset investor.

3. https://www.sec.gov/investor/pubs/assetallocation.htm.

4. http://www.aaii.com/o/assetallocation.

5. https://www.nuffield.ox.ac.uk/economics/papers/2009/w4/HF%20Working%20Paper.pdf.

6. Bob Rice, *The Alternative Answer* (Harper Collins, 2013).

7. https://www.baltercap.com/wp-content/uploads/2016/12/26.-The-Value-of-the-Hedge -Fund-Industry-to-Investors-Markets-and-the-Broader-Economy.pdf.

8. H. Kent Baker and Greg Filbeck, *Alternative Investments: Instruments, Performance, Benchmarks and Strategies* (Wiley, 2013).

9. ttps://www.cnbc.com/id/46191784.

10. http://www.forbes.com/sites/advisor/2013/05/22/what-is-an-alternative- investment/#1290702fdb81.

11. http://etfdb.com/type/alternatives/all/.

12. https://www.morganstanley.com/wealth/investmentsolutions/pdfs/altscapabilitiesbrochure .pdf.

13. https://olui2.fs.ml.com/Publish/Content/application/pdf/GWMOL/ Q1MarketQuarterly04172013.pdf.

14. https://www.pershing.com/our-thinking/thought-leadership/advisor-perceptions-of -alternative-investments.

15. https://www.thebalance.com/cryptocurrencies-are-the-new-alternative-investment-4048017.

Chapter 7

1. http://www.marketwatch.com/story/do-bitcoins-belong-in-your-retirement-portfolio -2013-08-29.

2. http://us.spindices.com/indices/equity/sp-500.

3. http://www.investopedia.com/terms/d/djia.asp.

4. http://www.nasdaq.com/markets/indices/nasdaq-100.aspx. All of the data pulled was total return data, meaning dividends were reinvested to show in total how an investor's wealth would have grown. Market indices were used, as opposed to ETFs, because these indices do not have management fees, similar to how the price of bitcoin does not incorporate management fees. If one wanted to invest in bitcoin or ETFs that represent these broad market indices there would be a diversity of fees among the instruments.

5. http://pages.stern.nyu.edu/~adamodar/New_Home_Page/datafile/histretSP.html.

6. This time period was used as it was the closest to a 5-year cut that the authors could derive given Facebook's recent IPO.

7. To represent U.S. bonds, U.S. real estate, gold, and oil, we used the Bloomberg Barclays US Aggregate Bond Index, the Morgan Stanley Capital International US Real Estate Investment Trust Index, the gold index underlying the SPDR Gold Shares ETF, and crude oil futures, respectively.

8. Minus the risk-free rate.

9. Using weekly returns to standardize for # of days scalar multiplier. All previous charts have used daily data.

10. http://www.coindesk.com/bitcoin-price-2014-year-review/.

11. http://corporate.morningstar.com/U.S./documents/MethodologyDocuments/MethodologyPapers/StandardDeviationSharpeRatio_Definition.pdf.

12. Market cap is an abbreviation of market capitalization.

13. http://www.aaii.com/asset-allocation.

Chapter 8

1. https://www.bloomberg.com/news/articles/2015-09-17/bitcoin-is-officially-a-commodity-according-to-u-s-regulator.

2. https://www.irs.gov/uac/newsroom/irs-virtual-currency-guidance.

3. https://www.sec.gov/litigation/investreport/34-81207.pdf.

4. Though debates still exist amongst these asset classes. For example, some people don't consider currencies to be an asset class.

5. http://www.iijournals.com/doi/abs/10.3905/jpm.23.2.86?journalCode=jpm.

6. http://research.ark-invest.com/bitcoin-asset-class.

7. This is a little more simplified for a cryptotoken within a decentralized application that leverages another blockchain. The decentralized application doesn't need to work directly with the miners of the blockchain; instead it relies upon another community and that community's cryptoasset to govern the miners and the associated blockchain.

8. http://research.ark-invest.com/hubfs/1_Download_Files_ARK-Invest/White_Papers/Bitcoin-Ringing-The-Bell-For-A-New-Asset-Class.pdf.

Chapter 9

1. http://factmyth.com/factoids/the-dutch-east-india-company-was-the-first-publicly-traded-company/.

2. Fernand Braudel, *The Wheels of Commerce*, Civilization and Capitalism 15th–18th Century, vol. 3 (New York: Harper & Row, 1983).

3. Nathaniel Popper, *Digital Gold: Bitcoin and the Inside Story of the Misfits and Millionaires Trying to Reinvest Money* (Harper Collins, 2015).

4. New Liberty Standard published an exchange rate for bitcoin of 1 USD = 1,309.03 BTC established using the equation based on the electricity cost and hardware cost of the machine to mine a bitcoin block. http://hikepages.com/history-of-bitcoin-the-digital-currency.html#.WMXcMxLytcA.

5. https://www.cryptocoincharts.info/markets/info.

6. https://data.bitcoinity.org/markets/exchanges/USD/30d. Screenshot taken February 18, 2017.

7. CryptoCompare, Log scale.

8. https://www.wired.com/2017/01/monero-drug-dealers-cryptocurrency-choice-fire/.

9. http://www.coindesk.com/chinas-central-bank-issues-warnings-major-bitcoin
    -exchanges/.

10. An example of increased regulation dampening liquidity and trading volume is the new
    regulation that came out after the financial crisis of 2008. Regulations like Dodd-Frank
    required much stricter compliance processes, and led to decreased trading volumes
    especially in the fixed-income market.

11. http://www.nytimes.com/2013/12/06/business/international/china-bars-banks-from
    -using-bitcoin.html.

12. https://www.cryptocompare.com/coins/eth/analysis/BTC?type=Currencies.

13. Technically, it is absolute returns minus the risk-free rate, which is commonly represented
    by the three-month Treasury bill.

14. We'll discuss the various investment options in the capital markets for investors in
    Chapter 15.

15. https://www.washingtonpost.com/news/wonk/wp/2017/01/03/why-bitcoin-just-had-an
    -amazing-year/?utm_term=.64a6cfdf7398.

Chapter 10

1. Edward Chancellor, *Devil Take the Hindmost: A History of Financial Speculation* (Farrar,
    Straus and Giroux, 1999).

2. Ibid.

3. http://www.perseus.tufts.edu/hopper/morph?la=la&l=speculare.

4. Benjamin Graham and David Dodd, *Security Analysis* (McGraw Hill, 1940).

5. Benjamin Graham, *The Intelligent Investor* (HarperBusiness [2006]).

6. https://blogs.cfainstitute.org/investor/2013/02/27/what-is-the-difference-between
    -investing-and-speculation-2/.

7. http://www.presidency.ucsb.edu/ws/?pid=14473.

8. Gustave Le Bon, *The Psychology of Revolution*, http://www.gutenberg.org/ebooks/448.

9. Niall Ferguson, *The Ascent of Money: A Financial History of the World* (Penguin, 2008).

10. Edward Chancellor, *Devil Take the Hindmost*.

11. http://penelope.uchicago.edu/~grout/encyclopaedia_romana/aconite/semperaugustus
    .html.

12. Edward Chancellor, *Devil Take the Hindmost*.

13. Ibid.

14. http://www.bbc.com/culture/story/20160419-tulip-mania-the-flowers-that-cost-more
    -than-houses.

15. Edward Chancellor, *Devil Take the Hindmost*.

16. http://www.economist.com/blogs/freeexchange/2013/10/economic-history.

17. http://penelope.uchicago.edu/~grout/encyclopaedia_romana/aconite/semperaugustus
    .html.

18. Edward Chancellor, *Devil Take the Hindmost.*

19. https://www.theguardian.com/technology/2013/dec/04/bitcoin-bubble-tulip-dutch-banker.

20. https://coinmarketcap.com/currencies/steem/.

21. https://z.cash/.

22. Recall that a coinbase transaction is the transaction that pays the miner with newly minted units of a cryptoasset in exchange for the miner having appended a new block to the blockchain.

23. https://cryptohustle.com/zcash-launch-breaks-records.

24. http://www.coindesk.com/bitcoin-breaks-700-zcash-steals-show/.

25. https://www.cryptocompare.com/coins/zec/charts/BTC?p=ALL.

26. http://www.zerohedge.com/news/2015-05-29/robert-shiller-unlike-1929-time-everything -stocks-bonds-and-housing-overvalued.

27. https://hbr.org/2014/01/what-alan-greenspan-has-learned-since-2008.

28. Edward Chancellor, *Devil Take the Hindmost.*

29. http://query.nytimes.com/gst/abstract.html?res=9806E6DF1639E03ABC4E52DFB667838 2639EDE&legacy=true.

30. http://time.com/3207128/stock-market-high-1929/.

31. Edward Chancellor, *Devil Take the Hindmost.*

32. Ibid.

Chapter 11

1. Edward Chancellor, *Devil Take the Hindmost: A History of Financial Speculation* (Farrar, Straus and Giroux, 1999).

2. http://www.thebubblebubble.com/mississippi-bubble/.

3. http://www.thebubblebubble.com/south-sea-bubble/.

4. Edward Chancellor, *Devil Take the Hindmost.*

5. Ibid.

6. Ibid.

7. Ibid.

8. Ibid.

9. Carmen M. Rinehart and Kenneth S. Rogoff, *This Time Is Different* (Princeton University Press, 2011).

10. https://www.washingtonpost.com/news/wonk/wp/2015/06/08/bitcoin-isnt-the-future-of -money-its-either-a-ponzi-scheme-or-a-pyramid-scheme/?utm_term=.39f7a8895637.

11. http://documents.worldbank.org/curated/en/660611468148791146/pdf/WPS6967.pdf.

12. https://cointelegraph.com/news/one-coin-much-scam-swedish-bitcoin-foundation -issues-warning-against-onecoin.

13. https://news.bitcoin.com/beware-definitive-onecoin-ponzi/.

14. https://www.fca.org.uk/news/news-stories/beware-trading-virtual-currencies-onecoin.

15. https://www.sec.gov/investor/alerts/ia_virtualcurrencies.pdf.

16. Edward Chancellor, *Devil Take the Hindmost.*

17. Niall Ferguson, *The Ascent of Money: A Financial History of the World* (Penguin Books, 2009).

18. https://dashdot.io/alpha/index_118.html?page_id=118.

19. Ibid.

20. Ibid.

21. https://coinmarketcap.com/historical/20170402/.

22. http://www.bitcoinmutualfund.net/.

23. http://www.digitalhistory.uh.edu/disp_textbook.cfm?smtID=2&psid=3173.

24. Edward Chancellor, *Devil Take the Hindmost.*

25. http://www.civilwar.org/education/history/faq/?referrer=https://www.google.com/.

26. http://www.nytimes.com/learning/general/onthisday/harp/1016.html.

27. Ibid.

28. https://www.forbes.com/sites/timreuter/2015/09/01/when-speculators-attack-jay-goulds-gold-conspiracy-and-the-birth-of-wall-street/#58d0b3afcda2.

29. Edward Chancellor, *Devil Take the Hindmost.*

30. http://www.history.com/news/the-black-friday-gold-scandal-145-years-ago.

31. Ibid.

32. Edward Chancellor, *Devil Take the Hindmost.*

33. http://www.history.com/news/the-black-friday-gold-scandal-145-years-ago.

34. Ibid.

35. Edward Chancellor, *Devil Take the Hindmost.*

36. Ibid.

37. http://www.nytimes.com/learning/general/onthisday/harp/1016.html.

38. Edward Chancellor, *Devil Take the Hindmost.*

39. http://www.usinflationcalculator.com/inflation/historical-inflation-rates/.

40. https://priceonomics.com/how-the-hunt-brothers-cornered-the-silver-market/.

41. http://www.investopedia.com/articles/optioninvestor/09/silver-thursday-hunt-brothers.asp.

42. John Kenneth Galbraith, *The Great Crash 1929.*

43. Edward Chancellor, *Devil Take the Hindmost: A History of Financial Speculation* (Farrar, Straus and Giroux, 1999).

44. http://www.nytimes.com/1991/08/19/world/upheaval-salomon-salomon-punished-treasury-which-partly-relents-hours-later.html?pagewanted=all.

45. https://dashpay.atlassian.net/wiki/spaces/DOC/pages/5472261/Whitepaper.

46. https://bitinfocharts.com/top-100-richest-bitcoin-addresses.html.

Chapter 12

1. Period is from fall 2016 to spring 2017.

2. http://www.cfapubs.org/doi/pdf/10.2469/cfm.v14.n1.2789.

3. https://twitter.com/VitalikButerin/status/832299334586732548.

4. https://steemit.com.

5. https://www.yours.org/.

6. https://swarm.city/.

7. http://www.gartner.com/newsroom/id/3412017.

8. https://coinmarketcap.com/historical/20170402/.

9. https://techcrunch.com/2016/03/16/why-latin-american-economies-are-turning-to
   -bitcoin/.

10. https://bitinfocharts.com/top-100-richest-bitcoin-addresses.html.

11. https://fred.stlouisfed.org/series/M1V.

12. This conversation purposefuly excludes M1, M2, and MZM as they are not relevant to
    cryptoassets.

13. https://www.gold.org/sites/default/files/documents/gold-investment-research/liquidity
    _in_the_global_gold_market.pdf.

14. Warren Buffet likes 12 percent, but we prefer 15 percent for risky stocks.
    https://www.oldschoolvalue.com/blog/investing-strategy/explaining-discount-rates/.

15. http://ethereum.stackexchange.com/questions/443/what-is-the-total-supply-of-ether.

Chapter 13

1. Ethereum will be switching from Proof-of-Work to Proof-of-Stake in the first half of 2018.

2. Hash rate charts for most cryptoassets are here: http://www.coinwarz.com/charts/
   network-hashrate-charts.

3. http://www.ebay.com/itm/like/262677542123?lpid=82&chn=ps&ul_noapp=true.

4. https://www.justice.gov/atr/herfindahl-hirschman-index.

5. https://www.justice.gov/atr/15-concentration-and-market-shares.

6. Ibid.

7. There are some that object to using the HHI to measure blockchain network mining
   concentration, mainly because many of these entities are mining pools that are actually
   composed of many entities. Therefore, the decentralization is actually much greater than
   registers through such network analysis.

8. https://litecoin.info/Spread_the_Hashes.

9. https://www.thebalance.com/bitcoin-mining-in-the-beauty-of-iceland-4026143.

10. Nodes are not the same as miners but are still a useful metric for determining the
    geographic distribution of the hardware maintaining and building a blockchain.

11. http://startupmanagement.org/2015/02/15/best-practices-in-transparency-and-reporting
    -for-cryptocurrency-crowdsales/.

12. Here are bitcoin's social repository points from CryptoCompare: https://www
    .cryptocompare.com/coins/btc/influence. You can substitute any cryptoasset symbol for
    "btc" in this address to see that asset's points.

13. https://help.github.com/articles/about-stars/.

14. To measure the days of existence, the following start dates were used for Bitcoin,
    Ethereum, Dash, Ripple, and Monero. Bitcoin: 10/31/2008, Satoshi's white paper release
    date. Ethereum: 1/23/2014, Vitalik's formal announcement on the Ethereum Blog. Dash:
    1/18/2014, the date the network went live. Ripple: 11/29/2012, the date Ryan Fugger made
    an announcement about the new team working on Ripple. Monero: 4/9/2014, the date
    thankful_for_today made an announcement about the impending launch of "BitMonero."

It should be noted that Dash's, Ripple's and Monero's start dates are more lenient than Bitcoin and Ethereum, as work was being done on all three of these before the chosen start dates, though because those dates are not easily ascertainable and to avoid controversy the most accurate announcement date of the new cryptoasset was used.

15. https://www.openhub.net/p?query=bitcoin&sort=relevance.

16. http://spendbitcoins.com/.

17. https://coinmarketcap.com/currencies/volume/24-hour/.

18. https://blockchain.info/charts.

19. https://etherscan.io/charts.

20. http://www.coindesk.com/using-google-trends-estimate-bitcoins-user-growth/.

21. http://www.investopedia.com/terms/m/mooreslaw.asp.

22. https://blockchain.info/charts/n-transactions.

23. https://etherscan.io/chart/tx.

24. Blockchain.info has done some analysis, which is what makes this an "estimated transaction volume," because some of the transactions using Bitcoin's blockchain are "change transactions," which sends a remainder back to a user and thus needs to be weeded out to get a more accurate estimation of volume.

25. Find Brian's research at https://www.therationalinvestor.co/ and on his podcasts on the Bitcoin Trading Academy at http://bitcointrading.net/podcast/.

26. https://www.cryptocompare.com/exchanges/guides/how-to-trade-bitcoin-and-other-crypto-currencies-using-an-sma/.

27. https://www.coindesk.com/bitcoin-traders-know-technical-analysis/.

Chapter 14

1. https://www.sec.gov/investor/alerts/bulletincustody.htm.

2. A famous early supporter of Bitcoin who has since tragically passed away from ALS, also known as Lou Gehrig's disease. Hal was the first person to grasp the promise of Satoshi's concept when it was first released as a white paper, and worked with Satoshi in late 2008 to refine the code.

3. Incorporating the hash of the previous block is what links together the blockchain and makes it immutable.

4. http://www.nvidia.com/object/what-is-gpu-computing.html.

5. https://en.bitcoin.it/wiki/Category:History.

6. http://garzikrants.blogspot.com/2013/01/avalon-asic-miner-review.html.

7. https://99bitcoins.com/2016-bitcoin-mining-hardware-comparison/.

8. http://bitcoinist.com/bitcoin-hash-rate-exceeds-1-ehs-for-the-first-time/.

9. To understand the specifics related to mining for other cryptos, use the calculator at https://whattomine.com/.

10. https://en.bitcoin.it/wiki/Comparison_of_mining_pools.

11. http://www.coinwarz.com/calculators/bitcoin-mining-calculator.

12. http://fc15.ifca.ai/preproceedings/paper_75.pdf.

13. https://www.genesis-mining.com/.

14. A site to evaluate the profit potential between mining for various crypto: http://www.coinwarz.com/cryptocurrency.

15. A listing of bitcoin-related hacks, exchange closures, etc., can be found at the following site (it's a bit dated, but interesting reading, especially regarding the "Wild West" early days): https://bitcointalk.org/index.php?topic=576337#post_toc_22.

16. Nathaniel Popper, *Digital Gold: Bitcoin and the Inside Story of the Misfits and Millionaires Trying to Reinvest Money* (Harper Collins, 2015).

17. https://www.cryptocompare.com/exchanges/#/overview.

18. There's no assurance that these exchanges will be operating at the time of this reading. Please do research prior to signing on with any exchange.

19. For more information on "socialized losses" related to bitcoin futures exchanges, please see https://www.reddit.com/r/BitcoinMarkets/comments/3gb9tu/misconceptions_regarding_socialized_losses_bitmex/.

20. http://www.marketwatch.com/story/why-bitcoin-investors-need-education-and-regulation-2014-12-12.

21. https://bravenewcoin.com/news/insurance-polic-now-available-for-bitcoin-exchanges/.

22. https://support.coinbase.com/customer/portal/articles/1662379-how-is-coinbase-insured.

23. https://www.coinbase.com/security.

24. https://commons.wikimedia.org/w/index.php?curid=1028460.

25. https://www.wired.com/2014/03/bitcoin-exchange/.

26. If valued at the $1,000 price at year end 2016, the value of the loss of 850,000 bitcoins would be $850,000,000.

27. Much of this Mt. Gox section comes from material in Robert McMillan's article "The Inside Story of Mt. Gox, Bitcoin's $460 Million Disaster," *Wired*, March 3, 2014, https://www.wired.com/2014/03/bitcoin-exchange/.

28. http://www.thedailybeast.com/articles/2016/05/19/behind-the-biggest-bitcoin-heist-in-history-inside-the-implosion-of-mt-gox.html.

29. http://fusion.net/story/4947/the-mtgox-bitcoin-scandal-explained/.

30. http://fortune.com/2016/08/03/bitcoin-stolen-bitfinex-hack-hong-kong/.

31. https://news.bitcoin.com/bitfinex-us-regulation-cold-storage/.

32. http://avc.com/2014/02/mt-gox/.

33. https://bitcoin.org/en/choose-your-wallet.

34. https://bitcoin.org/en/full-node#what-is-a-full-node.

35. http://www.dummies.com/software/other-software/secure-bitcoin-wallets/.

36. A more detailed list of these wallets can be found at https://en.bitcoin.it/wiki/Hardware_wallet.

37. http://www.ibtimes.co.uk/hardware-bitcoin-wallet-keepkey-integrates-shapeshift-1576590.

Chapter 15

1. https://www.americanbanker.com/news/from-toxic-assets-to-digital-currency-barry-silberts-bold-bet.

2. Actually, with fees and costs, the underlying value for each share was less than 1/10 of the value of a single bitcoin.

3. http://www.coinfox.info/news/company/2683-xapo-will-store-the-assets-of-the-bitcoin
    -investment-trust.

4. https://grayscale.co/bitcoin-investment-trust/.

5. The OTC markets including OTCQX are not to be confused with the Nasdaq market,
    which is a true stock exchange, like the NYSE, where trades are done with primarily
    automated systems. The OTC markets consist of a well-organized group of licensed deal-
    ers who set the price of the assets transacted there. While not as well known as the New
    York Stock Exchange or Nasdaq, OTCQX is a regulated marketplace, and investments can
    only be listed on it if they are sponsored and supported by companies with high financial
    standards and disclosures. https://www.otcmarkets.com/marketplaces/otcqx.

6. https://www.trustetc.com/self-directed-ira/rules/indirect-benefits.

7. http://www.cnbc.com/2015/03/04/bitcoins-golden-moment-bit-gets-finra-approval.html.

8. https://bitcoinmagazine.com/articles/bitcoin-investment-trusts-gbtc-begins-trading
    -public-markets-1430797192/.

9. http://performance.morningstar.com/funds/etf/total-returns.action?t=GBTC&region
    =USA&culture=en_US.

10. http://www.forbes.com/sites/laurashin/2016/09/06/tyler-and-cameron-winklevoss-on
    -why-they-fell-in-love-with-bitcoin/#209cc1f83a08.

11. http://www.businessinsider.com/the-winklevoss-twins-bitcoins-2013-4.

12. Nathaniel Popper, *Digital Gold: Bitcoin and the Inside Story of the Misfits and Millionaires
    Trying to Reinvent Money* (Harper Collins, 2015).

13. https://www.sec.gov/Archives/edgar/data/1579346/000119312513279830/d562329ds1.
    htm#tx562329_12.

14. http://www.CoinDesk.com/needham-bitcoin-etf-attract-300-million-assets-approved/.

15. https://www.scribd.com/document/336204627/Bitcoin-Investment-Trust-Spencer
    -Needham#from_embed?content=10079&campaign=Skimbit%2C+Ltd.&ad_group
    =&keyword=ft500noi&source=impactradius&medium=affiliate&irgwc=1.

16. https://www.bloomberg.com/gadfly/articles/2017-02-27/winklevoss-bitcoin-etf-bet-is-a
    -countdown-to-zero-or-less.

17. http://www.coindesk.com/sec-email-winklevoss-bitcoin-etf/.

18. https://www.sec.gov/rules/sro/batsbzx/2017/34-80206.pdf.

19. http://blogs.wsj.com/moneybeat/2017/03/10/lets-be-real-bitcoin-is-a-useless-investment/.

20. http://www.CoinDesk.com/solidx-bitcoin-trust-filing/.

21. http://money.usnews.com/money/personal-finance/mutual-funds/articles/2015/09/04/
    which-are-better-etfs-or-etns.

22. Although in theory, an ETN should track the value of its underlying index closely, an
    issuer has flexibility to issue or redeem notes in order to address market pricing of an
    ETN. For more info, read the FINRA investor alert on ETN at http://www.finra.org/
    investors/alerts/exchange-traded-notes-avoid-surprises.

23. http://announce.ft.com/Announce/RawView?DocKey=1330-502640en-0SJISU5E6EOFJU
    RBIMQU8C7OGS.

24. https://www.bloomberg.com/quote/COINXBT:SS.

25. Bitcoin Tracker One—Ticker: COINXBT; Bitcoin Tracker Euro—Ticker: COINXBE.

26. https://xbtprovider.com/.

27. https://bitcoinmagazine.com/articles/publicly-traded-bitcoin-fund-xbt-provider-resumes
    -trading-following-acquisition-by-global-advisors-1467821753/.

28. http://globaladvisors.co.uk/.

29. https://bitcoinmagazine.com/articles/publicly-traded-bitcoin-fund-xbt-provider-resumes
    -trading-following-acquisition-by-global-advisors-1467821753/.

30. http://www.cmegroup.com/confluence/display/EPICSANDBOX/Exchange+Traded
    +Instruments+on+CME+Globex.

31. http://www.ibtimes.co.uk/gibraltar-stock-exchange-welcomes-bitcoineti-1572361.

32. https://www.gsx.gi/article/8292/gibraltar-stock-exchange-welcomes-bitcoineti.

33. https://www.nyse.com/quote/index/NYXBT.

34. https://bitcoinmagazine.com/articles/new-york-stock-exchange-launches-bitcoin-pricing
    -index-nyxbt-1432068688.

35. https://www.ft.com/content/b6f63e4c-a0af-11e4-9aee-00144feab7de.

36. http://www.cmegroup.com/trading/cf-bitcoin-reference-rate.html.

37. https://www.cmegroup.com/trading/files/bitcoin-frequently-asked-questions.pdf.

38. https://tradeblock.com/markets/index.

39. Ibid.

40. https://www.thebalance.com/what-do-financial-advisers-think-of-bitcoin-391233.

41. https://www.onefpa.org/journal/Pages/SEP14-The-Value-of-Bitcoin-in-Enhancing-the
    -Efficiency-of-an-Investor%E2%80%99s-Portfolio.aspx.

42. https://www.thebalance.com/what-do-financial-advisers-think-of-bitcoin-391233.

Chapter 16

1. https://en.wikipedia.org/wiki/Moore%27s_law.

2. https://www.britannica.com/topic/Intel-Corporation.

3. https://en.wikipedia.org/wiki/Intel.

4. http://ben-evans.com/benedictevans/2015/6/15/us-tech-funding.

5. https://site.warrington.ufl.edu/ritter/ipo-data/.

6. http://ben-evans.com/benedictevans/2015/6/15/us-tech-funding.

7. http://www.forbes.com/sites/johnchisholm/2013/08/06/the-regulatory-state-is-strangling
   -startups-and-destroying-jobs/2/#1d88e9112651.

8. Try the same thing on http://www.indiegogo.com.

9. https://www.sec.gov/spotlight/jobs-act.shtml.

10. http://www.inc.com/andrew-medal/now-non-accredited-investors-can-place-bets-like
    -the-ultra-wealthy.html.

11. FINRA offers guidelines that investors should consider regarding Title III at http://
    www.finra.org/newsroom/2016/finra-offers-what-investors-should-know-about
    -crowdfunding.

12. https://www.crowdfundinsider.com/2016/08/88857-now-14-finra-approved-funding
    -portals-created-title-iii-jobs-act/.

13. https://www.forbes.com/sites/chancebarnett/2013/10/23/sec-jobs-act-title-iii-investment
    -being-democratized-moving-online/#6baf33b840f5.

14. http://www.huffingtonpost.com/josh-cline/the-six-things-nonaccredi_b_10104512.html.

15. https://www.sec.gov/news/pressrelease/2015-249.html.

16. http://www.huffingtonpost.com/josh-cline/the-six-things-nonaccredi_b_10104512.html.

17. http://venturebeat.com/2016/05/15/blockchain-startups-make-up-20-of-largest-crowd-funding-projects/.

18. http://www.coindesk.com/6-top-trends-coindesks-2017-state-blockchain-report/.

19. William Mougayar has put together a nice list of ICO resources and websites at http://startupmanagement.org/2017/03/13/the-ultimate-list-of-ico-resources-18-websites-that-track-initial-cryptocurrency-offerings/.

20. https://www.smithandcrown.com/icos/.

21. http://www.icocountdown.com/.

22. https://cyber.fund/.

23. http://nakamotoinstitute.org/.

24. http://nakamotoinstitute.org/mempool/appcoins-are-snake-oil/.

25. https://medium.com/@pavelkravchenko/does-a-blockchain-really-need-a-native-coin-f6a5ff2a13a3#.6u8xjtn55.

26. Don't let the use of the word "money" cause an investor to dismiss any applicability to digital currency or cryptoassets, as later cases have expanded the meaning of the term money.

27. https://www.coinbase.com/legal/securities-law-framework.pdf.

28. https://www.sec.gov/oiea/investor-alerts-and-bulletins/ib_coinofferings.

29. www.angel.co.

30. www.crunchbase.com.

31. https://angel.co/blockchains.

32. http://bitangels.co

33. http://bitcoinist.com/coinagenda-startup-winners/.

34. https://bnktothefuture.com/pitches/airbitz.

Chapter 17

1. Clayton M. Christensen, *The Innovator's Dilemma: When New Technologies Cause Great Firms to Fail Harvard* (Business Review Press, 2016).

2. http://www.aei.org/publication/charts-of-the-day-creative-destruction-in-the-sp500-index/.

3. http://research.ark-invest.com/thematic-investing-white-paper.

4. Don and Alex Tapscott, *Blockchain Revolution: How the Technology Behind Bitcoin Is Changing Money, Business and the World* (Portfolio/Penguin, 2016).

5. http://fortune.com/2015/11/04/jamie-dimon-virtual-currency-bitcoin/.

6. http://blogs.worldbank.org/peoplemove/impactevaluations/digital-remittances-and-global-financial-health.

7. https://siteresources.worldbank.org/INTPROSPECTS/Resources/334934-1199807908806/4549025-1450455807487/Factbookpart1.pdf.

8. http://www.imf.org/external/pubs/ft/fandd/basics/remitt.htm.

9. https://www.cryptocoinsnews.com/india-see-bitcoin-blockchain-remittance-new-partnership/.

10. https://news.bitcoin.com/why-volume-is-exploding-at-mexican-bitcoin-exchange-bitso/.

11. https://bnktothefuture.com/pitches/bitso.

12. https://usa.visa.com/visa-everywhere/innovation/visa-b2b-connect.html.

13. https://bnktothefuture.com/pitches/bitpesa-2.

14. https://ripple.com/network/financial-institutions/.

15. https://ripple.com/xrp-portal/.

16. https://www2.deloitte.com/content/dam/Deloitte/ch/Documents/innovation/ch-en
    -innovation-deloitte-blockchain-app-in-insurance.pdf.

17. https://augur.net/.

18. http://insidebitcoins.com/news/how-blockchain-technology-could-revolutionize-the
    -1-1-trillion-insurance-industry/28516.

19. http://www.businessinsider.com/us-bank-stocks-update-november-9-2016-11.

20. https://www.cbinsights.com/blog/financial-services-corporate-blockchain-investments/.

21. https://www.hyperledger.org/about/members.

22. https://www.hyperledger.org/.

23. https://www.hyperledger.org/industries.

24. http://www.coindesk.com/big-corporates-unite-for-launch-of-enterprise-ethereum
    -alliance/.

25. https://www.fastcompany.com/3017509/look-inside-google-garage-the-collaborative
    -workspace-that-thrives-on-crazy-creat.

26. https://www.irs.gov/pub/irs-drop/n-14-21.pdf.

27. https://www.sec.gov/oiea/investor-alerts-and-bulletins/ib_coinofferings.

28. https://www.irs.gov/uac/newsroom/irs-virtual-currency-guidance.

29. https://www.irs.gov/pub/irs-drop/n-14-21.pdf.

30. https://www.fincen.gov/sites/default/files/shared/FIN-2013-G001.pdf.

31. http://www.CoinDesk.com/cftc-ruling-defines-bitcoin-and-digital-currencies-as
    -commodities/.

32. http://www.cftc.gov/PressRoom/PressReleases/pr7231-15.

33. https://bitcoinmagazine.com/articles/tax-day-is-coming-a-primer-on-bitcoin-and
    -taxes-1459786613/.

34. Coinbase does provide a specialized Cost Basis for Taxes report to customers. See
    https://support.coinbase.com/customer/portal/articles/1496488-how-do-i-report-taxes-.

Chapter 18

1. http://www.pionline.com/article/20150921/PRINT/309219982/a-year-later-pimco-still
   -feels-effect-of-gross-exit.

2. http://www.foxbusiness.com/markets/2015/12/07/peter-lynch-25-years-later-it-not-just
   -what-know.html.

3. https://fbinsights.files.wordpress.com/2016/01/facebookiq_millennials_money
   _january2016.pdf.

4. http://www.businessinsider.com/millennials-dont-think-they-will-need-a-bank-2015-3.

5. http://www.thinkadvisor.com/2012/01/05/merrill-lynch-boosts-client-minimum-earns
   -experts.

6. http://www.transamericacenter.org/docs/default-source/resources/center-research/tcrs2014_sr_millennials.pdf.

7. http://www.huffingtonpost.com/david-seaman/strange-bedfellows-millen_b_10836078.html.

8. Each bitcoin can be divided into 100 million units, making it easy to buy 1/2, 1/10, 1/100, or 1/1000 of a bitcoin.

Index

About the Authors

CHRIS BURNISKE is a cofounder of Placeholder Ventures, a New York firm that specializes in cryptoassets. Prior to Placeholder, he pioneered ARK Investment Management's Next Generation Internet strategy, leading the firm to become the first public fund manager to invest in bitcoin. He then transitioned to focus exclusively on cryptoassets, paving the way for Wall Street to recognize it as a new asset class. His commentary has been featured on national media outlets, including CNBC, the *Wall Street Journal*, the *New York Times*, and *Forbes*.

 @cburniske

JACK TATAR is an angel investor and advisor to startups in the cryptoasset community, and speaks and writes frequently on the topic. With over two decades of experience in financial services, he was one of the first financial professionals to receive certification from the Digital Currency Council. He is the coauthor of one of the earliest books on Bitcoin, *What's the Deal with Bitcoins?*

 @JackTatar